PUNJABI CENTURY
1857–1947

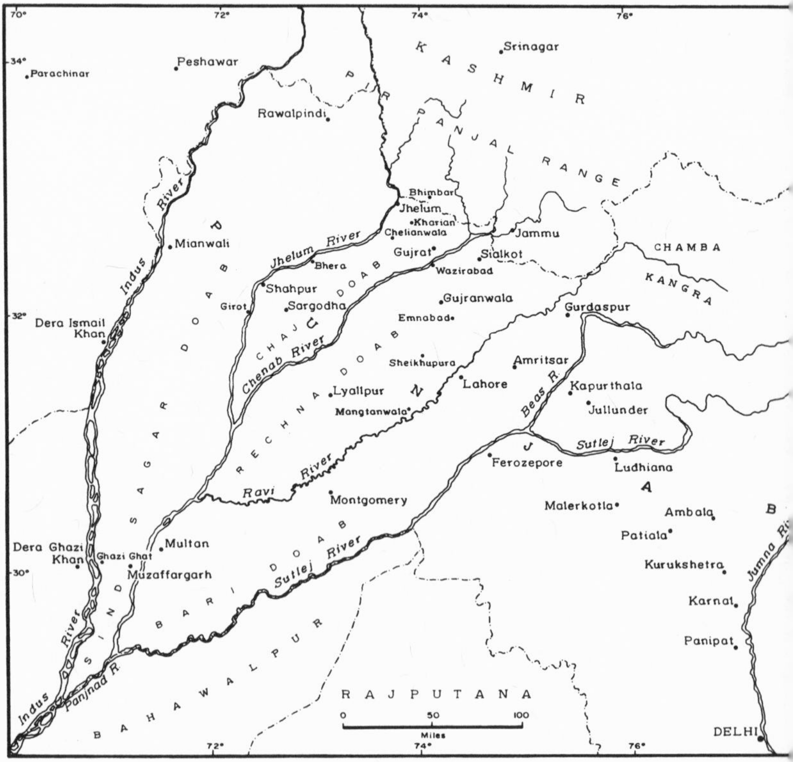

Map of the Punjab, c. 1920

PUNJABI CENTURY

1857–1947

By

Prakash Tandon

With a Foreword by

MAURICE ZINKIN

University of California Press
Berkeley and Los Angeles

First Published in 1961
by Chatto and Windus Ltd
London, England

Maurice and Taya Zinkin
for their inspiration
Ingegärd
for all her help

University of California Press
Berkeley and Los Angeles
ISBN: 0-520-01253-4
Library of Congress Catalog Card Number 68-25959

Printed in the United States of America
3 4 5 6 7 8 9

CONTENTS

ACKNOWLEDGEMENT

To Lady Ram Nath Chopra, the lady who was 'asked for' and was promised two years before she was born, for our talks about the charming engagement and wedding customs that have virtually disappeared; for interesting chats on the subject, to Mrs. Som Puri, her daughter, of my generation, who was already driving a car to drop in at her future husband's home; to Har Narain Batra, an excellent check whenever I was in doubt; to Maya, Manu and Gautam, our children, for whom this book was really written and whose comments were always encouraging. Maya of the next generation has new ideas, but with a Punjabi-Swedish practicalness she wants only a slightly arranged marriage while fully respecting the tradition of a dowry. To S. Natarajan for valuable corrections; to Cynthia Lisely for patient deciphering and flawless typing of the manuscript.

To Debu and Reba Mukherjee at whose charming bungalow in Mhow I began writing; and to Col. Sir Ram Nath Chopra at whose hut in the peaceful pine forest above Gulmarg I finished it.

Also to a friend of long ago, Donald Forsythe, who introduced me to English culture.

FOREWORD

by Maurice Zinkin

NOTHING IS more important to the illumination of history than good autobiography. It becomes particularly valuable in times of transition. Documents and statistics can give us the facts of change; only Cicero's letters tell us what the fall of the Roman Republic meant to those to whom the Republic mattered. Domesday Book gives us the figures, but how much would we not give for a Saxon peasant's reactions to the Conquest.

In the last fifty years India has been through the greatest transition in its history; the last twenty have been a time of revolution in the whole national life rarely equalled anywhere. Now, as India settles into its new, managerial world of industrialisation and State Capitalism, of feminine equality and family planning, the generation which is growing up to power no longer knows what the old India was like. They live in their own new ways, and they have the impatience with all others which is necessary if they are to renovate India at the speed they demand.

But there was a charm in the old way too; in its slowness, in the intensity of its family life, in the certainty of everybody's obligations, in the constant contact with the village and the farmer. It is Mr. Tandon's merit that, himself one of the most distinguished members of the new generation, he has been able to catch so exactly the flavour of the old.

The men of his generation, in changing their own lives, have transformed India. His own career is typical. Thirty years ago, when Indian chartered accountants hardly existed, he went off to England to become a chartered accountant. Over twenty years ago, when Indian officers in big British firms were rarer even than Indian captains in the cavalry, and when business, to young men of his professional class, had none too sweet an odour, he decided to go into business; and British, hard-selling business at that. His chosen business was the Indian subsidiary of Unilever, and, as he has made his way up, he has again and again been the first Indian to hold his post; the first Indian in Marketing Research, the first Indian head of a division, the first Indian on the Board, now the first Indian Vice-Chairman. This has been a common experience of his generation. As Indians have taken over from Englishmen all the keys of their own society, everybody one knows has become the first Indian to be something–a Major General, a Collector of Poona, a Governor. This in itself makes the experience of Mr. Tandon's generation quite different from that of his sons and their contemporaries, who are growing up in the comfortable knowledge that the keys of power are theirs by right.

This book does not cover the whole of Mr. Tandon's experience of the Indian revolution. Life in industry must await his retirement. The society he is describing, the British Punjab as it grew in the years after the Sikh Wars and the Mutiny, began to die in the 1930's; it was finally killed in the riots of 1947.

Mr. Tandon is talking of a past which is over, the flavour of which, had it not been for him, would soon have departed never to be recaptured. His memory, his sense of a scene as a whole, his capacity to recreate the past as it was and not as the present day would have it–these combine to give us the old Punjab as it lived, thought, ate and enjoyed itself. This is how marriages were made, this is how the Indian backbone of the administration got tired of the British, this is what the houses looked like and how one went out for a walk.

There is no comparable evocation of India as it used to be, except Kipling's *Kim*. *Kim* is one of the world's great stories, but Mr. Tandon writes from the inside.

CHAPTER ONE

OUR FAMILY were Khatris from the West Punjab countryside. For two centuries we had been moving along the banks of the Jhelum river, sometimes on its eastern and sometimes on its western bank, and for a while in the Himalayan foothills where the river drains into the plain.

We know about our past because in the Punjab it is possible to trace one's family for many generations, owing to the custom of maintaining family records at certain holy places, of which Hardwar on the Ganges is the most important. Whenever there is a death in the family, someone will go to Hardwar to immerse the ashes of the departed. There our family has its own panda, as these priests are called, who at his death is succeeded by his son. He maintains the family records in long, old-fashioned Indian ledgers, covered in red cloth, in which he writes down the length of the page. Every time someone goes he brings these records up to date by entering births, marriages and deaths, migrations and other information about what has been happening in the family. When I first visited Hardwar I had only to say I was a Tandon from Gujrat, and from a crowd of pandas our priest came forward and reeled off our whole family tree for several generations. He had met my father, uncles and elder brother when they had visited Hardwar. He has other Khatri families like ours whom he serves as priest, and whenever we visit we give him some money for assisting us with puja on the bank of the river. That is how he earns his living. The family ledgers are the precious stock-in-trade of these pandas, and they know the genealogies by heart. Having been trained from childhood, like their fathers before them, they develop phenomenal memories.

Other than at Hardwar, our family records are also kept at Kurukshetra, the battlefield of the great epic Mahabharat, and at Matan, in the valley of Kashmir. In the ledger at Matan, I read a message from a great grand-uncle who had walked up the old road from Gujrat over the Pir Panjal passes. The date of the Hindu calendar placed his visit at 1811, just one hundred years before I was born. He wrote in Persian about the arduous journey, the charm of Kashmir, and about our relations. I imagine he conformed to the custom of those days of bringing apples back to the plains, each apple tied in a knot in a turban, and distributed the rare fruit in halves and quarters to friends and relations as a kind of thanksgiving for his safe return. As a child I went to school for a time in Gujrat, where began the old Moghul road to Srinagar through Bhimbar and Muzaffarpur. The road was in use until the motor road from Rawalpindi was built. Tongas used to leave Gujrat railway station for Srinagar, a journey that took about a fortnight. I used to love climbing to the top of our house on cold winter mornings to gaze at the snow peaks of Jammu and imagine this uncle winding his way up, walking perhaps ten miles a day and taking twenty days for a journey that is done in a day by motor-car, and today takes less than twenty minutes by air.

During the Sikh period the family farmed and served occasionally with the Sikh armies. Father used to tell us that life was uncertain and sometimes precarious in those days. Although the Sikh empire at one time stretched over the Punjab, Himachal, Jammu, Kashmir and into Afghanistan, only during Ranjit Singh's reign did it wield any kind of central authority. Otherwise, justice was at a discount, for even in my days the word Sikha-Shahi (Sikh rule) still meant high-handedness in the Punjab. But the Sikh regime was never too repressive, and to us Hindus it was perhaps a welcome change from being inferior citizens under the Moslems. After all, we and the Sikhs stemmed from the same stock; most Hindus had Sikh relations, and intermarriage was common. In our own family my elder brother married a girl who was a Sikh on her father's side, but a Hindu on her mother's. Her youngest brother, a soldier in the British and later in the Indian army, married a great grand-daughter of Hari Singh Nalwa, the famous Sikh general who had marched into Kabul. His name had become a legend and we used to hear that even in our days, whenever a Pathan woman wanted to quieten a child she would say, 'Hush, Nalwa is coming.'

We and the Sikhs had the same castes and customs, and they were always members of our brotherhoods–biradaris. In the villages we lived together and celebrated the same festivals. Many Hindus, particularly our women, visited the Sikh gurdwaras to worship. Sometimes a married couple, who had lost hope of getting a son, would take a vow that if they had a boy he would be brought up in the Sikh faith. Although the Hindus got along fairly well under the Sikhs, at least as well as the Sikhs themselves, law and order were poor, and there were no opportunities for development. Local officials were arbitrary and often rapacious, and father told us that people tried to look poorer than they were so as not to attract attention. This had done my family some harm, for when the British began their system of land records we, like many Khatri farmers, refused at first to declare that we owned land. This later debarred us from the special rights which in the Punjab were conferred on the agricultural classes.

Father used to tell us about one of his grand-uncles who had fought the British under the Sikh banner at the battle of Chelianwala in 1849. He was a tall, well-built man in the prime of his life when my father was a boy, and at the festival of Holi he would dress as a lion and carry a whole goat between his teeth. He used to tell the village boys stories of the battle. At Chelianwala the British suffered heavy casualties, and at the cemetry constructed on the field, as late as in my childhood, professional mourners were hired on Saturdays for a few annas to beat their breasts and wail. This uncle used to say that when a British soldier fell down he would put blades of grass in his mouth and say, 'Hamen nahin maro, ham gai hai. Dekho, ham ghas khata hai.' (Don't kill me, I am a cow. Look, I eat grass.) 'How could one kill a cow?' he would ask.

The Punjabis, as old people used to say, were puzzled at the first sight of the Englishmen because they had never seen any people look so implausible. They were used to Pathans, and some of their own people were fair, occasionally with light hair and grey eyes–we had a cousin with ginger hair and a skin that reddened instead of tanning, which he considered a great misfortune, as he was always compared to the posterior of a monkey! But never had they seen people so incredibly red-faced, and dressed in such quaint tight clothes displaying their bottoms so indecently.

Never had they seen women who went about barefaced in equally incredible clothes, and spoke to strangers with the confidence of men. Their children they found unbelievably beautiful.

The villagers were, to begin with, frightened of the new conquerors. Women would hide their children. But fear soon gave way to curiosity and then to controversy. What were these Angrez log up to? Their ideas were quite unlike those of rulers in the past. They began by doing the oddest things, like consulting each peasant about the land he possessed and giving him a permanent title to it, with a fixed revenue which was remitted in years when crops were bad. The officers moved about freely, unguarded and without pomp and show. The visiting officials pitched their tents outside the villages, and held their office under a tree where anyone could approach them. Accompanied by just one or two persons they would ride on horseback for hours, inspecting and talking to people. Most of them had learned Punjabi well, some quite fluently. Their women, whom we soon began to call mem sahibs, also moved about freely, asking the village women and children questions. The officers and their wives had insatiable curiosity about our habits and customs and seemed never to tire of getting to know us. Their manners were strange but kindly and considerate, seldom hectoring or bullying. In their dress, manner or speech there was nothing of the rulers, as we were used to, and yet it was soon obvious that there was no authority lacking, and that they had a peppery temper.

I think what impressed our elders most, and what they still spoke about when I was young, was that in the past there had been rulers who were virtuous and mindful of the rayats welfare, but never a whole system of government that was bent to public good, with no apparent personal benefit to its officers. These and many other things at first intrigued the people, and later pleased them.

We Punjabis were fortunate in escaping the rule of the East India Company. For the few years before 1857 Punjab was governed by the Commission under Lawrence and a set of officers whose interest was development rather than trade. We started our British chapter under the new government with no hangover from the Company. In this virgin field, with no regrets from the past, the government settled down to the task in which our family, like many others, was to play a small part, of building an administration; giving the province a new judiciary; for the first time a police; instituting land records and a revenue system; education department; building irrigation canals which changed deserts into granaries; and providing many other services that laid the foundation of a peaceful and prosperous countryside. It was a benevolent bureaucracy which gave much opportunity for building and therefore attracted men who liked pioneering under conditions of scope and power.

When I was at school our textbooks dividing Indian history into three periods, Hindu, Muslim and British, ended with a short chapter, 'Angrezi Raj ki Barkaten'–Blessings of the English Raj. This was always a standard question in our examinations. There was a list of about a dozen blessings like law and order, irrigation canals, roads and bridges, schools, railways, telegraph and public health. In my generation these things were taken for granted, but my father used to explain that while he, too, was born in an era of peace, to his elders the new law and order really meant something. Having lived through the break-up of the Sikh empire, human rights and respect for life and property were an unfamiliar concept to them. They really understood what it meant not to be harrassed any more by marauding groups of disbanded soldiers. They had the legends of Jehangir's march to Kashmir in their memory, when his army of two lakh soldiers and camp followers passed through the country like a locust swarm, leaving a line one hundred miles wide that was denuded of all food. The Punjabi language was full of words and proverbs that bore testimony to its tough rulers in the past. 'Never stand behind a horse or in front of an official!' And now, suddenly, the soldiers stopped marauding and foraging. In fact, many soldiers of the Sikh armies, who might otherwise have rampaged around, were engaged in the new armies and given a regular living. The British soldiers were simple, and instead of helping themselves paid fancy prices. If our generation began to be amused at the textbook blessings of the British Raj, my grandfather's generation took them seriously and praised unreservedly. So did my father and his generation, at least to begin with.

I think we must have found something in common between us and the Englishman which made us get on well together from the start. For one thing, there was little or no orthodoxy in us, nor the aloofness and complexity of the southern brahmin. We were willing to accept the foreigners as man to man. Our society was extrovert and adaptable. It had, while retaining its internal structure, adapted itself to each change until, like the exposed cross-section of an archaeological excavation, it showed layers of characteristics piled one upon the other from each external impact. And this, the British impact, was comparatively so gentle and persuasive that the Punjabi for once enjoyed the process of change and adaptation.

Muslim domination of a thousand years, often intolerant and usually zealous, had rubbed off the outward signs of Hinduism, and what was left was driven inward, making it more a belief and a certain way of life than a practice of orthodox rituals. In our names, clothes, food, language, learning, perhaps even in our attitude to women we borrowed freely from the Muslims. Our cooking is mostly Muslim; our names a mixture of Sanskrit, Persian and even Greek; the salwar kameez of our men and women and the semi-purda were also imported. Of my first names, one is Sanskrit and the other, Lal, Persian. Some boys were named Sikandar (Alexander), and some were even called Walayati, a name for foreigners, which became synonymous with the English. This word was later adopted by the English soldiers as 'Blighty' for England. In our language a man who always gets the better of you in an argument is called Aflatoon (Plato); and one who was legalistic in discussions was called a Rattikeen, after the name of a famous English chief judge of the Lahore High Court, called Rattigan. In all this borrowing we may have lost something but we also gained much, at least in directness and adaptability and it was probably that which appealed to the British and made them enjoy their task as builders and teachers, and made us apt and eager learners.

My grandfather, Maya Das, became the first member of the family to join the new government service. The eldest of three brothers, he was born at Kala Serai on the west bank of the Jhelum in about the year 1840, before the British took over the Punjab. He went to a small school in the village Sikh dharamsala, where they taught children how to read and write Persian, and simple arithmetic. Persian was still the written language of the Punjab. After leaving school he was taken on as a kanungo, a minor official, in the Revenue Department at a small salary, I imagine about twenty rupees per month. As his work dealt with the farmers, it meant gifts of vegetables, ghee and other produce, for it was considered a normal thing to offer such gifts; in fact, the farmers regarded it as no imposition if it was left at only that.

The early years, when the new services were being organised, were, according to our father, full of problems, some human and amusing. One aspect of the British which was not understood, was their sense of discipline–something quite new and alien to the people. Our grandfather related the story of one of his colleagues who was appointed a patwari. It was a simple enough job and required the barest of training in maintaining a register of land records and transfers. But like all jobs in the new regime, it imposed a type of discipline which this man found hard to grasp. He was asked to maintain a diary in which entries were made of his daily work, but he was told that every Sunday was a holiday, when he need not work. There were, of course, the festival days which were also holidays, but the idea of not working on Sunday, which up to now had been a day like any other, was new and one which this man never quite understood. Some time later, the British revenue officer paid an inspection visit and looked into his diary, and found that very little work had been done, and that ineptly. What, however, disgusted the officer most was a frequent entry: 'Today a Sunday was celebrated.' The officer decided that the wrong man had been recruited and discharged him. This man did not mind very much losing his job, as in those days of simple wants and plentiful food, living in a village without a job was no particular hardship, but what really upset him was the Sahib's lack of appreciation of his gesture in celebrating this Christian holiday with such flattering frequency.

The dismissal of this colleague of my grandfather was something odd to everyone at the time. Surely one has to consider things in their proper perspective. A funeral, an illness, a wedding, a call for help from a neighbour or relation are all things which must receive preference over work in hand. It may require several days' absence from one's work, but these are duties which must be performed unquestioningly. You just lay down tools or tether the bullock, strap your horse and go. This poor man was merely following the custom of his society, of course taking advantage of the new rule which allowed holidays. Dismissal was, therefore, a punishment wholly undeserved. What would the widowed aunt say if he did not turn up for at least two days to attend the head-shaving ceremony of her son; more so now that he was a government official and a man of some importance. His presence was necessary, and he went, but he took the wise or, as it turned out to be, unwise precaution of treating the absence under the new rules as a Sunday and entering it meticulously in the diary.

Looking back, I suppose that for discipline to grow gradually in a society as the result of changing economic and occupational conditions is one thing; for it to be imposed suddenly must have been totally incomprehensible to our people, and could only be regarded as an idiosyncrasy of the rulers. It did not begin to be really understood until my father's generation.

My grandfather died young. Having started modestly in a profession he had keenly felt his lack of education and realised that going to a dharamsala school was not enough. People were now talking of the new high schools where they taught the English language, the key to new skills and professions. He decided to send the brightest of his younger brothers to Gujrat, forty miles away, which had the nearest high school. This was the school to which my father and uncles and we brothers and cousins all went later in continuation of the new process of professionalisation that had begun in a small way with grandfather.

My grand-uncle, Thakur Das, was born in 1850, the year after the British fought their last battle in the Punjab at Gujrat. According to custom we never take the names of our ancestors, as far as we know, but this grand-uncle was named after an ancestor six generations ago. The reason for defying this ban was strange. Our great-grandmother had a dream while she was pregnant, in which this distant ancestor Thakur Das appeared and told her that he was going to be reincarnated in her womb. When she bore a son, he was named Thakur Das in deference to the wishes of this ancestor. In the family records at Hardwar I could only see this one instance of a name repeated.

Thakur Das grasped the opportunity for education that grandfather gave him, and studied with avidity like most Khatri boys of his time who for generations had been deprived of their right to opportunities in service. He was the first in the family to pass matriculation, and we were told that there was great jubilation in the village. He was immediately given the title of Babu. This title had been brought by Bengali and U.P. clerks who came with the British to man their services, but so far there had been few Punjabis to acquire enough education to earn it. He was a bright pupil and was noticed by the English headmaster who after school took him on as a teacher.

At this time, in about 1870, the government was encouraging the practice of law in the newly formed courts. Through the influence of his headmaster, grand-uncle was offered a year's legal training in Lahore. To our village this was indeed the wonder of all wonders of the new times. He was probably the first from the village to travel as far as Lahore, but to study in that town, in one of the new colleges, to learn to argue, defend and cross-question before an English judge, was indeed something to talk about. What was more, he was supposed also to have acquired a knowledge of the English language. He could 'git-mit git-mit', as they said when they first heard English spoken. A year later, my grand-uncle finished law and with great pride and ostentation displayed a painted metal board with a wooden frame, declaring his name and profession in an arc in English letters and a straight line in Urdu underneath. Fifty years later, we used to decipher the faded

English lettering. It said, 'Lala Thakur Das Tandon, Pleader, Gujrat.'

The process of professionalisation was now proceeding rapidly. Next door another pleader soon set up his board, a Kochhar Khatri, who later caused much admiration in the town by giving college education to three of his sons, the eldest of whom became one of the first Indian judges in the Punjab, the second a pleader, and the third a doctor who joined the army. The small town would indeed have marvelled had it known that his granddaughter would marry an army officer from far away Maharashtra who was to become Chief of Staff of the Indian Army.

Innovation was also fast catching up. As his practice prospered, grand-uncle left the city and built a house just outside the city wall, facing one of the gates. It was built in a new style, which bore the first traces of influence of the British bungalow. Houses had so far been built inside the city wall, usually two or three storeys high. With pressure on the limited space, they seldom had only a single storey, and rarely more than three, with an open room or two on top to catch the breeze or escape from the rain when people slept out on the terrace on summer nights. With peace and safety, people began to leave the city, though no one as yet dared to go as far as the civil station, where the English officers lived in large bungalows. They could not have gone to live so far away from their people, virtually into the jungle, nor would they have had the courage, even had they been allowed to do so by the sahibs. The first move was to go just outside the city wall.

Our grand-uncle's house had a high wall around it which was blank on three sides, while on the fourth side, facing the road, it had open arches and a high old-fashioned studded gate, barred at night from inside. These arches were rented, partly as a source of income, but also for protection since the house was outside the city wall. As the house faced the main city gate, its front soon became a tonga stand from which these two-wheeled horse carts went to the railway station of Gujrat, to some neighbouring small towns and villages, and to Kashmir. Inside the main gate of the house, as you entered, there was a rectangular courtyard with rooms on two sides, a shed for grand-uncle's tonga, and a stable on the right, and a blank wall opposite the entrance. The rooms were occupied by grand-uncle's clerk, servants, some nondescript distant relatives, people from our village, and his clients. It was customary for clients from villages to sleep at the pleader's house, though they boarded outside. A courtyard full of resting and sleeping clients was a visible sign of a pleader's success.

In the left corner of the courtyard, through the blank wall, there was another gate that led to the inside of the house where the family lived. Just within this gate was a dark vestibule called a deohri, which was as far as the tradesmen could go uninvited. In it there was also a deep well, known as a baoli, from which the family drew water. Through another door at the top end of the deohri you entered the house, which was also built around a square courtyard. On the opposite side of the entrance was a wing with kitchen and store rooms; facing it was a wing with living rooms; on the right a blank wall, and on the left a room which occupied the full length of the wing and was used as grand-uncle's sitting-room and office. This room had a door opening to a passage by which the visitors and clients came in from the outer courtyard without going through the family quarters. The passage ended in a small square sunken garden behind the house, which had a grove of fruit trees and some jasmine and rose bushes to provide grand-aunt with flowers for her morning puja. The garden with its oranges and mangoes was a great temptation to us, but we never dared to go beyond picking fallen fruit. The luxury of a private garden, adjacent to the house, was a novelty. Some city people had fruit orchards, but these were outside the city and more like farms.

The house was built of the old, thin, hard Punjabi brick, more like a small tile compared to the later thick English brick. Afterwards they stopped building houses like grand-uncle's. As the pressure of population grew inside the city suburbs began to spring up. When they saw the first Indian officers living in government bungalows in the civil station, some people took courage and moved out to their vicinity, into bungalows of English style. Others went to the suburbs and built houses rather like those in the city but with ugly modern touches. The style of grand-uncle's house somehow went out of favour.

Inside, the house was spacious, with high ceilings, cool in the summer but so very cold in the winter that you tried to keep close to the kitchen fire or a charcoal brazier. It was sparsely furnished, with string charpoys or niwar, cotton tape, beds and low string and niwar stools, called pirhis. They all had gaily lacquered legs. In the main bedroom, faded with age, was a rather elaborately worked pirhi with a high back. It had a coloured string seat and ornately turned sides and back studded with mirrors and ivory pieces. It was the pirhi which grand-aunt, like all Punjabi brides, brought in her dowry. Near it was an old bed of elaborate design which had been her bridal bed. This furniture was very like the style still seen in Gujerat and Saurashtra. In our own house we had a very old bed on which our father's grandmother had lain on her wedding night. The rest of the furniture consisted of many steel and wooden trunks; there was the very large steel trunk in which grand-aunt brought her dowry. They contained clothes, linen, blankets, shawls, quilts, utensils of copper and silver, jewellery and ornaments, and tapestries called phulkaries.

The sitting-room called baithak, literally meaning where you sat, was an impressive long room furnished in the old style. It served as a study, office and reception room. The entire floor was covered with a cotton carpet, durrie, with a white sheet, known as chandni, meaning moonlight. On it were placed flat white cushions to sit on, and tubular cushions, known as gao-dum (cow-tailed) takias, to lean against. Near the cushions were low octagonal, ivory inlaid mango-wood tables and brass spittoons. At the head of the carpet was a large divan-like cushion where grand-uncle used to sit. Near this was a low ornamented hooka with a long stem. The whole effect of the room was one of extreme neatness, cleanliness and chasteness. Before entering you left your shoes outside. In the walls there were small modelled and arched recesses with shelves, some of which had shutters of carved rosewood, while others were open. The walls were lime-washed in white, and the inside of the open cupboards was washed in green.

At the north end of the baithak there was an alcove with a low thara, a brick platform, also covered with durries, chandnis, and gao-dum takias. This part of the room was used for an office and had modern revolving wooden shelves containing uncle's law books. It also had some low desks with sloping sides for writing. On the desks were ceramic ink-pots containing rags soaked in Indian ink. The pens were cut from hard reeds and sharpened to a point at one end. There were also modern English pen holders of porcupine quills with metal nibs. For blotting the ink there were brass cups with perforated lids to sprinkle sand.

The alcove had a number of pictures hung in a line, all tilting forward from the wall. The pictures were quite a fascination to us children. They were prints of the royal family of Travancore by Ravi Varma, who painted a large number of Indian mythological subjects, depicting practically the whole story of the Hindu faith. The settings were the lush jungles, hills and waterways of Travancore, which in dry dusty Punjab looked unfamiliar but very beautiful. The women in the pictures, the Shakuntalas and Damyantis, the Sitas, Lakshmis, and Saraswatis, were large, handsomely proportioned fair women looking more like women of the north, but presumably modelled on the lovely grey-eyed Tia women of the Cannanore coast.

Interestingly enough, the place of honour in the drawing-room was given to an English coloured print, which was as popular as the Ravi Varma pictures for nearly fifty years. This was a picture of life in steps of ten years till they reached the prime and then descended. It began with birth and ended with death, both events being blessed by angels. On the first step there was a baby in a cradle, and on the next a flaxen-haired girl playing badminton. She was soon a young woman in the arms of a smooth-faced young man, saying a shy yes to him. On the next step stood a bearded man and this ripening woman, both looking fondly at their baby in a cot. Then came the top step with a greying man and woman as proud parents of a family. After that the steps went down, through grandparenthood to decrepitude, till a very old woman was sinking into the arms of an angel. This was life, though depicted in foreign symbols, some to us seemingly immodest, like the young couple in each other's arms. Mercifully they were not kissing, as then the picture could not have been displayed at all. It was much appreciated and always caused wise comment by my grand-uncle and his visitors.

Our grand-uncle, with white hair and a square cut white beard, was a distinguished looking man in my childhood memory. He always wore loose white pyjamas, a white shirt, a cream cotton or grey woollen long coat, a starched loosely-tied white turban, and strong Punjabi shoes. He had a very courteous manner and spoke to us children with old-fashioned politeness, which was very flattering but made us giggle. It was the custom in those days for elders to receive and talk to visiting children as if they were grown-ups. But grand-uncle always amused us because in his polite speech he always addressed us as langoors, long-tailed monkeys, an affectionate reference to Hanuman's monkeys who in the Ramayan followed Ram and Lakshman in their battle with Ravan. We were pleased at this reference too because in the local annual depiction of the Ramayan we boys tried hard for parts in Hanuman's monkey army.

Grand-uncle's day began early. He would sit in his office, and the munshi, his clerk, would bring in the clients whose cases were coming up for hearing in court that day. A client, usually a simple villager, would at once begin a long account of the wrong done to him, his complete innocence and the equally complete perfidy of the opponent, his full faith in grand-uncle, who next to God must know the whole truth, and his confidence that justice was going to prevail–in his favour. And so these clients would declare at length as grand-uncle went through his preparatory notes on the case, asking some questions and instructing the munshi to impress upon the clients not to say more than what had been agreed upon.

After working till about nine o'clock in the winter months, grand-uncle would go in for his meal, a breakfast and lunch together. During the winter he ate in the inner courtyard in the sun. His food was always cooked by grand-aunt and served by one of the children if they were about. The custom of servants cooking and serving came later. Usually, grand-aunt cooked outside and my uncle sat near her. After the meal he had a quiet pull at his hooka in the courtyard, or in his office if he had some last-minute work at the cases. At about ten o'clock he would tie his turban, put on his coat and shoes and leave for the courts. His tonga was waiting outside and solemnly he and his munshi would get in with the law books and files. Making much unnecessary but quite musical noise with the foot-bell, fixed in the dashboard, the syce would drive away very importantly, for there were few private tongas in Gujrat in those days.

We never quite knew what happened in the courts; how the cases were argued; what the judges did. But in the afternoon grand-uncle would return at four o'clock, and after some sweets or fruit and milk, or in the summer almond or some fruit juice – tea was unknown in those days except as a remedy for chest troubles–he began his work again, usually receiving new cases. At night he worked again after dinner in his office, consulting the law books and preparing the cases. In the summer months the courts began at seven in the morning and sat till midday. He then did his preparatory work very early in the morning and in the cool of the night.

Every evening water was sprinkled on the dusty brick-paved floor of the outer courtyard, and grand-uncle would sit there in a reed chair which later gave place to an English deck-chair, smoke his hooka and receive visitors. His friends, relations and clients would drop in for news, to chat, or to seek advice. The relatives would also drop in on the family in the inner courtyard. He was over seventy when I first remember him. He spoke in clear Punjabi laced with chaste Urdu and Persian and an occasional English word, punctuated with much conscious wisdom and many Punjabi, Persian and Urdu proverbs. At that age, everyone expected him to speak with the dignity and wisdom of age, education and experience. He was one of the first to receive higher education, to travel outside the Punjab, and to speak with the English in their own tongue. These things, combined with age, gave him a natural position of leadership in the town and community.

He was a man of considerable interests. He collected old coins and was reputed to have a rare collection at a time when few Indians went in for such hobbies. On special occasions, when he came across anyone who showed an interest in the subject, he would take out his collection from a locked cupboard in the drawing-room. My uncle, who had once been present, said that it was quite a ritual. Grand-uncle kept the coins in cloth bags tied with strings, and would take out one coin at a time. Uncle said he did not trust the visitor with his collection; but then this uncle did not like him and was the first in our family to rebel against the authority of an elder. He was later to break away from grand-uncle altogether, something then akin to apostasy. Another interest of grand-uncle's was to trace the family history. For this he did a considerable amount of research in the villages along the Jhelum and often spent his holidays at Hardwar with the pandas, delving into family records. When I first went there in 1950, the panda had heard from his grandfather of old Lala Thakur Das and his researches. I do not know what happened to his records over which he spent much time and care.

Grand-uncle was over eighty when he died in 1931. Till the end he regularly took his walks in early morning and in the evening, along the Bhimbar road. On cold winter mornings, muffled in his grey coat and a thick shawl, he used to walk through the avenue of leafless shisham trees. Above the trees, catching the early rays of the sun, were the peaks of the first line of the Himalayas, a rose pink against the deep blue of the foothills. In the evening he gazed at them again as he set out, but then they looked a light mauve above the very deep mauve, sometimes purple, of the North Indian winter line. In summer the hills were hidden by the dust except after rain when the air was washed clean. He loved his walk, which was often punctuated by people joining him, if they wanted some private advice or to get their side of the story in a family quarrel first, which they found difficult to do at the evening gatherings in his house.

He loved his life, which was something new and exciting. His generation was the first span of the bridge that began in 1850. With my father began the second span and with me the third. Grand-uncle was born seven years before the Raj began, and father died seven years after it ended.

CHAPTER TWO

MY FATHER, Ram Das, was born in 1876 in Kala Serai, three miles from the town of Jhelum. He was only about twelve when our grandfather died, leaving him the eldest of four brothers and two sisters. Normally, as an orphan, he would have hung around the village, but the custom of familial responsibility came to his rescue. In this case there was also an old debt. My grand-uncle had been educated under similar circumstances by my grandfather; it was now his turn to educate my father. This debt my father repaid, when his turn came, by educating his three younger brothers.

Father moved to Gujrat to live with his uncle who put him into his old school. In district towns government had opened high schools, and in smaller towns middle or primary schools. About the same time the English Protestant missions were also starting schools in the Punjab, and some of them built a great reputation for themselves. The high schools in my father's time still had English headmasters, who in their own way did much pioneering work in evolving curricula, translating textbooks and writing new ones. My father used to speak highly of his headmaster, who must have worked hard for a small pay, so far away from home. This admiration he was often to express for many of the Englishmen he came across at school, college and in service. Most of them had no doubt been put there by circumstance, having been born in India, and had they even wished they had nowhere else to go. But he looked at it in another way. They could have behaved like unhappy exiles and done just enough to keep their heads above water; but he admired those, and there were many of them, who seemed to love India and threw their roots deeply into its soil and from whose suckers grew many trees in my father's generation.

Some of them could have left India but stayed on through choice, sometimes in obscure corners of the country. A fine example was Dr. Taylor who, after resigning from a successful career in the medical service, settled in a small village, Jallalpur Jattan, about ten miles from Gujrat, where he began to practice eye surgery. He rejected the idea of working in the comparative comfort of even a district town like Gujrat where he would have had the company of his compatriots because, he argued, Gujrat already had a hospital and he could do more good in the country. He made a great name for his charity and his skill, and patients came to him not only from Gujrat but sometimes from several hundred miles away. His name became a legend. He specialised in the cataract operation where through simple surgery he restored sight to many. He was not the only one; there were many like him. There was Miss Brown who started a women's hospital in Ludhiana which was later to become, I think, the first women's medical school in India.

Father's life in his uncle's home must have been quite hard. While, thanks to the system of family responsibility, poor relations, particularly young ones, were taken care of, they were actually barely tolerated and their dependence was often made clear to them every day of their life. Women were perhaps the ones to blame. Men were indifferent, and they might not give the same affection to the dependent child as to their own children, but the women were adept at making the dependant's life miserable. While grand-uncle treated father with kindly indifference, so long as he filled his hooka properly–a chore which must have put him off smoking for the rest of his life–grand-aunt monopolised all his spare time outside school hours for running errands and doing shopping. She made sure at the same time that he was kept constantly reminded of his position.

Years later, when our father was well settled, we children used to call on grand-aunt and listen deeply impressed to how she had looked after our father, how she had swathed the poor boy with affection and care so that her own children sometimes felt envious. She would express lachrymose doubts whether our mother felt for us the way she did for our father. We used to be touched by this eloquent expression of an affection of so long ago and envied our father as a little boy. We thought of the many good things we missed in life for, according to our aunt, while she firmly believed in not spoiling her own children, she made sure that the poor orphan never went without anything he ever wished for. She conjured visions to us of our austere, stern father spoiled and doted on. It was only when we grew up that we began to discover the humour of the situation, but one who knew it all the time but never saw the joke of it was our mother who, being in the position of a daughter-in-law, dared not retort. Back home she used to be very upset. Our father never said anything.

At school father did well. Despite the many chores his aunt gave him, he worked hard at studies when he could. This was the age for hard work. Boys were avidly soaking up the learning that was being imparted in the new schools. There were stories of boys who literally mortified themselves to learn. To prevent sleep, they would tie their top knot with a string to the ceiling so that each time they nodded with sleep they woke up in pain when the hair was pulled up with a jerk. To prevent their eyelids from closing with the heavy sleep of youth they would put drops of acrid rape-seed oil, which smarted and burnt their eyes but kept them awake. In the cold freezing winter nights they woke up at three o'clock in the morning, went out of the warmth of the quilts and the closed rooms and bathed in icy water to wake themselves up thoroughly and then settle down to long hours of study until day-break. They would do hard physical jerks and exercises to keep awake. The privilege of education came virtually free, and the results it was leading to in the shape of new careers were so glittering that they studied with a dedicated obsession.

The English headmaster of the Gujrat government school may have thought that this was perhaps going too far, but he must have been secretly satisfied, I imagine gratified and touched, by this naïve and hungry desire to learn. The boys had coined a Punjabi expression, remembered even in our days, wishing that they could grind the books into a pulp and extract the knowledge out of them and drink it. They could learn so much more that way, for it would become a part of their system. If it is wondered what kept men like this headmaster going, one only has to think how moved they must have been at the response they evoked. People wanted more and more of them; their needs and demands were limitless. In India, service, genuine and freely given, soon becomes elevated to saintliness. Saintliness is never conferred; no formal declaration makes saints; they are made by popular opinion. Some of the early pioneers of education and social service in the Punjab acquired such haloes.

My father held his generation of schoolboys as an example to us. This was not just a case of the nostalgia of each generation for its past, for his generation did work hard all through life. Education and opportunities were new and they fell on virgin soil, which blossomed soon into a meadow of a very industrious, able and conscientious professional class. The Punjabi Khatris had for generations been deprived of their right to administration; and now suddenly opportunities were thrown before them, anyone's to pick up. The Khatris, and soon the other castes, ran forward to grasp them. The Khannas, Kapurs, Chopras, Malhotras, Sahnis, Dhawans, Talwars, Puris, to mention only some among the Khatris: Batras and Kumars notably among the Aroras: soon they spread all over the Punjab government civil list, the medical service of the army—the first commissioned service open to Indians—and the professions of lawyers, barristers, doctors, scientists and professors. Many rose from the lowest ranks through sheer integrity, hard work and self-teaching. One of the earlier Indian deputy commissioners, nearly fifty years ago, had joined the revenue service forty years earlier as a satchel bearer. Many of them even left India and went across the forbidden black waters to the Mauritius Islands, Fiji, Malaya, Burma and East Africa, in search of greater responsibility and better opportunities. Many young munshis, as they taught English probationers Urdu and Punjabi and explained Punjabi life and customs to help them pass service examinations, were also teaching themselves, quickly and assiduously, till the pupils discovered the talent of their teachers and assisted them, sometimes to reach high posts.

After passing matriculation from Gujrat, father went to Lahore to join the Dayanand Anglo-Vedic College. Before finishing college he decided to compete for the entrance examination to the Roorkee Engineering College. This college had been started in 1844 for training of the Royal Engineers and was run by that corps. After the consolidation of the Punjab, the government began to take on a few British and Indian civilians for manning the newly created department of public works, with its branches of irrigation, and building and roads. This department expanded so rapidly with the growing network of irrigation canals and roads in the Punjab and western United Provinces that the demand for engineers soon necessitated reserving the whole college for training civil engineers.

The Thomason Engineering College at Roorkee had a succession of able teachers, and a stiff competitive examination for admission. The number of entrants was limited, and each one who passed was assured service. This made entrance to Roorkee a coveted prize. Father travelled to Roorkee without mentioning it to grand-uncle. He was anxious to make his way quickly, but he missed admission by one place. Putting aside his disappointment, he went up to the principal and asked if he could not squeeze in another student. The Englishman was somewhat taken aback by this simple country boy suggesting such an innovation, but to father's surprise he was at least not visibly annoyed, and asked him to come back the following day. Fortune favoured father, for the next day one of the boys decided against joining the college, and so there was a vacancy which fell to him. His uncle was very pleased and agreed to pay for the two years' course. It was a very expensive education for those days; it cost thirty rupees a month.

He sometimes spoke to us of his stay at Roorkee as a dream. The thought that in two years he might become an engineer–he had never in his life met one–in one of the coveted government services, with a fixed salary of an amount he would hardly know what to do with, spurred him to work as he had never worked before. The end of studies seemed near and the reward of a post within his grasp. It would also mean the end of his dependence. He would go back to Gujrat and to his village with an air of importance, the first engineer from his village and the second from Gujrat. It is difficult to imagine his elation, and I find it hard to compare with anything in my life. Perhaps my joining a British commercial firm marked among us something just as new and daring, though without the aura of government service.

In 1898 father qualified as a civil engineer and joined the irrigation department of the Punjab government. His uncle's pride was justifiably great. He had repaid the debt to his elder brother. His aunt felt that her anxious care was the factor most responsible for his success.

At the time my father began his career, the service rules, like the Indian caste system, were clearly defined, well understood and fully accepted. You accepted them as the natural order of things. There were three grades in service, virtually like the Hindu castes, because entry was preordained and determined by birth. There was a grade for the British-born, which was the seniormost; followed by a middle grade for the locally born British, pure or mixed; and a junior grade for Indians, irrespective of their caste. Between the English-born and the Indian-born British we were unable to make a distinction. They all looked the same, spoke the same language and seemed to live alike. The difference was too subtle for us to appreciate. It could only be inferred that those who were born in England belonged to superior families and received better education than their local kinsmen and therefore were better qualified for superior posts; but strangely enough, the locally born talked of 'home' with the same nostalgia.

My father's generation for two reasons accepted the position without any resentment. First, the initiative lay with the British officers, who were developing the country and the services, and it therefore seemed only right that as teachers and leaders they should enjoy a superior position and the privileges of gurus and mentors. We are used to giving our gurus and seniors respect. In the primary school my father went to, the boys swept the teacher's house, did the shopping, tended the cow, chopped wood and brought daily offerings of milk, curds, vegetables, grain and fruit. In fact, this is how in kind and service the teachers used to be paid, but even later, when school fees were given in cash, the custom of service and gifts continued for a long time. Even I took milk and curds to the master besides the English newspaper to which my father was one of the few in the town to subscribe. Thus, the British were not begrudged this privilege which they were entitled to by their special position. It was when the position gradually changed and they no longer were the teachers–when many of them were being trained by Indians–that their privileges began to be questioned. But that was to come later. When my father joined service the order was unquestioningly accepted. I wonder sometimes if the British during those first fifty years were so busy teaching and building that they did not look ahead to the time when their pupils would be mature enough to demand equality; or were they convinced that that stage was never going to be reached and the teaching would somehow continue for ever; a trust in perpetuity, where the ward would never become his own trustee. Actually the process took its natural course, jerkily but always upward. At each stage of transition there was a jerk, a delay and some frustration, but soon someone would jump the cataract and begin to swim steadily upstream towards the higher reaches of responsibility and power. My father having started low struggled hard till he reached the nirvana of his service, the cadre of the Imperial Service of Engineers.

All that he had endured in his early years–the dependent life of an orphan, the concentrated effort to equip himself for a profession, and the strain of reaching the upper rungs of his career – made father into a quiet, determined and taciturn man. He was conscientious and meticulous at work to the point of being a perfectionist. From the first month at Roorkee College when he sat at the drawing boards he maintained a spirit of never being satisfied with whatever he did, drawings, calculations or discharging obligations. He always felt that he could do still better. His only enjoyment in life was work, and I do not even know whether he really enjoyed working. Perhaps it was the only thing he knew how to do, and he did it well. But most of his colleagues that I knew were also like that; they lived and talked only about their work, though they envied the ability of their English colleagues to combine it with rest and play. Father, who never relaxed from work, explained it to us by saying that the Englishmen could afford to relax because if things went wrong they managed to explain it to each other, and took the attitude that things do sometimes go wrong. But when an Indian made a mistake the reaction, if an understanding one, was that the job perhaps was too difficult for him; 'after all they did not have the skill or the experience; one must be careful with giving responsibility too soon; perhaps one should have kept a closer eye'. Such quite well-meaning remarks hurt, even when there was no imputation of negligence. Being always on test like this made him, if possible, even more conscientious and punctilious. He thus worked and worked, and took his first holiday twenty-eight years after joining service. He had taken odd short spells of leave to attend funerals and weddings, but leaving work to rest and relax he did only once in the thirty-five years of his service. By then his career was assured and he was senior enough not to worry about others. So he took six months' leave, and he and I went trekking in Kashmir. We walked, waded and climbed, and he never spoke about work. We followed our great grand-uncle's footsteps and brought the family ledger at Matan up to date.

For years father was so busy at work that he never gave any thought to religion. Our home was not irreligious; we feared God and invoked His name, but there was no daily worship or ritual, or much visible influence of religion on our daily life. We were only conscious of our religion at festivals and fasts, weddings, namings or death; and then only in a mechanical sort of way. Sometimes my mother performed a kind of ceremony, as for instance on my recovery from chicken-pox, when some simple offerings were made to Durga, the goddess of small-pox. For big functions, requiring more complicated ceremonies, a brahmin was called in, who usually appeared to us almost as ignorant as ourselves.

There had never been much formal religion in our homes and villages anyway; invasions and the bigotry of the invader had erased much of it from the surface. Furthermore, my father and most others of his generation had been too absorbed in learning their professions. From a simple boy in a village he had become an engineer doing complicated trigonometric calculations–a transformation where religion had played no part. Through his school and college days and his early working life in the jungles he remained disinterested, but when he was first posted in a town both he and my mother came under the influence of the Arya Samaj. This reformist movement, started by Swami Dayanand Saraswati, had found a more receptive soil in the Punjab than in the home of the founder in Kathiawar, or even in progressive Bombay and Poona. To our new professional class it provided a western social reorientation combined with simple Vedic belief and ritual. Its opposition to orthodoxy and idol worship, and its revival of Vedic ritual in modern form, without temple and priest, made a direct appeal to the Punjabi intelligentsia. Actually two schools of thought had developed within the Arya Samaj; those who harked back to a purely Vedic education, known as the Gurukul party, and the others who wanted to combine the Vedic with the modern, and became known as the College party. The former founded an old monastic type of teaching institution in the Kangra hills, called Gurukul Kangri, with an emphasis on Sanskritic education. The Anglo-Vedic school made a wider appeal, and its focal points, the Dayanand Anglo-Vedic High School and the College by the same name in Lahore, commonly known as the D.A.V. School and the D.A.V. College, became the backbone of the progressive section of the Punjabi Hindu community. Its emphasis on modern education, its opposition to child marriage, and its sponsoring of widow remarriage were in line with the modern concepts in which my father had been trained. We began to profess this new creed and attend the mandir, which did not look like a temple, but more like a lecture hall with a pleasant open courtyard and a garden. Worship took place in the courtyard or in the open hall. There were no priests except visiting swamis who were modern, educated men. The prayer, sandhya, was Vedic, as were the hymns; and in the centre of the congregation a votive fire was lit with incense and sandalwood. The whole ceremony was simple and beautiful. Men, women, and children prayed together, and afterwards there was an informal sermon from a swami or a member of the congregation. We also did the sandhya twice a day at home, in the morning and evening. But this zeal did not last very long, and after some time my father began to lose interest even in the mild discipline of the Arya Samaj and did his sandhya irregularly, nor did he often go to the mandir, though in the house we continued to follow the Arya Samajist rites.

The Arya Samaj had a certain polarising effect on my father's already somewhat unconventional thinking. Even in his class he was ahead of his time. He set his face against many old customs, important and unimportant, and it was characteristic of our society that he was seldom censured for it; in fact, there was even some grudging admiration. When, for instance, he arranged the marriage of our cousin, his dead sister's daughter, with a boy from Bahawalpur, whose language and custom were as far removed from ours as to be almost non-Punjabi, it caused at first considerable consternation in the family, but at the wedding many realised that it was a very good match, and that was what really mattered. He had even allowed the boy to visit our home and meet the girl before the marriage. He was opposed to ostentation, to gold and jewellery, lavish spending on weddings and ceremonies; in fact, to all the non-productive expenditure in which our Hindu society commonly indulged. He was willing to be considered mean rather than to accept such, in his opinion, senseless obligations. In all this he was helped by our mother, though perhaps somewhat hesitatingly since she felt that on occasions he was callous in his beliefs. She thought it selfish of him to believe that everybody should move at his pace; others without the advantages of his education and position in the community could not, in fairness, be expected to ignore custom as he did.

A characteristic which also led him into difficulties was his flat refusal to secure jobs and favours for relations, who considered it quite natural to turn to him for help, and equally unnatural that he should withhold it. If he turned away his relations they could not very well turn to others who, after all, had their own obligations and demands to fulfil. This was a dilemma in which many of his generation were placed, the difficulty of fitting a new definition of integrity into the traditional pattern of duties towards the family and caste. Father used to envy his English colleagues who, being far away from home, had no relations demanding favours. He also attached much importance to the honesty of his service. The new administration in the Punjab had acquired a reputation for incorruptibility, at least at the level of its officers. At the lower levels the traditional graft continued, though in a subdued way, but in the higher ranks there was hardly anyone who was corrupt. But, as he explained, desisting from corruption was easy enough.

You were under no obligation to a stranger to do him a favour and accept his money. It was the importunities of the relations that were difficult to refuse, as when your widowed aunt came and sat at your doorstep and left her young son in your care to provide for. Once we had a cousin living with us for nearly two years, till even he got tired of the free support and went away in disgust.

As children we did not understand our father's problems, and we saw him as an austere, colourless person, without any relaxations or enjoyments that we could share, interested only in his work and our future. He continually exhorted us to work and looked upon play as an exercise which you needed at regular intervals in order to work even harder. He continually advocated simplicity in clothes, food and thought. Explaining to me the proverbs in Nesfield's English Grammar, he paraphrased the whole list in his own way of thinking. The one I remember particularly as being at variance with what our teacher had explained was 'wine in, wit out', which he carefully explained meant losing your wits as soon as a drop of wine went in. I protested that that is not what Nesfield could have meant because the English were known to us for their fondness of liquor. That nettled him, for although he held them in high regard for their many virtues, their conscientiousness, sense of responsibility, industry and integrity, he was inwardly sorry that they drank. He almost felt they let him down. He must have tackled one of them on the subject, and I think he must have been told that they did it only for the sake of their health, because soon afterwards a half-bottle of Hennessy brandy appeared in our house which he began to take in medicinal doses with hot water on winter evenings. It never became a habit, and after a while he gave it up, finding the taste too unpleasant and also, I suspect, because we began to ask questions.

There was no contradiction or ambivalence in his make-up; he was all of a piece and lived up to what he preached. His generation founded the new Punjabi middle class and added some modern values to the old Punjabi character, but what they lost in the process was the colour of my grand-uncle and his age.

My mother was a Vinayak Khatri, whose family came from a small town, Hadiabad, in Kapurthala State in East Punjab. It was rare in those days for someone to marry so far away, nearly two hundred miles, from home. When we asked mother about this unusual thing, she would only shrug her shoulders and quote the Punjabi saying, 'You go wherever your grain and water takes you.' She did not belong to the plains, for she was born and brought up in the mountains and lived there till she left to marry father. Her own father was a post-master who spent most of his working life in the hills of Kangra and Chamba. It was a delightful source of wonder to us that she had been familiar with mountains, forests and snow, things we had never seen. She would describe to us how snow fell, but we could not quite picture it. She must have found the early years of her life in the plains somewhat trying, but the canal post near Madhopur headworks, on the river Ravi, where she first joined father, was near the foothills and from there she could see snow peaks. Although it never snowed the water in the canal was always ice-cold.

She had the build and complexion of the hills: she was small, wiry and pale-skinned, and for years she spoke with the accent and diction of the hill Punjabi which, free from the influence of Urdu and Persian, was nearer to Sanskrit. She was brought up simply, but was given education in Hindi, which for those days was unusual for women. Her father had belonged to the orthodox Gurukul wing of the Arya Samaj and had sent her only brother to the Gurukul seminary in the Kangra hills. The education they gave was amazingly out of tune with the changing times, and he always remained very unworldly. Our mother was more practical; she was remarkably firm and determined, and could take care of herself in most circumstances.

Father must have tried in the early years of married life to expose mother to English influence. For a while he must even have persuaded her to wear English clothes, because in an old photograph of theirs we saw her incredibly dressed in a European blouse, long skirt and shoes, and with her head uncovered. Father's experiment could not have lasted long, or perhaps it went only as far as this photograph, because we could not remember seeing her in anything but Punjabi clothes. His attempts at modernising her eating habits made no headway at all. She belonged to the very strict school of vegetarians that would not even tolerate onions in cooking. Her food was consequently cooked separately from ours, and while she did not mind onions entering the kitchen, meat and fish had to be kept and prepared outside. On nights when we children wanted to snuggle into her bed and be kissed by her, we would share her food. She did not say no, but we knew she did not like us smelling of meat. I could tell the way she kissed that she found it distasteful.

She quite enjoyed meeting the wives of father's English colleagues, but often twitted him that they were not as rational as he made them out to be. They were as full of contradictions and conservative as we were. She admired them tremendously for their ability to bear separation from their children for the sake of their husbands. To put children to school in England, and be separated from them for three or four years at a time in order to be near their husbands struck her as a great sense of duty towards both children and husbands. When my brother, and later I, left for England for our higher studies, her eyes did not even look misty. I learned afterwards that when she returned from the station she went and lay in bed and sank into deep coma for many hours. This was a strange habit with her: she seldom complained or lost her temper, but when she could stand things no longer, she would quietly go to bed without anyone knowing it, and lie there in a faint, sometimes for several hours. We would go about the house in a normal way, and hours later she would slowly open her eyes, get up and go about her work as if nothing had happened. She did not like to be asked how she felt.

Mother had an uncanny sense of premonition of danger. This was something that never failed to intrigue us, for she was unerringly right about future events, especially deaths in the family. There were occasions when she told father that she must leave at once because someone was about to die. Father scoffed but she went, and she was right. Usually she did not share her premonitions with us, though sometimes we could tell from her restlessness that some bad news was on the way. She woke up one morning and said she knew that our youngest uncle, still in his thirties, recently married, and perfectly healthy as far as we knew, was going. We received news of his sudden death the same day.

After the short experiment at westernising her father must have left mother alone, but she kept pace with his development, though at her own distance and without letting go anything she cherished. Generally speaking, throughout the process of change, our women showed enough attachment to tradition to prevent the change from swamping old values. Our fathers changed rapidly, our mothers slowly, and between them my generation managed to learn the new without entirely forgetting the old.

CHAPTER THREE

AFTER JOINING the service, my father moved about the Punjab from one canal post to another. We lived in small canal colonies–at some headworks, a new construction project, or at operating posts along a canal. I was born in one of these colonies, at Bullokee, where a headworks was under construction to take a new canal out of the river Ravi. It was for those days a large project, designed and patiently built in brick and mortar without the aid of any plant and machinery. The whole barrage was made by hand, brick by brick, joined with hand-crushed brick mortar and lime. There were no trucks, earth movers or Euclid dumpers; only men and beasts. The animals used were always donkeys, who were more manœuvrable on the rough sites than bullock carts. The donkeys threaded their way through dumps of materials and construction work carrying their loads in two bags slung astride. Dams then were small but took many years to build. Bullokee was one of those small dams on which my father, as a young man of thirty-two, was posted. My recollection of Bullokee was solely a beautiful solid gold watch which he received as a gift commemorating the construction of the dam and the part he played. Father told us that on the day they opened the sluice gates to let the first water into the new canal, everyone from the chief engineer in charge of the project to the workmen received a gift. The watch had a white enamel dial with Roman figures in blue and finely shaped gold hands. On the inside of the gold cover at the back was an inscription which I still remember: 'Presented to Ram Das, Sub-Divisional Officer, by the King Emperor of India, for service on the construction of Bullokee Headworks.' It was considered too precious for everyday use, and for years it remained locked up till some burglars stole it. Of all the things we lost in the burglary, father tried hardest to trace this watch, but the police only discovered that the thieves had sold it for seven rupees. We offered to buy it back for much more, but it could not be traced, although ironically we got back some old clothes.

When the project was finished father was transferred down the new canal to a small colony near a village called Mangtanwala. Our nearest railway station was the famous Sikh Gurdwara of Nankana Sahib. We lived here till I was seven, and its memories have stayed with me for ever, so clearly etched that time has neither diminished nor effaced much. It was a lonely, flat, unbroken and dusty country, but as my childhood in these surroundings was happy and contented I have continued to love this kind of vast and open countryside. Dust and flatness have never depressed me. I love the treeless west Punjab country, with its far horizons, as much as the mountains, in whose distant acquaintance I later lived in Gujrat. Small towns like Gujrat I do not mind, but life in big cities I have never cared for. And yet, with this aversion I have had to live the last many years in Bombay, and before that in Manchester. I suppose with no choice in the matter, I became attached to them both, but my heart is still in places like Mangtanwala.

Our colony was half a mile away from the canal bank. A road led from a point where a fall had been built in the canal to allow for the gradient in the land. Its rushing noise could be heard on still evenings from quite far. It was a big canal, some two hundred and fifty feet wide, and we were not allowed to go into the water, but our uncle, whenever he came home on holidays from his college in Lahore, used to organise swimming parties; he and his friends sometimes gave us a dip in the grey swirling waters under the fall. Occasionally the man who lived in a brick cabin at the fall and took readings of the canal caught a fish and sent it to our house. This was a rare treat which somehow always coincided with the visits of our young uncle, who would himself clean and fry the fish for our evening meal. On those days we were not allowed to drink milk or eat any milk preparation, for it was believed that mixing milk and fish caused leprosy.

The colony was built in a square. On the front, where the road from the canal joined it, there were three bungalows, the first a rest house for visiting officers, the second the residence of the executive engineer under whom my father worked, and the third our home, which stood in complete contrast to the other two houses. The first two were built in the style of dak bungalows of the late nineteenth century, red baked-brick structures with wide verandahs and flat roofs in which old steel rails were used as rafters, with brick paved ceilings in arches. Our bungalow, the oldest of the three, was unusual as it belonged to the earliest style of British bungalows in the north. Its high walls were made of sun-baked mud and straw bricks, and lime-washed. It had gables and a sloping roof covered with a very thick straw thatch. The single-storied thatched cottages I occasionally saw in England always reminded me of our old bungalow.

Behind the row of bungalows were the office buildings, a dispensary, staff quarters, workshop and telegraph office on one side, and fruit and vegetable gardens on the other. The colony was well planted with a variety of trees and flowering shrubs, both local and exotic. There were mangoes, rosewood, flame of the forest, coral, Indian laburnum, pipal and avenues of eucalyptus. Pleasant and shady, trimly maintained, like all other canal colonies and bungalows it bore the stamp of successive English officers. Having its own water channel from the canal it was well watered and green, and during the hot months an oasis in the dry parched country around. The drinking water we drew from our own wells. There were no shops, and one had to go to the village of Mangtanwala a mile away for simple necessities, while for other shopping our nearest place was Nankana Sahib, and the nearest big town Lahore.

As the canal system was first started and for many years run by officers of the Corps of Indian Engineers, its organisation was based on military lines. Our colony was the Headquarters of a division which extended about fifty miles on either side along the main canal and included its lateral distribution channels which carried the water to the fields. The whole division was connected by its own telegraph, and later by a telephone system as well, which also connected us with our neighbouring divisions. In our own division there were two more sub-divisional officers like father, but they were posted away and lived in their own colonies, smaller but set up like ours.

Father was responsible for operating and maintaining his part of the canal. After a certain amount of water had been received, he had to ensure its flow with the minimum of losses. From the main canal smaller channels, and from them still smaller channels took the water into the fields. At the distribution points men were posted to let out water at fixed intervals. The farmer waited at the appointed hour, day or night, to receive the water in his field, and for the whole of his turn he stood guard to make sure that his neighbours did not divert the water to their own land too soon. He stood there with the spade over his shoulder ready to strike. Water was his life blood, and quarrels over it often led to murder, almost as commonly as quarrels over women. A Punjabi proverb attributed all troubles in life, feuds and murder, to zamin, zan, zewar –land, women, gold.

All along the canal men were also posted at such key points as at falls in the canals and at the junctions where the smaller channels left the main line. They were on round-the-clock duty to take readings every few hours which they telegraphed to father's office. All day long and till late in the evening, and sometimes even in the middle of the night, these telegrams would keep coming in, but the calm way in which father read them and put them aside intrigued us. But sometimes he would leave his meal to go into his office room and send for a clerk or an overseer to telegraph a message to some operating point. In an emergency he would go away himself. Run on a strict regimen of constant communication and speedy action, our colony was on duty the whole time and always in a state of alert.

Occasionally there was an alarm, as when there was a breach in the canal bank, and then it was truly like a battle. A canal would break its bank and water rush into the fields, flood the country, and keep on advancing. The farmers around the breach were in a panic and would run with their cattle to dry ground. Their standing crops might be ruined; land waiting for the next crop or land just sown might be flooded; mud huts might collapse and altogether much loss could result. If the flood was serious, in this flat country it might cause water-logging for a whole season. The farmers at a distance on the other hand might benefit by the unexpected supply of water, provided it was timely, and breaches in the canals were therefore sometimes suspect.

S.O.S. messages were telegraphed to the divisional headquarters and to the circle superintending engineer. Aid was rushed from all directions; farmers from the neighbourhood were pressed into emergency service; and large numbers of men fought ceaselessly to fill the breach. Thousands of sandbags, brushwood and earth were dumped into the breach to stem the rushing water. It sometimes took days to patch a breach. In the meantime the flow of water in the canal would have been closed, but if the breach was at a long distance from the head it would take some days before the flow was exhausted.

A canal breach was something to talk about for a long time in a colony, but while the fight was on there was hectic activity at the base. Men and material were rushing out, and the base was denuded of all staff except the telegraphist and an odd clerk. All operating staff, the overseers, sub-overseers, mates, workshop men, labourers, in fact all able-bodied men would be rushed to the spot. Couriers dashed backward and forward from the temporary base at the breach to the headquarters carrying messages for the telegraphist to relay upward, and to carry instructions received from the circle officers to the breach base.

Slowly the news would begin to arrive that the men were getting the upper hand and the gap was closing. Until then the men at the breach had been too busy to think of sleep or food—just eating scratch meals of dal and chappaties from the field kitchen. Now the families would despatch some food from home, and the men had their first decent meal. When the breach was filled our father would arrive back slumped half-asleep in the saddle, worn out, unshaven and caked with mud. His return was the sign that the crisis was over, but there was still plenty of work ahead. Reports had to be made and arrangements put in hand for the permanent work to restore the water flow.

Father was a big-set man of strong constitution that took seemingly unlimited strain. Over forty years later, when he was an old man of eighty, paralysed by a stroke, I watched him once shuffling from his bedroom to the bathroom, holding the wall as he moved across a distance of ten feet in almost as many minutes. We never helped him till the end, because independent movement, however slow, kept him going and retained his pride. On this occasion my mind flashed back to seeing him in a state of virile fatigue, and I reminded him of it. I said, 'It took you ten minutes to walk ten feet; what was the longest you ever rode?' The courageous man that he was, he brightened at the question and said he was once in the saddle for twenty-four hours and must have ridden well over a hundred miles. And instead of rueing his fate, he avidly began to describe the occasion.

Maintenance work on the canal went on the whole time. There were bridges, falls, breakwaters and masonry work to be looked after, banks to be trimmed and their berms repaired, roads on the sides to be kept serviceable, and many other jobs for the proper care of the canals. There was always some new construction work and remodelling, surveying and designing; and whenever the canals were dry the work that could not be done otherwise had to be quickly finished before the flow began again.

The colony was self-contained and provided all its own services. We had our own doctor, and father had also engaged a schoolmaster. On festival days there was much excitement, especially at Diwali when everyone lit lamps at night, and at Besakhi, the end of harvest festival when we all put on new bright clothes and went to the canal bank. Sometimes there was a wedding in the colony, and then there was great festivity. The girl's father would ask permission to hold the wedding there because it was cheaper than going home. Everyone helped by lending utensils, cots, bedding and by serving the guests. The wedding party would arrive from Nankana Sahib railway station in tongas and on horses, with its own brass band. A gas-lamp at night created a brightness we had never seen before. At births, illnesses, occasionally deaths, the colony doctor came into prominence. He was usually a simple man who continued to apply with diminishing skill whatever he had learned many years ago. Some doctors were bold enough to experiment, but most of them relied on an array of ten bottles, numbered serially, which were dispensed according to the diagnosis, and sometimes tried in turn.

For us the most exciting place in the colony was the telegraph office with its gadgets and instruments. We were mystified by the morse code which conveyed messages many miles away and brought the reply back instantaneously. The decoding of the tick-ticking by the 'tar babu', the telegraph clerk, never failed to thrill us. Some years later when the telephone arrived and we could hear a squeaky voice from points many miles away, our excitement knew no bounds. Another place of interest was the guard-house where an iron chest, called the treasury, was kept. The guards were under the command of a barquandaz, 'the one who wields lightning', as the artillery men were then called. Our guards carried swords which had never been used to anyone's knowledge. The barquandaz was a very distinguished looking old man with a beard dyed red and a well tied turban from which hung a gold embroidered flat tassel. He spoke to us with clipped dignity, and his flattering address of huzoor and janab always made us giggle.

In front of the guard-house was a wooden tripod with a flat gong on which the guard on duty beat the hour melodiously. At night it gave a feeling of security to the whole camp to know that the guard was on watch. There were also two chowkidars who did the rounds. To announce their presence, both to those sleeping in the camp and to possible intruders, they used to utter some blood curdling yells. A really good night watchman had to have a powerful voice that could strike terror in a thief. He always developed his own style of announcing his presence every quarter hour or so. One of our best chowkidars, a one-eyed puny bhayya from the U.P., though known for his unprepossessing physique and presence, was yet a man transformed at night. Few intruders, even if they knew him well in the day, would dare to cross his path at night for fear that the magic of his nocturnal voice might have given him some demonaic strength unsuspected by day. Every quarter hour he would begin by clearing his throat in a stentorian manner, then hold the phlegm, of which he could produce prodigious quantities, for several minutes and finally spit it out with an ear-splitting noise. This was enough to scare most strangers. He would then proclaim loudly in a voice that could be heard in the village a mile away, that those who were sleeping should continue to sleep; others beware!–'sone walo sote raho, baqi khabardar'. It was a testimony to the day's toil that everyone did continue to sleep. His imprecations were also a clear warning to the intruder that he was directly taken note of as not being asleep. After that Lachhman would make a suitable pause to let his warning sink in, and then suddenly hell was let loose. He yelled a long blood-chilling ha, ha, ha, like a pack of howling hyenas. This set all the pariah dogs as far away as Mangtanwala barking and sent the neighbouring jackals in full retreat. But the colony continued to sleep. Once we had a burglary, and in the morning we found Lachhman gagged and tied. He never lived down the indignity and eventually resigned.

There was much bustle when the superintending engineer arrived in camp with his staff of clerks, orderlies, guards, horses and camels. For days ahead the colony was tidied up and made spick and span. While he stayed in the rest house, tents would be put up for his large staff. His orderlies and guards looked resplendent. To add to all the excitement, the superintending engineers in those days were always British, and in an out of the way place like ours theirs were the only English faces we ever saw. Looking back, it is interesting to think that here in a large government colony of a technical nature, in a country ruled by the British, as far back as before the First World War, one seldom saw any Englishmen. The executive engineer in charge of our division, his three subdivisional officers and the entire technical staff were already Indian.

We children led a happy existence. There was no school, and we had only a private teacher who taught us under a tree or in the sun, according to the weather, with none of the irksome discipline of a regular school. There was plenty of time to play and a lot of space to play in. Our games had always something to do with the work of our fathers. One of us would be the horse, with a string round the shoulders and under the arms, the others would be the officers and overseers, and we would go on inspection tours. An English officer had to speak with accented Hindustani, with the tongue rolled in the mouth, and the others had to call him sahib the whole time.

We also greatly looked forward to the visits from relatives, especially our young uncles, who being brought up by our father used to spend their school and college holidays with us. Life would then be very exciting. They would organise sports and games and in the evenings tell us tales of Lahore, a strange and fabulous city where there were motor-cars, shops, many-storied buildings and rare fruits and sweets.

A few times in a year we accompanied father on tour. This was the greatest event of all. The night before, a string of camels would arrive at the bungalow to load the baggage, which meant practically half the household. First the office desk would be dismantled, and in the drawers of the two cupboards of the desk were carefully packed files, stationery, red and black inkpots, drawing instruments, pens, pencils, diaries and paper-weights. The cupboards would be slung over a camel and the desk-board tied on top. On the other camels were loaded the trunks, bed rolls, crates containing cooking utensils, crockery and glass, foodstuff and luggage of the staff. There was much commotion in loading the camels as each animal was made to sit down to strap the baggage. Willing and patient as camels are, they grumble a great deal when they are made to sit or get up, and keep up a constant barrage of protesting noises. When the caravan was ready, the barquandaz with his sword in scabbard would stand in front of the first camel, which had a bell and a lantern hanging from its neck, and at a signal from him the train started, accompanied by the guards and followed by the servants and father's riding horse. The first camel as the flagship carried the khazana, the chest with money, which was to be disbursed in payments and salaries. With the solitary swaying light and the tinkling of the bell, the camelcade travelled through the silent night and arrived at its destination in the early hours of the morning. Some sleepy dak bungalow would suddenly come to life as the camp was set up.

We would wake very early the next morning to savour the excitement of our departure to the full, and hope that no last-minute telegram would delay the start. We would run to the stables and watch the horse harnessed and hitched to the tonga, a two-wheeled trap with a seat in front and a seat at the back on which people sat with their backs to each other. Our father, the syce, a servant, we brothers and father's black-japanned despatch-case would set off after breakfast to the first dak bungalow ten or twelve miles away. We drove along the canal, on the road built on one of its banks. On the canal side there was a protective berm while on the other side the bank sloped steeply outwards and was flanked by a regular row of shisam trees. The surface of the road was kutcha but well dried and smooth and the tonga sped along, but never for very long. There were always interruptions on the way. There would be work going on which father had to inspect; the overseers met him on the way to discuss their work; the records of the check posts had to be examined. These to us were dull delays; but more interesting were the supplicants on the way. Farmers would hear that the engineer was passing their way, and individuals, groups, sometimes large parties of them, would wait for him. Their requests were usually of two kinds, either to increase the size of the water outlet, or a remission of irrigation revenue because the crop had been poor. Sometimes they would come with personal complaints and grievances, which they felt any government officer ought to be able to redress.

The interesting thing about these delegations was their style. A group of stalwart Muslim or Sikh farmers, bearded, with large loosely tied turbans, long home-spun shirts, brightly coloured tehmads wrapped round their legs, and sturdy Punjabi shoes with turned-up leather spurs, would move forward, bow and stand with old-fashioned courtesy of hands folded over their stomachs. Slowly their spokesman would begin reciting the grievance or the request in old-fashioned Punjabi, embroidering it with some very flattering remarks mixed with great hopes and choice blessings. 'Janab,' he always began, 'huzoor, we are in great distress. Only you, the generous supporter of the poor can help us.' And so he would continue, considering it unmannerly to come to the point too soon. At suitable moments an elder in the group would prompt him, sometimes by underlining a point, at other times by politely disagreeing with him. The latter was a practical gambit. 'No,' the elder might say, 'not at all, huzoor will understand the thing himself; he is so wise and perspicacious that now that he knows our predicament he will insist in his wisdom in giving us a water outlet twice the present size and not one and half times that we ignorant jats are asking for.'

These peasants were men of dignity and charm, shrewdness and much cunning, but centuries of oppression had taught them to be self-effacing. That is why they always began with professions of great distress which made the task of an officer somewhat difficult. He never knew how much to discount, and some discounting was essential if one were to be fair to others. A curious weakness with them was their pride, usually tinged with boastfulness. A cousin told me a story which is an amusing illustration of this pride. As a young magistrate visiting a village he was approached by two men with a dispute about a buffalo. One of them claimed that he had left the buffalo with the other when he had gone away, but now that he had returned and demanded it back the other man refused to give it. My cousin tried in such cases to bring about a settlement instead of taking official cognisance which would lead to a long-drawn suit. He asked if they were interested in a peaceful settlement, or preferred to fight it out, in which case he had to demand their presence at his court in town which they would have to attend several times.

The prospect of travelling to town for several hearings and engaging pleaders had a chastening effect upon both; but, said the defendant, while he admitted that the buffalo had been left behind with him–in fact he had never denied it–the animal had been in a wretched condition at the time; and yet look at it now! He had fed it and looked after it like his own beasts so that today it was one of the best buffaloes in the village. Had the original owner continued to keep it, the buffalo would have died long ago. He rightly refused to return the beast, at least not until he had been paid for all he had spent on it, both in care and money. He would be reasonable and buy the buffalo at the price the animal was worth at the time he took it over. The argument now resolved into deciding a suitable price.

The original owner naturally started with a price which the present custodian thought outrageous, and one he could never pay. He simply did not have the two hundred rupees that the owner asked, and the buffalo was not even worth half that sum anyway. The owner was adamant about the price and refused to believe that the other could not afford to pay two hundred rupees. He informed my cousin that the other men had just taken his groundnut harvest to the market and sold it for three hundred rupees. How could he then deny that he had not enough money? This apparently went straight home. This farmer was one of the first in his village to grow groundnut, and he was very proud of his yield, which was well above what the agriculture department people had told him to expect. That he should be told before the magistrate, and in full hearing of the village, that he had only been able to get three hundred rupees, when in fact he had got nearly twice as much, was an insult he could not bear. 'Huzoor,' he shouted, 'this man is a liar. Mine was no mean little crop like his; I grow groundnuts, not grams. I harvested twice as much from my land as this liar, and I cashed not three hundred rupees but six hundred. Huzoor, here is this liar's full price for the buffalo; here is two hundred rupees. I will not have my groundnut crop run down by anyone.' And the slighted groundnut grower insisted on paying the full amount because his farming pride was deeply hurt.

These West Punjab farmers could also be very violent, and the canal officers had to handle them carefully. Water to them was life. In a dry country with scanty rainfall, irrigation canals had created some of the best farming land out of desert and scrub. Rain came from above as God willed it, in plenty or otherwise, and nobody could stand face to face with God and demand adequate rain, but one could go up to a canal officer and demand water; all he had to do was to enlarge the outlet. And so the eternal demand for more water went on.

In three or four hours we would reach the bungalow, having covered only ten miles. In the bungalow, which had lain deserted since the last visit, there was much activity. Our camel caravan had arrived several hours earlier and camp life had begun its routine. The house was open and ready to receive us. Father's office looked exactly like at home; the bedrooms were ready; in the dining-room the next meal was waiting to be served; the bathrooms had jugs and tubs of cool water drawn from the well; there were flowers in all rooms and a large basket of fruits and vegetables from the garden to show the skill of the mali. Outside, the staff, clerks, peons and guards were installed in their quarters, and life in the camp hummed with activity. To us it added to the excitement that everything revolved round the centre of authority that was our father.

If it was summer, we would feel drowsy and after lunch go to sleep. Somehow the lunch, cooked by the same man who cooked everyday at home, and perhaps not so well in camp, tasted so much better. In the afternoon, while father worked in his office and saw an interminable string of people, we nosed about the camp or went swimming in the channels, which were just deep enough for us. We would dive and play in the muddy water, while the village children watched us with curiosity. Soon they would throw off their clothes and take running dives in the Punjabi fashion, folding their knees in the air. They were born swimmers and divers.

Father's day began early next morning. In camp in the summer he was up before five and out on inspection before six. He would go in the tonga or ride his horse, visiting the spots where farmers had complained and petitioned. He returned at eight or nine and did office work till one o'clock. After a meal and rest he worked again in his office from four till seven. He would then go for a walk or visit another site. After dinner he worked again for an hour or two. When the gong struck ten and the chowkidar began his rounds the camp turned off the lights and went to sleep. On summer nights we slept on the high terrace where lying in bed you had everything below you and only the sky above. You did not see the trees or buildings but looked up into the vast dome of the sky, velvety black on moonless nights, studded with uncountable bright points of scintillating light. The whole country stretched around like a flat black saucer, featureless and immense. Its silence was broken in the early night by distant voices from the neighbouring village, an occasional barking of a dog. The continuous sound of the crickets, of the water in the canal rushing down the fall, hastening to its destination of thirsty fields, all merged into the silence of the night. The sound of cascading water in this flat dry country was a music born with the canals.

CHAPTER FOUR

THE FARMER boys among whom I grew up were a remarkable lot, well made, self-confident and fearless. They would jump from trees, dive into the canal from high overhanging branches, ride horses bareback, drive a herd of buffaloes cursing and swearing like grown-ups, and try to tie their turbans like their fathers. They grew on a simple diet of milk, curds and ghee; wheat and maize chappatis; cooked and raw simple vegetables; gur and fresh cane. It was healthy though unvaried. During the dry season, when there were no vegetables, the farmers would have just curd, butter, salt and bread for lunch, bread and dal for dinner; and last night's bread with butter and churned curds for breakfast.

When the boys grew up some of them went into the army, others stayed on the land, while very few went to towns. Their childhood was short as they were put to work at the age of three or four, even if it was only taking a horse to water or grazing the cattle. In the evenings they played gulli danda with a stick and a bail sharpened at the ends, or kaodi. In this game two teams were ranged against each other across a line. A boy from one side would run into the other side calling kaodi, kaodi in one breath. The opponents would try to tackle the runner as he pranced about trying to touch someone. If he managed to return to his own side of the line without losing breath, any that he had touched were out, but if the other side made a successful tackle he would be pinned down till he lost his breath, and then he was out. Among other exercises a favourable pastime was massaging and wrestling.

As small boys they sometimes played with girls, mostly hopping and running, but soon they became self-conscious and stopped mixing, and if a soft boy wanted to continue to play, the girls would peck him away with their sharp tongues and with slaps. While the boys were confidently growing into men, the girls were cockily developing into self-assured Punjabi women. There was no purda and growing girls went about freely, but as past playmates met at the well they would be seized by shyness, conscious of the change in each other. The girl he had fought and whose pigtail he had pulled had acquired new contours of rounded softness. She had lost her level, cheeky gaze and now looked on the ground or aside at her girl friends, upon which they would all burst into a titter. The boy whose face she had scratched and clawed now looked hard and angular, his voice had become husky. He seemed anxious to help her draw water when she could pull the bucket as well as he. At other times there would be bantering between boys and girls, and as long as the whole crowd joined no notice was taken, but as soon as a boy and a girl exchanged glances which showed the slightest signs of individual interest, someone would immediately warn the parents, who took it as a sign that it was time to think of arranging her marriage. 'Youth has come to your girl,' some neighbour would tell a mother; 'it is time you "had her asked" by a good family.' Engagement is charmingly known as 'being asked', mangna. Marriage would follow within a year, usually after the next winter harvest when the wheat was in.

As soon as the girl had been asked boys stopped looking at her. She acquired a new status in her family and especially among her girl friends who would talk to her about the future when out fetching water. She would listen but never join in the conversation, for that would be immodest. If the boy was from the same village she would know him; if he was from another village she might not even know what he looked like. Her friends would tantalise her by sometimes painting the picture of an ogre and sometimes of a prince. She was innocent enough to accept both and be frightened by one and thrilled by the other. At times she would cry at the uncertain prospect before her and the parting from her family and friends when she would have to go and live in another village. The girls would try and console her. 'Don't worry, he is tall, taut and handsome; he will come riding on a horse, with a high plume in his turban. He will seat you behind him, and as soon as you have put your arms around him he will spur his horse and gallop away. We know you will be crying, but you will soon forget your tears and all of us. A few days later he will bring you back but you will not be the same; he will not bring back the girl he took. And you will no longer play with us or tell us what happened to you. And then you will return only occasionally, till one day you will come big and heavy, waiting to fill the apron of your shirt.' 'Stop it, you immodest girls, have you no shame?' would protest the betrothed girl, hot with embarrassment but yet excited. She would say protestingly, 'How do you know all this; you should not be thinking of these things; you are telling lies.'

In this bantering talk were woven their own day-dreams, longings and fears. Their playmate has been asked for; their turn cannot be far behind. Deeply attached to their mothers, the girls have been taught from a very young age that parting is inevitable. The mothers have referred to it in anger, admonition and gentleness. Each time the girl made a mistake, burnt the food or dropped a stitch, the mother would say, 'What are they going to say–is this how I taught you.' From mother and father it is always 'they'. They, who will come to take you away one day. They, to whom you belong. They, to whom we must turn you over, well endowed and well trained. And now, with the betrothal, 'They' have asked for her and she has been promised. From now on she is 'Theirs'. She is already part of another family. If anyone insults her, 'they' will avenge it, arriving with sticks and spears. And there may even be murder if the insult is great and the family proud. Her own people would join in the revenge, if they had not already taken it themselves. If the boy's family came to suspect that the girl's parents had not taken enough care to guard her modesty, or if there was the smallest suspicion that the girl was immodest herself, the betrothal would immediately be broken off. Such girls brought shame upon their families. It was best to return the shagan, the gifts received at the engagement ceremony.

Illicit love between the unmarried was rare, and if it happened the only recourse for the boy and girl was to elope. This was a risky business for they would soon be missed and chased on horses. It was difficult for this flat, featureless country to hide a runaway couple. The girl would be dragged back home 'by the hair' which, to teach her a lesson, in the old days was cut off and her face blackened. Irate father and brothers might even kill her. Chances of pre-marital love were also made small by the early marriages.

Virginity was sacred, and girls were married before there was much chance of their losing it. Illicit love was more common between married men and women or married women and unmarried young men, and the rendezvous usually the tall millet or sugar cane fields. Such affairs were few but not so rare, and a fruitful cause of crime. The husband would go into a towering rage, pick up his axe or spade and rush out to seek the man and cut him down on the spot. He might also kill his wife if she confessed the affair and seemed brazen about it.

There were sometimes rapes and abductions, but mostly with the woman's consent or connivance. It usually became known as rape if they were caught, and abduction if she changed her mind after eloping. When in love, it was not uncommon for a woman to poison her husband. The country abounded in poison-lore, and with the help of some old woman, a married girl would poison her husband to be free to marry her lover. At other times the lover might murder the husband. In this fertile, otherwise peaceful canal country the passionate nature of a virile farming stock led to love intrigues and murders, poisoning and witchcraft.

The country like its people had its varying moods. It quivered under the blazing heat of summer, when temperature in the day could hit one hundred and twenty-five in the sun, and in the winter at nights a white blanket of hoar frost covered the ground and temperature dropped sometimes to the twenties. A change in temperature over a range of a hundred degrees made both farming and farmers hard. After the bitter cold of winter nights and the many wet days, when a piercing wind blew from the Himalayas, spring came gentle and balmy, with the first touch of warmth, which gradually rose to the crescendo of dry searing summer when man and beast panted breathlessly for the relief that the rainy season would bring. After the rains came the freshness of autumn containing the first touch of winter, crisp in the morning and chill in the evenings. Our Punjab country had five seasons: winter, spring, summer, rains and autumn.

Spring harvest was the climax to the farmers' toil and hopes.

For days whole families worked out in the fields harvesting, threshing, winnowing and bringing in the corn. Women, tall and slim, would stand on low wooden stools, erect like taut bows with their breasts pointing upward, their arms stretched high above their heads holding flat reed trays. Like the opening movement of a dance, when from stationary feet a movement would shiver upward and end in the finger-tips, these women would gently tilt the trays with a quivering movement into the wind and shake them like bells. The wind would sweep the chaff while the grain fell into a heap below. The wind outlined their supple bodies as it swept their clothes back. Few sights are more graceful than women winnowing, except perhaps women walking from the wells with pitchers of water on their head. They walked along narrow banks of twisting and turning ditches and channels, talking, laughing, gesticulating and occasionally stopping to pick out a thorn from the foot. Their bodies swayed in a rhythm, arms swung freely, but the pitchers filled to the brim never lost a drop. Another typical sight, one of greater interest to the menfolk, was the women walking at noon to the fields carrying victuals. They carried flat reed baskets on their heads with thick oven-baked unleavened bread wrapped in a napkin and some cooked vegetables. On the basket rested a small pitcher full of lassi, buttermilk. Tired and hungry, the man kept looking towards the village till he caught sight of his wife. From afar he would recognise her and keep turning his head to look at her. He stopped work when she came near and walked to his well under a tree, leading the bullocks in front. He watered them and spread some straw before them and after a wash himself sat down to eat his meal. She sat in front of her man and helped him to the food, but never ate herself; she always ate alone when she returned home. He ate silently while she talked about the morning's happenings, the children, the neighbours, in restful, small talk. After she had seen him eat his fill she collected the food left over and started to walk back. There was no farewell but a simple, 'Achha main chalni han–right, I am going.' The farmer eating under a tree, his wife sitting beside him and a baby lying on the ground was one of the first stories we read in our Urdu textbook.

When the harvest was over and the grain was in, there was leisure. In the canal lands the crop was usually good, because the canal water, unlike rain, seldom failed. And now it was time to think of chores, digging ditches and repairing bunds, a well or the house, buying new bullocks or a horse, marrying a daughter. But first there was the Besakhi festival.

Besakhi was a secular festival, the only one of its kind in which Hindus, Muslims and Sikhs all participated alike. Though celebrated both by town and country, it was essentially a farmers' festival, a kind of thanksgiving, but of a bacchanalian kind; an orgiastic feast to relax the tensions of months of hard work at the rabi, the main crop of the year. It was held on a river bank to which families trekked on foot, on horse, in bullock carts and in tongas. The men were dressed in new clothes and brightly dyed turbans; the women in new salwar kameezes, and dupattas as brightly dyed as the men's turbans; the boys dressed like their fathers and the girls like their mothers, but the very little boys had special clothes. I can remember exactly how I was dressed one Besakhi. A pill-box red velvet cap with gold embroidery, a brightly striped shirt, new white pyjamas, cut out at the bottom and in front to save my mother the trouble of carrying spares, and embroidered red leather Punjabi shoes, which being new hurt the whole time. I do not know how proud my mother felt but I certainly was really happy.

The farmers went about in groups. Some of them were drunk, others pretended to be, or, as they said in Punjabi, had just wetted their whiskers with it. They danced the bhangra to the rhythm of a double flute, and a wooden rat fixed to a stick which went up and down the stick as it was pulled by a cord, making a clacking sound. The rat and the double flute were the only instruments beside a drum, but the jats made up for that with a great deal of vigour and vitality as they danced in a circle. The tune was a long simple descending recitative melody which was picked up at the end by a shout and then went on again. Their movements were curiously feminine, in fact, hermaphrodite. They would start by holding both arms stretched high above their head, not unlike the graceful movement of women winnowing, and dance backward and forward. The left hand then held the loosely tied tehmad round their legs, while the right arm was held above with the hand drooping down gracefully, and first one foot was put forward and then the other. They danced like that to a low melody on the flute, almost softly, with a lithe and sinuous grace; but suddenly the flute lifted up to a high note and with a yell their bodies burst into a masculine, powerful whirling dance. Danced by strong bearded men, Sikhs or Muslims, it was a curious sight, at first ludicrous but soon beautiful. The ludicrous touch was deliberate, and the name bhangra has come to mean merriment with a lot of noise and chaos.

Many years later bhangra was adopted as one of the folk dances at the Republic Day celebrations in New Delhi, and a team of Patiala Sikhs toured the country. Although many other dances had far greater artistic value, it proved the most popular item. I saw them in a Bombay drawing-room, a tall, handsome lot, their beards tightly tied and their clothes colourful. The sight of these men starting with the feminine opening movements of bhangra was curious. I was looking at the faces of the people to see their reactions, and noticed with interest that while the women soon came under the spell of the dance the men were less impressed. The gentle opening followed by the triumphant, powerfully suggestive yells, seemed to fascinate the women. That these tall sinuous men could be as soft one minute and as strong the next seemed to stimulate them, as indeed is the whole purpose of the dance.

The sandy bank of the river was used as a fair ground. Hundreds of shops made of bamboo and gunny bags were erected. The shops sold a variety of goods but commonest were the booths with highly coloured sweetmeats and drinks. After a ceremonial dip in the river we had a picnic meal and then set out to enjoy the fair and spend our money. The village women could not be torn away from the general merchandise shops which attracted them with an assortment of colourful glass bangles, bead necklaces, mirrors and combs, kohl, highly perfumed hair oils, and such other luxuries that they could not buy in the village shops. The children were thrilled by the wooden hand-painted toy birds, animals and carts. The mechanical Japanese toys had not yet arrived. The villagers wandered about, gaping at the sophistication of the town shops, while the shopkeepers leered at them and tried to pull them in.

There were numerous other attractions: wooden giant wheels, merry-go-rounds, acrobats, conjurors, animal tamers with bears, monkeys, snakes and mongoose, and medicine men. The latter applied their skill with amazing boldness. A dentist would virtually hypnotise a group and then proceed to pull out perfectly healthy teeth, quite painlessly, of one person after another. The proof of his skill was the painless extraction, whether needed or not; no one questioned the necessity but everyone admired the way he did it. An optician would fit old men with second-hand glasses, testing their sight by the simple process of trying two or three pairs and then asking with which of them they saw best. An occulist cured all eye troubles with some drops whose great merit was their fierce stinging action. For minutes the victim would contort his face in pain and press his eyes, while all the by-standers watched the effect of the drops. When the pain gradually disappeared and the man at last opened his eyes he was so happy to see daylight again, having fully expected the painful darkness to stay for ever, that he shouted happily that he had never seen so well before. There were a variety of one-pill-or-powder healers who convinced everyone who stopped to listen that he was positively ill. One farmer will admit to backache and dizziness when he stands up after digging a ditch; another is caught with the disease of urinating whenever he excretes. At this revelation the doctor will challenge them all to deny that they suffer from the same complaint, for he can tell from their faces; and they all nod assent. Another quack who specialises in women's diseases will not be perturbed by the fact that he has only men in his audience. It is easy enough to convince them that their women suffer silently.

Astrologers and amulet sellers also had their market, but the weirdest of all these benefactors displayed a revolting array of dead iguanas, small lizards, baby crocodiles, snakes, animal skulls, all pickled in a trayful of oil, out of which he dispensed in small bottles for rubbing on rheumatic joints, for general massage, or as aphrodisiac.

The favourable spot for men at the fair was the wrestling pit, where anyone could compete, though the greatest interest was aroused by the professional bouts. There were games, kaodi and gripping the wrist; gatka, where one man would fight several opponents with short sticks; and then there were horse races where simple jats raced on a variety of horses and ponies, yelling and shouting and waving their arms, with more enthusiasm than speed.

Troubadours and bards sang and recited ballads and legends; professional entertainers specialised in parody, mimicry and farce. On the singing and nautch girls men showered coins whenever they rendered a particularly touching verse or a suggestive dance movement in a confusion of tinkling ankle bells. When the girls cast longing glances or flicked them with their long silk handkerchiefs, the farmers wished that they had not brought their wives, who were busy shopping somewhere but would soon come to drag them away.

As the spring afternoon paled, tired, hot and dusty families began trekking back to their villages. The bullocks groaned and snorted as they pulled the heavy creaking carts over the sandy river bed. While the crops were ripening, and during harvest, the bullocks had little work to do, except to pull the persian wheel for an hour or two a day, to water the vegetable patch and to fill the bathing and washing tanks. The threshing of corn was easy work, for they had just to walk round and round unhurried on a bed of harvested stalks. Now that the men had leisure the bullocks were going to be busy. Grain and enormous piles of straw had to be pulled to the market; the wedding season was coming, and after that they would start the next ploughing.

The time had come for weddings, and the country echoed to the beating of drums. Gaily dressed women and children, packed in bullock carts, with the men riding or walking in procession, happy, shouting, bantering and raising much dust on the village roads was a common sight everywhere. The guests arrived at the wedding house with voracious appetites. If they gorged themselves they would be twitted for not having enough to eat at home, but a barat, wedding party, that did not eat well was criticised for being finnicky. So they usually put up with it good-humouredly and vied with each other in stuffing themselves. In between meals the men played games and took exercise in order to do justice to the next meal. The young and strong among the visitors would challenge their hosts to wrestling and games, and the two sides competed earnestly to uphold the honour of their village. In the evenings there was drinking and dancing girls, story-telling and boasting about houses, fields and cattle. The hosts could not retaliate easily; in fact, they had to restrain themselves. But their case was taken up by their village mirasis, the professional clowns and entertainers, who had the traditional liberty to exercise their sharp tongues upon the guests.

On the third day they packed the dowry, and with the bride in a palanquin the procession of bullock carts and horses started back for home. Swathed in red, the bride, a mere girl of fourteen or so, sobbed and cried as she left for a strange home. Consoling words from friends and parents were forgotten in the loneliness that gripped her as she sat huddled in the rocking palanquin which passed fields and villages she did not recognise. When the party reached the village a procession of women would come out to receive the bride and bless her. They would raise the curtain of the palanquin and lift the veil to see her face. If she was beautiful there would be unreserved admiration, she would be compared to the moon; but if she was plain there would be a chill praise which made their opinion equally clear. The groom strained his ears to discover what his bride looked like, while she tried to look from the corner of her eye through the uplifted veil to get a glimpse of her man.

When the excitement died down and the over-fed guests went to catch up with lost sleep the little palpitating red bundle was led to the innermost room in the house where the groom was nervously waiting. Before closing the door his mother would say, 'Son, take care of her.'

When the weddings were over, there were trips to the market to sell the grain. In fact, a few trips had already been made to settle with the money-lender and to raise cash for the weddings. There was an air of fursat, leisure, of the year's job done. Spring was losing its balminess, the sun was rising earlier and setting later every day. The days were becoming warm, but the nights were still pleasant. At first people moved out of the rooms at night to sleep in the verandahs, then into the courtyard, but with the first signs of real summer they moved their cots on to the roof terrace at night. On moonlit nights the country became ethereal and unreal. Sometimes you would wake with a large, bright white moon staring down in your face. The full moon would stare at couples sleeping on roof terraces. It would make the shy bride feel guilty in her husband's embrace as this intruder looked shamelessly on her body which she was just discovering for herself. In all poetry around the moon, masculine in our lore, legend has him condemned to eternal sleeplessness because he once pried on his mother bathing. His brother the sun, more modest, his mother said, will rest peacefully every night. But the moon was nevertheless, perhaps just because of his boldness, the favourite. With the face of a moon, is how the mothers like their babies to be described. The moon's face framed in black clouds, is how the poet describes his beloved lying on a pillow with her black hair loose.

When nights became hot and still and the summer gathered full strength, the dust storms arrived, sometimes followed by a cooling shower. Everyone would wake up with a start, and then there was commotion on all the roof terraces in the village. Drunk with sleep, people staggered down with their beddings and cots to the verandahs below.

During the day, under a hazy sky the country burned and languished. High whirlwinds raced across the land picking up dust and dry leaves along their path. The cattle herded together in the shade, and the farmers sought the pipal trees near the wells. These were most trying days for both man and beast. Healthy and strong men suddenly crumpled up from heat stroke. Cattle died of no seeming illness. The days got hotter and hotter until men felt they could stand it no longer. Dust storms of various colours would blow out of nowhere. They were usually brown, but sometimes yellow, red and even black. The black sand-storms were frightening, for the hard white daylight of an afternoon would suddenly become almost pitch black so that you could not see a few feet ahead. The red storms were the colour of blood and awesome; in the yellow storms there was an eerie amber light.

When the earth could stand no more and the parched soil cracked; when the air was so dry that one could drink a large pitcher of water in a day without a drop of sweat but only some grains of salt on the brow, the horizon would darken one afternoon, and instead of the hot dusty breeze there came a cool fresh wind with the smell of moist dust. The sky became covered with seething billowing, white-edged clouds, which approached like an angry army. Peals of thunder and long forks of lightning rent the sky, and large rain drops began to fall, at first slowly and deliberately but soon racing madly down to earth till they were like long needles of glass bursting as they hit the ground. They beat a terrible tattoo on the dry caked earth, and the noise swelled to a deafening roar. The rain storm lashed the hungry earth which seemed to delight in its violence. Big trees which had stood for years fell like toys, sometimes over men and beasts cowering under them. Little rivulets ran gurgling with red-brown liquid everywhere. Slowly the fury of the storm began to abate, and the rain settled down to a more gentle persistence. The farmers praised God and gave Him several grateful names as the peals and flashes became more and more distant and receded into the western horizon. By the evening the frogs croaked, the sloping banks of ditches were touched with tender green, and there blew a cool and fresh breeze. 'Zameen noo vatar aa giya,' the farmers said. The soil has received the proper moisture, and with a little sun would be right for the plough. The wet spell would last for three or four days and then one morning when the sun shone bright out of a blue sky, flecked with white fleecy clouds, the farmers lifted their ploughs and led their bullocks to the fields singing their simple yodelling songs. The earth yielded softly to the plough and the clods broke easily. The new cycle of growth had begun.

Savan was the poetic month of rains. It was the month for picnics by canal and river banks, when large parties went swimming for the day and cooked their food outdoors. It brought friendly clouds and nourishing moisture, but also floods from swollen rivers which, while doing damage to standing crops and villages, added another layer of alluvial topsoil. About drought, floods or locusts the Punjabi farmers complain mildly. If God gives He is kind; if He does not give He has merely withheld. They were not an especially religious lot, Hindus or Muslims, but they were god-fearing. Canals gave greater certainty to their lives and a plentitude they had never known before, yet they thanked God for timely rains. They were a contented lot.

When the rains stopped the sun shone every day again but now it had lost its fierceness. It rose lower in the sky and the days got shorter. Mornings had a pleasant touch of cool turning into cold. People who had left the terraces at the beginning of the rains now found it cool even in the verandahs. First the blankets and then the quilts came out of the big trunks. It was also a season of illness. The stagnant water bred mosquitoes which brought malaria. People shivered with cold and ached, then became hot and broke into perspiration. Sometimes the fever came every day, at other times every other day, and it took its regular yearly toll of life, young and old.

The autumn became chillier but there was no leaf fall, for the leaves had fallen at the end of winter. Autumn was only a season of change between summer and winter, and one day the wind would blow cold from the north. It came from the fresh snows of the Himalayas. Winter was the pleasantest time of the year in the Punjab. The invigorating air brought life and vitality back to bodies drained by the desiccating summer. The mornings were cold and misty; often there was frost, and sometimes the water in the ditches had a thin film of ice. The sun would rise like a big orange in the mist, and as it rose higher and gathered strength the mist would slowly dissolve. Days were crystal clear, and everyone warmed himself in the benign rays of the golden sun. There was much work in the fields, and many crops grew in these winter months. Sugar cane was ready in early November, but wheat, barley, grams, peas and mustard ripened through the winter. Near the towns there was much market gardening as well. It is the season when the flat Punjab country looks at its best with the rich lush green of the growing crops. In a single well-watered field there may be as many as four different things growing together.

While the men worked in the fields in the wine-like air, the women sat in the afternoon sun spinning and embroidering while they sang together, before starting to cook for their men. They embroidered phulkaris, literally meaning flower work. They were tapestries of red handloom cotton cloth embroidered with silk thread of gold, blue and green. The designs were traditional and geometric, in long diagonal stitches. The really beautiful ones, called bagh, garden, were a closely embroidered field of gold with a small red border left at the ends. They took many months to finish. Phulkaris were never sold but handed down from mother to daughter, and were worn wrapped like shawls on auspicious occasions beginning with the wedding day.

It was the season of healthy appetite and rich food. The Punjabi love of food, of curds, buttermilk, thick chappatis and sarson sag, the cooked mustard leaves, knew no bounds. Women put extra lumps of ghee into the sag and big chunks of freshly churned butter on the yellow maize chappatis. It was the season to feed the men. Fresh cane juice boiled off into gur, plain or spiced, was eaten in large quantities. Special sweets, pinnis, made of equal quantities of sugar, ghee and roasted gram flour were considered essential to resist the cold. 'Feed him and give him strength in this season,' was the older women's advice to the young women, and as the young ones snuggled with their men under thick quilts at night they felt that food had given them a new vigour. It was also the season of mating horses and cattle.

In the middle of winter arrived the Arabian monsoon, short, useful but bitterly cold. For days the sky was leaden and low, the air damp and chilling to the bones, but the farmers were happy; it provided moisture to the crops. And when the sun shone again the wheat and mustard were standing high and waving joyously in the breeze. The green rippling waves of wheat contrasted with the pure gold yellow of the mustard flowers–a sight I have felt the need to see every year, even if for a day. Like people returning to their mountains, valleys or seashore, I long to return to the Punjab to see its flat land clothed in its exuberant colours of growth; its many greens, the green of the chilli fields, the green of the wheat, of the gram and rice; and its yellows of mustard, cotton and snogra, the Punjabi flax.

As the wheat yellowed and the mustard flowers bleached and formed into seed, the winter's pace began to slacken. The sun became warmer and rose higher each day. Spring was heralded by the festival of Basant. Men and women dyed their turbans and mantles yellow in honour of the ripening corn, the mustard flowers, the yellowing pods of peas and grams, the yellow flowers of cotton, and all the bounties of nature associated with yellow. Yellow halva and yellow sweets were eaten in large quantities. Winter was over and with it the worst the weather could do to the crops, which would now ripen safely. And when the harvesting is over and grains are taken in will come again the boisterous festival of Besakhi.

The flowering trees added their own contribution of colour in spring. They shed their leaves, and against the bare tracery of branches the corals burst into their blood-red spiky bunches of flowers; the dhak, known as the flame of the forest, with its long flowering branches packed with velvety pink petals; amaltas, the Indian laburnum, with its drooping cascades of incandescent yellow flowers; the big siris, the rain tree, with its small, delicately formed brush-like pink flowers. They all dabbed their patches of colour on the country in one last heroic effect before summer spread its withering fingers.

Our language, Punjabi, has no script and hardly, until lately, any except religious literature. For centuries the Muslims had used Persian which the Sikhs continued as their court language. The Sikhs had evolved the Gurmuhi script for writing Punjabi by modifying the Sanskrit alphabet, but this they did to avoid the sacrilege of recording their holy book, the Granth Sahib, in Persian script, the script of the Muslims against whom they had revolted. Persian however continued to flourish as the language of culture and communication. Educated Punjabis were therefore bilingual, speaking Punjabi and reading and writing Persian.

The British brought Urdu with them from the United Provinces and Delhi, and supplanted Persian. At the same time they brought English, and from then on education was imparted both in Urdu and in English. Persian, along with Sanskrit and Arabic, became a classical language, and we had the choice of one of them. By the age of ten I was learning English and Persian, my curriculum was in Urdu and I spoke Punjabi at home and outside. Official business was transacted in both languages, at the higher levels in English and at the lower levels in Urdu. The district level was the dividing line. My father, when he was in the districts, had a stenographer for English and a munshi for Urdu.

Hindi, in the Devanagri script, arrived later and was confined at the beginning to the Brahmins and to our women, the latter through the influence of Arya Samaj. Literacy among our Hindu women thus began with Hindi, and this created some amusing situations, because in my mother's generation there were many women who could not communicate with their husbands when they were away from each other, as they could only write in Hindi and their husbands only in Urdu or English. In our generation the same problem was solved by the middle class girls learning English. At home, like their parents, they spoke Punjabi with their husbands, but their correspondence was in English. The girls were in fact trilingual as they spoke Punjabi, wrote in Hindi to their mothers, and in English to their fathers and husbands.

In the early years the Englishmen were also trilingual. They spoke in English to the westernised Punjabis, in Urdu to the Punjabi with ordinary education, and in Punjabi to the rayat. In fact, the English official then had a rather better knowledge of Urdu, and usually also of Punjabi, than the average educated Punjabi had of English. This helped both sides, but particularly the Punjabis. Speaking in Urdu or Punjabi gave them a poise and a dignity which later suffered badly during the early period of anglicisation; a poise which only those recovered who achieved mastery of the English language and familiarity with its culture.

A snob value began to be attached to knowing first Urdu and later English, and Punjabi was relegated to the home, the women and the illiterates. The language consequently began to lose its purity, and by my days it was so mixed with Urdu that except for the verb endings and prepositions it was almost Urdu. The well educated went further by adding English, and their speech became a mixture of a little Punjabi, some English and much Urdu. I have often wondered what effect it has had upon Punjabi character to have no language of our own, only an unwritten dialect and that also heavily mixed. I imagine it has helped to make the Punjabis what they are, practical, not overcultured, at ease when transplanting themselves.

Punjabi is a quaint language, slow, indelicate and lusty. When the U.P. babus came with their refined speech and manners, we became acutely aware of our crude ways and indulged in self-depreciation, which however in Punjabi make-up goes hand in hand with boasting. A Punjabi will often refer to himself as a yokel, a jat, and an ox, but somehow manage to make it sound like a boast. He will firmly run himself down, but always in a frank, open manner, without any trace of selfconsciousness. Equally, he will boast with the casualness of making a self-evident statement. The language lends itself to both.

Punjabi excels in love and in abuse. Its abuse is of the genealogical kind which can trace one's family history in the most revealing and incestuous terms. Father used to relate the story of an English colleague who appeared for his departmental examination in Punjabi. The examiner asked him whether he subscribed to the popular view that the Punjabis were a rude and rough people. In reply the young probationer burst into such choice Punjabi, tracing both the legitimate and illegitimate ancestry of those who held such a view, that the examiner interrupted him to say that quite obviously the candidate's knowledge of the language was both classical and sufficient for the department's normal requirements.

Our language is worth listening to when a villager prods a particularly stubborn bullock under a plough, or when he chastises an unwilling buffalo out of the pond. The animal will listen contentedly as the man improvises particularly lurid situations out of its ancestral past, and offer just enough resistance to keep the flow of words from changing to serious use of the stick.

A classical use of the language was made by women quarreling with a neighbour. Such quarrels were an institution that provided a relief to the dull routine of their daily life. A quarrel would always begin in the afternoon, when morning chores were finished, but before the evening's work began. One of the parties, the aggrieved or the offending one, would come to the platform in front of her house and begin to mutter vaguely as a warm-up till the opponent felt it was time to take notice and come out to her platform to take up the challenge. The neighbouring women would hastily put away their work and appear on their thresholds. And now the quarrel began in right earnest. The preliminary sparring was over, the audience had settled down to an afternoon's fun, and there was no retreat. Minutest details from the past were brought out and painted in word pictures of the most damaging colours, with ogress, eater of her dead children, eater of husbands, immodest, burnt, drowned, all generously used as adjectives. A great accusation was meanness, which in the Punjab is a cardinal sin. Stories, true or imagined, were remembered and embellished of meanness to guests, meanness at births, weddings and funerals, meanness to relations and neighbours' children; in fact, meanness of all kinds was treasured like scandal to be used on some such occasion.

As the afternoon wore off, the quarrel ran its course like a mountain stream, angry and rushing, as it swept past each obstacle. The neighbours listened approvingly or disapprovingly as the contestants cleared a hurdle or baulked at it. The liveliest to watch were the quarrels between two equally matched opponents, but of rare interest were those between an older woman and a young one, where experience clashed with inexperience and astute thrusts were met with headlong impetuosity. Each stroke of the experienced woman was known to the neighbours, but there was excitement in the possible contribution of the beginner. Occasionally, when cornered, youth would fall back on the weakness of age and having found the delicate spot turn the weapon mercilessly. Such weakness might be the lost looks of a wife and the roving eye of the husband.

Like the stream, the quarrel went on. The Punjabi language and its idiom would rise to heights to be remembered for many a day, perhaps made use of in a future bout. Sometimes in the heat of the fray, a casual thrust might draw blood from a spot unknown and unsuspected by the person dealing the innocuous blow. The victim would burst into a long wail and sob bitterly. An old hurt or a healed wound would suddenly gush, and the quarrel was at once over. The neighbours would rush to the side of the defeated in genuine solace, while the victor was left shamefaced with a hollow victory, protesting that she did not realise. Such dramatic endings were rare though.

As the afternoon lengthened and the time approached for the return of the menfolk, the quarrel would begin to flag. In South Punjab one of the parties might dash in and bring out a reed stool and lean it upside down against the front door. This meant that the quarrel would be renewed the following afternoon. There was no retreat now unless the other party felt she had had enough, in which case she disappeared, and no upturned stool picked up the gauntlet. Back in the house, the woman decided whether the husband was going to be drawn in or not. Usually they did not involve their husbands.

If a woman decided to bring her man into it, she would with great adeptness create an atmosphere of complete gloom to meet him when he came home. She would sit in a corner and sulk, the light would not be lit, and hearth left cold, there would be no cooking, the children left unfed, so that the man came home to an air of desolation which immediately made him sense that something was wrong. And slowly, never all at once, the story would come out. Usually the man would shrug his shoulders and consider it wise to ignore the affair; sometimes he would talk to the other party's husband, and both of them would make some wise or cynical comment about the ways of women and leave it at that.

Vivid in quarrel, Punjabi can equally convey its vigour in love. In Heer Ranjah, in Sohni Mahinwal, in Sassi Punna, in its ballads and folk songs, it has been enshrined in all its simple, but vigorous poetry. But whether in the ballads, the improvisation of the peasant in the field, or the women quarrelling in the mohallas, its purple passages are those tinged with the facts of life. They are earthy and direct. Love and death to the Punjabi go together. 'May you die,' is what the peasant says to his valuable ox, the mother endearingly to a naughty child, and the lover to his beloved. 'May I die,' is her ecstatic reply to each caress. The Freudian death wish is common in Punjabi; in love, in disappointment, in culmination, in frustration, in triumph and in defeat.

Although not written down until Urdu came in the last century, Punjabi has through the ages accumulated a great fund of folk tales, folk poems, fairy tales, heroic legends and old stories, tales which were passed down through the professionals when they were in verse and through the families when in prose. There was a great variety of bards who sang the ballads to their own tune on a simple string instrument. Stories were told us at nights by parents and elders, at home and in the squares, till we knew them by heart. On winter nights we would sit huddled in our thick quilts, with only our faces peeping out, and in the summer we sat on our cots on the terraces listening to these stories, embellished and animated by the skill of the story teller. It was customary to sit in a ring in front of the teller, who before starting would appoint someone in the audience an 'anghara bharne wala', whose duty it was to keep the story teller company by making suitable interjections like, 'yes; and then what happened; and so the prince said.' As children we always competed for this task.

These stories fell into different categories. There were fairy tales of enchantment, with a princess as the reward of adventure, usually living under a spell in an underwater palace guarded by a snake or ogre. A variation on this theme was the famous Gul Bakavli, where the quest was for a flower with magic properties of cure. There were heroic tales of adventure and drama, and humorous tales. They told of princes, princesses, ailing mothers and fathers who could only be cured by a certain remedy; stepmothers, either revengeful, if they were old, or in love with a younger member of the family, if they were young themselves but were married to older men; ogres, ogresses, jinns and giants; birds and animals as companions to the prince. An unusual character in some stories was a half brother who always insisted on accompanying his elder brothers on their adventures. He was not half in the sense of relationship but literally half. He had only one eye, one ear, one arm, one leg, and so on, but that did not deter him from setting out with his brothers. He made up for his deficiencies by distinguishing himself in an emergency in an amusing manner.

Stories were always told at night because there was a belief that if you told stories during the day travellers would lose their way. We always said that this was a ruse to put us off from bothering the grown-ups in the day time, but our elders genuinely believed in this superstition and would only relate stories at night, when everybody was safely home after the day's toil and travel.

Another interesting pastime was conundrums, mostly in quite beautiful couplets. Some were meant to teach us the complex system of relationships by asking us to guess the relationship that was involved in a complicated chain. In Punjabi each relationship, even the wife's father's sister's husband has a specific name, and we have to learn them all. To our great amusement the answers to the conundrums were sometimes something as simple as father or mother, but you arrived at this solution by a tortuous route.

CHAPTER FIVE

We Tandons are a sub-caste of the Kshatriya caste, or the Khatris as they are called in the north. We belong to the first group of twelve Khatri houses, known as the Bahris; these are followed by another fifty-two houses, thus called the Bunjahis; and then the Sarin Khatris. Originally these sub-castes must have been the equivalent of tribes or clans, and they continued to maintain a kind of tribal cohesion. We usually married among the Bahris, and the other groups among themselves, but while you could accept a daughter-in-law from a sub-caste lower than yours, you never gave a daughter to an inferior sub-caste. Sons could marry 'beneath' them but never daughters. As all marriages were arranged these rules were seldom broken.

There were other restraints on marriage. We could never marry into another Tandon family, even if there was no known relationship. Consanguinity was also strictly barred, and we could not marry the most distant cousin. All cousins, however remote, were your brothers or sisters. These were eugenic precautions which worked well to maintain the stock free from the usual signs of interbreeding. But I suppose such strictness will only work as long as marriages are arranged.

Caste pride among us did not lie in arrogating privileges or exercising authority; it took mainly the form of a code of conduct in regard to marriages and hospitality. To a Khatri a daughter was a debt which must be discharged honourably. She must be married into a caste of equal or higher status; a dowry must be raised; and having got her married, one must never accept anything from her or her in-laws. Parents, and even brothers, sisters or relations, unless they were younger than her, would never stay at her house. When they visited her they would not accept any food or drink, but if under any circumstances food had to be accepted, it was scrupulously paid for, and at a generous rate. An elderly aunt made such a fuss that she was a joke in the family. At the end of a half-day visit to her married daughter she would count up a long list of items that she would insist on paying for; one anna for a glass of water, another two annas for using the mat to sit on, and so on. We always reminded her that she had not paid for visiting the closet.

The marrying of a daughter was called kanya dan, literally, the gift of a daughter. It was a sacred duty, and having performed it one never took anything back that might savour of repayment. In its own practical way it was a precaution against the wife's relations, particularly the mother, imposing upon her, but like the eugenic precautions it was carried to a meaningless extreme just to rule out all chances of its ever happening. Having too many daughters was clearly a misfortune among us, for even after they had been married and provided with dowries, usually beyond one's means, gifts in cash and kind had to be provided by the parents and brothers on all possible occasions. And if the daughter or her in-laws were calculating enough, this could become an intolerable burden.

Hospitality with us was equally a matter of pride and social obligation, and its rules were inculcated from a young age. If a person from your village or a relation was visiting your town, but was staying with someone else, you went formally to invite him and his family. Etiquette made them protest by saying that wherever they were they were eating your food, so why should you trouble. You insisted and they protested, but after the procedure had taken its conventional course they very modestly agreed. There was a fresh protest when you asked them to both meals of the day. That really was too much trouble, they would say, but you always retorted that you were Khatris, not Sonars, that you should ask them to one meal only. The Sonars were the goldsmiths, who as a caste had been dubbed mean.

Formalities of the invitation settled, someone of the family, usually one of us children, had to go to fetch them even if they knew their way. Unless they were close relations, they came only just before the meal, which always began with a sweet, never with a salt dish. You always 'sweetened the mouth' at the start. The meal was literally a battle between the hosts and the guests, in which the latter must, after much seemly protesting, eventually lose. Men and women ate separately, our mother eating alone, last of all. After lunch one of us would walk back with them, and again fetch them in the evening for the second meal.

When we boys were sometimes staying with relations, other people in the town used to invite us. When we returned home mother would ask searching questions about where we had been invited, and make sure that all those who ought to have invited us had in fact done so. From the full account we gave she also made certain that we had gone through all formalities properly. Did we protest the right number of times; did we suggest that one meal would be enough, and did we accept only after the Khatri-Sonar analogy had been given; did we pretend at the meal that we were not hungry; did we begin the meal by eating the sweet; did we put forward our hands with fingers outspread over the plate when the hostess wanted to help us to more? These and many other questions were asked to make sure that we did not behave as we would have liked to by accepting the invitation with alacrity and falling upon the food like young wolves.

Next to our Khatri caste were the Aroras who were usually merchants and traders. They had their own sub-castes, but among them there were not the same strict gradations. They could marry in any sub-caste they liked, but of course the strict rules of consanguinity, common to Hindus, applied. Their rules about marrying daughters were the same as ours, but with an interesting exception. They could sometimes 'exchange' daughters, that is, marry a brother and sister to another sister and brother. Such a custom the Khatris frowned upon for two reasons. It introduced an element of bargaining in your daughter's dowry, because at the same time you were receiving a dowry from the other house for your daughter-in-law. While this went against our Khatri pride, there was a shrewd and practical reason as well. The invariable misunderstandings between the bride and the mother-in-law in one household could have repercussions on the other.

Khatris and Aroras were the two props of our Hindu society, and around them was built the structure of the service castes, both Hindu and Muslim. All the service castes were hereditary. Some of them worked on the jajmani system whereby each family was hereditarily attached to a group of jajmans–families to whom they ministered. We had a family barber, whose father before him had been our family's barber, and so the barber's family and ours were indissolubly bound. Good or bad we could not get rid of him, nor could he refuse to serve us, unless we went to live in another place and adopted a local barber family. But whenever we returned to our home town the old barber was there, and there was no changing him.

The first and most important in the jajmani system were the Brahmins. That they could be the leaders of society, in a position of privilege, I only discovered when I went to live outside the Punjab. With us the Brahmins were an unprivileged class and exercised little or no influence on the community. Perhaps the Muslims had so discouraged temples and external worship that the Brahmins had no place left from where to exercise their authority. In towns like Gujrat, and more so as you went further west of the Jhelum river, there were very few temples of any size. Only in Lahore, and that in the deep heart of the city in Hindu mohallas, did one come across any big temples; mostly our temples were holes in the walls or little shrines under pipal or banyan trees, easily demolished and just as quickly set up again. The importance of the Brahmins was therefore limited.

Our Brahmins did not as a rule even have the role of teachers, because until the British opened regular schools teaching was done by Muslim mullahs in the mosques or by Sikh granthis, scripture readers, in the gurdwaras. Our Brahmins were rarely erudite; in fact many of them were barely literate, possessing only a perfunctory knowledge of ritual and knowing just the necessary mantras by heart. As the occasions requiring their aid and knowledge were few, to earn their living they had developed a system of charity. Every morning members of a Brahmin family would visit the homes of their jajmans to collect cooked food–a chappati, some cooked vegetable or lentils, and buttermilk. The food would last the Brahmin family for both meals of the day; sometimes there were chappatis left over which they would dry and eat later soaked in hot milk. Handa, as such gift of food was called, was always in cooked food. It could never be claimed in its equivalent of raw food, for that our women would have considered an imposition.

While mother could always manage the handa out of whatever was cooked for the family, to give it raw would have meant dipping into her stores. While the handa took care of the family food, gifts in money and clothes on ceremonial occasions helped the Brahmins to eke out a thin living. It was a frugal life, and there were rarely any affluent Brahmins.

Without erudition and because of their daily dependence on the other castes, there was a touch of mild derision towards the Brahmins. The very address 'oh Pandita' or 'oh Brahmina' had gentle sarcasm about it. They were never elders of the community, nor was their advice sought on mundane matters. On the other hand some respect was shown to the astrologer pandits, who were the élite of our Brahmins, or the learned pandits who gave religious discourses, but astrologers and learned pandits were few. To the astrologers we went for establishing auspicious moments for betrothal, marriage, a business venture or a journey. They interpreted the almanacs, called jantris, and advised on the influence of the heavenly bodies upon individuals. These jantris, produced by the great pandits of Banaras and Hardwar, were essential for Hindu homes, sometimes the only book a family might possess. They were calendars with information about stars, planets, the moon and the sun, whose interpretation was the specialised task of astrology. The basis of each individual's life, as it was governed and influenced by the heavens, was his horoscope which the astrologer cast at birth and consulted before all important moves and occasions in life. Astrology was the preserve of Brahmins.

The other Hindu service castes were the artisan castes of Sonars, the goldsmiths; Tarkhans, the woodworkers; Jhewars or Mehras, the cooks, chars and water carriers; and Kalals, who sold liquor and were on the fringe of the social scale. Of these only the Jhewars were included in the jajmani system, and were in daily contact with us. A woman or girl from our Jhewar family would come every morning to clean and wash the utensils, while a man would bring water from the nearest well, and later from the hand pump on the ground floor. At weddings, or when we had a lot of guests, their men came to do the cooking.

The goldsmiths and carpenters were independent and dealt with whoever needed their services. The Kalals, before the British introduced liquor, sold opium, hemp and other narcotics. Liquor among us was practically unknown and addiction was mainly to eating opium, although even that was an uncommon habit.

There were no Hindu untouchables in the West Punjab, and such work as that of sweepers, skin-flayers and leather workers was done by Muslims. They were presumably untouchable Hindus who had at one time become Muslims to escape their lot, which they apparently did not manage to do even though they acquired some kind of theoretical equality with their Muslim brethren. They had the right to worship in mosques and to mix at an uneasy distance with poor Muslims, but they were compelled to retain their unwelcome professions.

As a boy I would feel quite ashamed when my mother, asking for a glass of water at some Muslim house, would be told with ingratiating courtesy that both the glass and the water had come from a neighbouring Hindu family. But slowly I saw the change come in. Our father made no bones about eating with Muslims and bringing them home. Interestingly, this problem was solved in our home, as in many other homes where a similar change was at work, by the introduction of chinaware. Our women, who objected to Muslims eating off our metal utensils, willingly shared china plates, cups and saucers. These were somehow considered uncontaminable. Their gleaming white, smooth surface, from which grease slipped off so easily, somehow immunised them from contamination. My mother would not at first use the chinaware herself and reserved it for the menfolk and for Muslim, Christian and English guests, but she soon began to weaken. This led to the next stage, that of accepting unpeeled fruit in non-Hindu homes.

Then followed the acceptance of tea and manufactured biscuits and the English bottled lime cordial, but mother never reached the stage of eating cooked food with Muslims or even with my father's English colleagues. This also used to puzzle me, because I could understand the traditional taboo on Muslim food, but how did this taboo attach itself to the English? I think it came from the discovery that like Muslims they ate beef, and that only Muslim cooks would serve them. As a child I could never understand how the Muslims and the English swallowed such insults from us and did not retaliate. It took the ideal of Pakistan and a separate Muslim nation in the 1940's to create an occasional feeling in Punjabi Muslim minds that they should also not accept food or water from the Hindus. The English, I suppose, just left it as one of our idiosyncracies and bothered no more about it.

There were a number of other Muslim service castes who plied hereditary professions. Two of them were in the jajmani system. I have already mentioned the barbers. In addition to his professional chores of haircutting, shaving and some surgery, the barber enjoyed the important function of go-between for arranging betrothals. At the weddings the barber, Raja, as he was always courteously called, had a place of honour second only to the Brahmin. As a barber we children of course never took to him because he always knew better than we how our hair should be cut. Just at that time the English style of hair-cut, known to us as the 'Bengali fashion', was becoming popular, but our Raja insisted on giving us a close crop. To add insult to injury, he said it was good for us because it did away with the need for dressing the hair and thus losing valuable time every morning which might otherwise be spent on studies. We despised him, but dared not say so, and in any case his argument about work appealed to our father. But whatever his skill as a barber, the Raja enjoyed much prestige among his jajmans for arranging betrothals, when he literally held the honour of a family in his hand.

Another Muslim caste in the jajmani system was that of Mirasis. The Mirasis beat drums and played the shehnai, a flute with a trumpet end, at weddings and other auspicious occasions, but their speciality was wit and repartee which they could exercise with traditional immunity on the highest and the lowest in the society. The victim could not take umbrage at the Mirasis' wit. They would come to weddings and other gatherings, invited or uninvited, and begin to poke fun at guests and hosts alike. Their wit was inherited down the generations and practised from childhood; it was sharp and very quick, and at times brilliant. Woe betide a man who tried to retaliate and get the better of them, for they could reduce him to rags before a company. A problem with the

Mirasis was how to send them away satisfied; anything short of that would lead to a special session against the poor host; and it was the respected custom to let the Mirasi say whatever he liked without showing anger and rancour. In any case, retaliation could only lead to an admission of lack of humour; the Mirasi had nothing to lose. The Mirasi women also worked, playing small drums and singing, but they never excelled in wit, only in vulgarity. Men and women sang praises of the family and recited its genealogy at weddings. They were also the vehicle of old ballads and songs. The word Mirasi in the Punjabi language has come to mean witty and funny in an overdone, vulgar manner. They lived as a close community in their own mohallas. Although Muslims, other Muslims never inter-married with them. Their women were slim and attractive in a brazen way, and of easy virtue.

The Mirasis moved with the times and took to brass bands, an influence from the army, which gradually replaced the shehnai and the drum at weddings. Dressed in the quaintest uniforms which were a mixture of those of the regimental bands and of the court dress of the King Emperor as shown in pictures, the Mirasis led the wedding processions and gave their customers the maximum value out of their new instruments, drowning the din of the party and even challenging the fireworks.

Not far removed from the Mirasis were the Kanjars, the community that bred prostitutes and singing and nautch girls. They were of course not in the jajmani system. Their men lived like drones, condemned to this because illigitimate birth of such low origin prevented them from going into any occupation. They were also Muslim, although the ranks of prostitutes drew castaways and fallen women from all communities. As with the Mirasis there was no inter-marriage between them and other Muslims. The professions of singing, nautch and plain prostitution were graded in that order in their community, on account of the requisite skill and talent required. It took only good looks to make a prostitute, while dancing, despite the low level to which it had dropped, still required some years' training and a lithe figure; but singing needed both talent and intensive training of many years. The singing girls were the élite of their community. They were no common prostitutes, and gave their favours only when they wished. The Mirasis provided them with musical accompaniment.

Other professional castes of interest were the Bhands, Bazigars, Saperas, Madaris and Behroopis. Bhands and Rasdharis were a community of clowns and jokers whose specialities were farce and impersonation. At weddings and parties they gave traditional performances or improvised skits on the company present. They were ingenious in both humour and farce, and never performed anything serious or classical. The word Bhand in Punjabi is synonymous with clown.

Bazigars (acrobats) and Madaris (jugglers) were also hereditary professions. They moved from place to place, the Bazigars as a troupe but the Madaris always single. Sapera, the snake charmer, must also have formed his own caste, but somehow one never knew where he came from.

A Behroopia's speciality was to disguise himself and act a role in such a realistic manner that people did not suspect it to be play-acting. He might arrive at a party as an old toothless hag, and no one would know until the end, when he suddenly threw away his garb and declared that he was a Behroopi. People used to be so taken in that they would gasp with wonder and reward him suitably. They were consummate artists. The word Behroopi in Punjabi has come to mean someone with a deceptive appearance. Rasdharis on the other hand went about in groups and put up plays and dramas. Dressed in colourful costumes they would arrive in a town and give short performances of old legends, stories or plays at street corners and at weddings.

The trades of weavers, tailors, washermen, blacksmiths, potters, oil pressers and vegetable growers were also practised only by Muslims. In some cases there was probably no question of caste involved, for when the British brought Hindu regimental tailors and barbers, some Punjabi Hindus also took to this work. To some trades like blacksmiths and weavers, resistance was broken by the arrival of machines; but to others like oil pressing, pottery and vegetable growing the Hindus never took. Even the agricultural Hindus never practised market gardening. For this there was a special Muslim caste of Arains who only grew vegetables. An ordinary farmer might grow some vegetables for himself but never a surplus for sale.

All these castes did not make ours a multi-layered society; it would be more apt to describe it as a multi-unit society, in which each caste had its functional place without oppression by a higher caste. The different castes were united into biradaris, literally meaning brotherhoods. There was an overall Hindu biradari; there was a Khatri biradari, an Arora biradari, and biradaris of sub-castes and of each service caste, Hindu or Muslim. These biradaris were loose and undefined, but in time of need they formed themselves into close-knit groups. They gave you certain rights and expected some duties. They were led by elders of the group, not formally elected but just the senior and most respected men. Your rights were your duties. At weddings and funerals everybody helped the family ungrudgingly. At a daughter's wedding the biradari members served the guests and helped with many chores; at death, when the immediate members of the family were too stunned to be of much use, the whole biradari was a source of strength.

The biradari also had a useful legislative function, that of altering customs which with changing times had begun to be onerous. At one time our Khatri wedding parties used to stay for a whole week at the girl's house. With rising costs and urbanisation this became an imposition, but no one dared to 'lose his nose' by asking the guests to stay for less than seven nights. Ultimately the Khatri biradaris reduced the number to three, and once this was sanctioned we could all follow suit. Later the three nights were reduced to two and then to one. The biradari also served as a forum for disputes between its members. If a difference could not be settled between two parties someone would suggest that they might put it before the biradari. The biradari would either hear the complaint in public or appoint an arbitrator. The rulings of the biradaris, whether on disputes or on obsolete customs, usually relied upon persuasion for their implementation. Occasionally they might pass a stricture or utter a caution. Only rarely, when either wilful defiance or serious immorality was involved, did they resort to the extreme penalty of excommunication, which consisted in stopping hooka pani. No one would then offer or accept a smoke or a drink, enter into a marriage alliance, or have any social intercourse with a person thrown out of the biradari, but fortunately such complete ostracism was rare. If your own biradari threw you out, no other biradari, even of a caste lower than yours, would accept you. How could you belong to a biradari which was not yours by natural right? The worst effect of such excommunication was that it made also your children unacceptable, both socially and in marriage. The sons might yet move to another town to settle and marry there, but the problems of marriageable daughters brought most recalcitrants to heel.

Stopping hooka pani was such complete punishment that it usually did not last long, provided you made amends for your misbehaviour. You went to some elders and begged their pardon, suggesting that the biradari might gather to reconsider their decision. Gatherings of the biradari were interesting affairs and provided lively entertainment to the community. The meetings took place in the evening after dinner in the open square of a mohalla, and all members could attend. The accused and the complainant, if there was one, were called to appear before the biradari panchayat, the five elders, which sat in a group at the head of the congregation. The meeting might last one or more evenings until a decision was reached. There was much lobbying and many private discussions in between. Witnesses were called; anyone could charge, accuse or defend, the whole procedure an open forum with the community sitting in judgement, guided and tempered by the elders. Often the mere public ventilation of a grievance, the sympathy it evoked and the condemnation aroused, was sufficient to satisfy the complainant or the biradari, and a mild regret closed the matter. On more serious occasions, such as the awarding or a revision of the hooka pani punishment, the guilty person would take off his turban, the repository of his honour, and place it at the feet of the panchayat. This was an expression of the deepest regret and humility, before which the biradari must by convention relent. Although women did not usually attend the biradari meetings and were not members of the panchayats, they exercised great influence from behind the scenes.

I remember a particular case of stopping of hooka pani soon after the first world war. There was a Khatri who had made a very large fortune during the war, and in the first flush of his new wealth he decided to remarry, even though his first wife was still alive, in sound health, and had borne him sons. Members of his own biradari, and even of the lower castes, refused to consider such an alliance, but he found an old man in poor circumstances who agreed to give his very attractive daughter, much younger in years than the wealthy suitor. The old man felt that this was an excellent match for his daughter, far beyond his best expectations. From poverty she would rise to living like a rani, in luxuries undreamt, with untold silver, gold and servants. Besides the suitor was a high class Khatri and a very generous man, who offered to see that the old man and his sons would want no more.

When people heard of the proposal they were outraged. It was an injustice to the first wife, also a woman from our town. Had she not borne him sons and was she not, besides, still young and fertile? She was good enough for him, in fact originally better than his station; she came from a better family, and was married to him when he was still struggling in life; what if he had amassed a fortune since? Had she died or become mad, or had she been barren, or had she produced only daughters, remarriage would have been understandable, but here there was no justification at all. Self-respecting families had rejected his offers and now he had obviously lured this wretched old man into giving his daughter. It was clearly a case of selling a daughter, a black mark which no forehead of a Khatri in living memory had worn. Elders of the biradari tried to dissuade the old man from this transaction, but the betrothal went through and a date was fixed for the wedding. There was nothing the biradari could do to the rich man as he came from another town, and in his own town he was too big to care. But on the wedding day, when the bridegroom's party arrived at the railway station, it was met by a jeering crowd which drowned the half-hearted music of the brass band. The old man was ostracised; no one came to the wedding; no one helped to receive and serve the guests; and all the way back to the station the next morning the party were jeered again. In fact, the barat only stayed for one night. Knowing the reception they were going to get from the town they 'stole in like thieves at night and crept away before dawn' – a metaphor which was reserved for morganatic and ostracised weddings where a small barat would come late in the evening and leave by daybreak because it dared not show its face to the town.

The rich man never came again to our town; he died a few years later. The old father lived a despised unhappy life despite his new affluence which turned bitter in his mouth. Occasionally his daughter visited him, but no one went near her and her wealth and pomp were scorned. The first wife was treated with added respect and sympathy. The incident was never forgotten, and the lesson was not lost on the town.

There was another interesting case of biradari punishment where a member of the panchayat decided to break the rule that he himself had agreed to introduce. The Hindu biradari of his town had decided to ban fireworks at weddings on the ground that they were a wasteful expense. This wealthy man, a pancha himself, decided to hold a most lavish wedding for his daughter, for which he ordered fireworks specially from another town. The biradari reminded him that it looked ill for a pancha to break a rule, but he proudly ignored their advice. When the barat arrived there was consternation, for not a soul turned up to receive and to serve, except a few immediate relatives. It taught the man a lesson. All the elaborate arrangements he had made, the pomp and show which should have drawn great applause turned to dust. Worse still, he was reduced to insignificance in the eyes of the visitors who naturally wondered what sort of a family their boy was marrying into. But if it taught him a lesson, the biradari learned its lesson too, for soon afterwards the ban on fireworks was relaxed. It was a harmless, though wasteful, custom, and people liked their fun at weddings, which it was unwise for the biradari to interfere with.

Even when the biradaris were powerful, they were seldom harsh or vindictive, nor were they easily influenced by the well-to-do and powerful members. Through centuries people had learned to rely upon them. The panchayat elders would forfeit respect and confidence if they transgressed the limits of natural justice. A strong man could defy the biradari for a while, but ultimately he had to get his sons and daughters married, and sometimes he had to take out a funeral. He could not therefore afford to stand apart for too long.

Our lawyer uncle used to explain that the weakening of the biradari system began when the British brought codified laws, impersonal courts, professional advocates and judges, high stamp duties, rules of evidence and procedure. Though the new justice was impartial, it was cumbersome and costly. The judges at first were unfamiliar with the ways of people, but as they began to understand them people also learned that this new impersonal justice could be deceived by casuistry and false evidence. It was difficult to sustain a lie before a biradari–if you were not found out then, you were bound to be caught later–but before a judge, to whom you were merely a plaintiff or a defendant, perjury was only actionable if it was found out at the trial. Time came after the First World War, when the farmers made so much money from a good crop that a man might publicly declare that he was going to put aside so many thousand rupees to settle a score by murdering someone, and later fight it out with the help of a leading criminal lawyer. And get away they often did.

If the introduction of law courts deprived the biradari panchayats of their function to adjudicate and arbitrate, the growth of western education and the movement away from home weakened their social importance. People developed personal standards which made them decide social issues in an individual light rather than according to custom. Our father lived most of his life away from our Khatri biradari in Gujrat, and altered custom as he saw best in the light of his newly acquired western education, which naturally challenged many of the old beliefs that had so far been taken for granted. He began to apply, in fact, the same procedure which the biradari has applied collectively and over a period, the changing of outworn customs; but in his case it was he who decided when the custom was outworn. The weakening of the biradari system meant in time a weakening of the caste system, as obligations to your caste were enforced by the biradari through the restraints that they exercised by day to day contact, backed ultimately by the threat of sanctions. But once you moved away from your town the biradari ceased to have a hold on you. In the new place you formed new friends, and sometimes new relationship, and although you tried to keep contact with your original biradari the ties soon began to weaken. You might join a local biradari, but somehow its ties were never quite so strong.

CHAPTER SIX

GUJRAT IS the place I came to regard as my home. I have no recollection of Kala Serai where the family originally came from. The canal colonies we lived in had a transitoriness about them, but Gujrat with our own house, our biradari and relations, was a home to us. In the Punjab your home, whether referred to in the simple Punjabi word, ghar, or in the more poetic Persian word, vatan, meant a lot. It was the first question you asked a stranger even before you asked him his name or caste; and if you both came from the same place or nearabouts a relationship was immediately formed. In a strange town you made a biradari of your two families with all its obligations and rights, and exchange of gifts of fruits and sweets on ceremonies, festivals and weddings. If his wife came from your town she became your sister, if he came from there, he was your brother, and if the wives came from the same town, they became sisters. The children referred to them according to the acquired relationship.

Travelling in a train you might suddenly discover that a man in the compartment hailed from the same village or town. There would be an immediate shout of 'Lao, tusan te sade vatni hoay, sade apne ghar de, sade bhara, wah, wah!' 'Take it, you are our countryman, from our home, our brother, well, well!' A feeling of warmth welled up, especially if you were a long way from home. Everyone in the compartment felicitated you on this coincidence. In a strange part of the Punjab you both regarded yourselves as exiles, and commented on the air, water, milk, vegetables, the size and sweetness of cabbages and cauliflowers, dialect and everything else as being not quite what you were used to. You were abroad and such differences were to be expected, but it was good to have someone from your home. The locals would accept it all in good part, and remark that it was but natural that things away from home are never the same. Gujrat provided the anchor in our itinerant life.

Gujrat was founded, probably in the twelfth century, by a dynasty of cattle-rearing tribes, known as Gujars, who also founded the state of Gujerat. Its population in 1917 of under twenty thousand was probably less than it had been in its days of glory. It lay on the Grand Trunk Road of Sher Shah, between Peshawar and Lahore and between the rivers of Jhelum and Chenab. To the north, about thirty miles away, began the foot-hills of the Himalayas, to the west, at the same distance, the low hills of Pabbi, where the plateau of Puthowar began to rise towards Rawalpindi. Gujrat was thus situated in a triangle of flat land with hills at the apex and rivers on two sides, while at its open base the flat plain of the Punjab stretched endlessly to the south. Its strategic position can be easily realised. After the invaders from the north-western passes crossed the Jhelum and descended down the Pabbi they came upon Gujrat, a walled fortified town built on the only hill for miles. It was the only well fortified town up to Lahore.

The city was built on a kind of right-angled hill, one side of which rose steeply. The town sloped from the small crown of the hill down to the plain below. There was a city wall all round with five gates, in addition to the main gate on top of the hill. Being contained by the wall it remained for centuries very congested, and it was not until the end of last century that the first houses, among them grand-uncle's, were built outside the wall. Thirty years of uninterrupted peace, which looked good for a long time to come, tempted people for the first time to venture out. Inside, the city had remained unchanged for eight hundred years, perhaps longer, since its strategic importance was such that there must have been some habitation even before the Gujars founded it; they perhaps only renamed and rebuilt it into a strongly defended town. Apart from its age we knew nothing of its history.

The city had a kind of defensible planning. It was divided by three main streets in the shape of a bow with an arrow. One of these streets ran roughly north south connecting two gates, like the string of a bow; another ran from the eastern gate to the citadel on the crown of the hill, like the arrow in the bow; the third street went in an arc from the vicinity of the northern gate to the southern gate like the bow itself. These main streets were quite narrow and contained the shops, which were ranged in groups of the same kind. There was one bazaar of gold and silversmiths, another of confectioners and cook shops; then there were groups of dry grocers, dyers, metal workers, cloth merchants, general merchants, book shops and stationers, shoe shops, and so on. In the side streets were groups of potters, weavers, and odd professions like brass bands. In one area lived the prostitutes and nautch and singing girls, and in another the Mirasis.

Inside the sections made by the three main streets were mohallas, small blocks of houses opening on to a square. The mohallas had usually two openings, a lane leading in at one end and leading out at the other, though some mohallas ended blindly. The lanes, called gallis, were quite narrow and had houses on both sides. One called the bheeri galli, the narrow lane, was indeed so narrow that if you saw someone coming from the other side you waited to let him come out first. Two grown-ups could not pass each other even sideways. It was just about two feet in width, and on both sides it had high blank walls. The walls must have been several hundred years old, and the old thin brick had been rubbed through the centuries up to a man's height into a smooth lacquer-like surface that shone black. There were other lanes not quite so narrow where two persons could just pass each other. Many of these lanes went through two or three small mohallas, eventually ending in a cul-de-sac. The mohallas were purely residential and had no shops. They were originally occupied by people of the same caste, but this tended to disappear in our time, though most Hindus and Muslims still generally lived in separate mohallas. Our small mohalla was a mixed Hindu and Muslim locality. The service castes had their own mohallas.

Because of the limited space within the city the houses were high, nearly all of three stories, more than which it was difficult to build with bricks and timber. Each house had a platform in front with two or three steps leading up on either side. The main door was in the centre of this platform, which was called thara and served several purposes. Women sat there in the afternoons spinning, sewing, embroidering and gossiping or quarrelling. From their respective tharas they could talk to each other without leaving their own domain. Upon the thara the itinerant merchants spread their wares while the women looked at them from their windows above, coming down only if they became interested.

You arrived in Gujrat by railway train. The station was about one mile from the city, and outside it was a large cluster of tongas. Red-shirted coolies took your luggage to the tonga shed where you were at once surrounded by all the tonga-wallas and dragged in all directions. You could either take the whole tonga or share it with others. After piling up the luggage you had the inevitable argument with the coolies, the usual rule being to offer a low amount and gradually raise it. Four people with some children in their laps settled in the tonga, and it started towards the town. Half way, the Grand Trunk Road from Peshawar crossed the city road, and there you were stopped at the octroi post to pay toll on anything unused that you brought in. Passing through the eastern gate the tonga would go by one of the main streets and stop at a small well, called Khari Khui, because its water was brackish, an uncommon phenomenon in this part of the country. Here we alighted from the tonga and found someone to carry the luggage. The lane twisted and turned past tall houses, at places barely five feet wide between the projecting platforms, till we reached Kuanungo Mohalla, a small mohalla with two tiny squares. The narrow lane connecting these squares was about thirty feet long and went between the blank walls of two houses like a tunnel. These two houses joined on top forming a roof over the lane, which then led to the next square and stopped there.

Our three-storied house in the second mohalla was typical of other middle class houses, but perhaps more ornate than most, both inside and outside. It had a large wooden door, fretted and chiselled, with carved wooden knobs with iron studs in them. At night a stout rectangular wooden bar let into a recess in one wall was pulled behind the door and slid into a recess into the opposite wall. This old safety device, known as erl, was common in our homes. Each storey had windows and fanlights with small panes of coloured patterned glass. The windows were painted a light blue, and the facade of the house was plastered in mat pink. The whole facade was symmetrical, ornate, and quite attractive. It was a square house with an open well in the middle, and the rooms on each floor opened into a verandah, running all round the well. On the first floor the well was covered with a wooden frame with iron bars; on the other floors it has a wooden railing fence around it. As the house had blank walls on all sides, except the front, where the entrance was and some windows, the purpose of the well was to provide light and ventilation and to keep it cool in the summer. In winter, to prevent the cold wind from outside from blowing through the house, we had to keep all windows closed. During the rains the water poured into the well and flushed out through the drains into the street, and in early spring when it hailed it made a carpet of white on the ground floor. Thus in the congested heart of the city, the house was open to the elements.

The entrance door opened into a vestibule known as deohri, which was a sort of reception room for strangers and hawkers. Nobody could proceed beyond this room unless invited. On the left of the deohri a door opened to a narrow staircase leading upstairs. Small at the base compared to the height, the old Punjabi houses had to have steep stairways with very high steps, and a rope to hold on to as you climbed up. On the right-hand side of the deohri another door led to the ground-floor rooms, and if the two doors were closed the deohri itself could be left open. The ground-floor rooms around the well received little direct light, and the blank walls at the back made them totally dark. We used them only as store rooms. On the ground floor there was a tube well with a hand pump. A pipe went up to the floor above so that water could be pumped up.

When visitors and traders knocked at the door with the padlock chain, if the men were out mother would look out of a window from upstairs to see who it was. If the visitor was a relation she would come down, but traders were never allowed upstairs, nor would they have found it easy to carry their loads up the narrow steep steps, so mother would either go down herself or would lower a basket by a rope, or ask the man to leave the stuff. If the men were at home during the day the deohri door was left open, and it was customary for visitors to call from downstairs and be told either to come up or to wait outside or, if the weather was inclement, inside the deohri. Women visitors just called and climbed upstairs, as also relations or close friends of the family.

The deohri had another and tragic use. On a death the men

coming to condole waited out in the street or sat on the platform, but the women came into the deohri. Relations and close friends of course went upstairs. When the body was brought down it was placed in the deohri for arranging the bier. On the days following the women called every morning and sat in the deohri to mourn.

At weddings the deohri also had its use. The bride, as she left home, tarried there awhile to take a last farewell from her parents before she stepped into the palanquin. When she reached her new home the deohri was her reception chamber. After the first few days when the initial shyness had grown into intimacy the young bride would run downstairs to open the door, in the hope of a quick embrace from her husband in the dark deohri. An understanding mother-in-law would tell her to go down and open it. Girls in young unrecognised love would sometimes stand in the deohri behind the entrance, and make some sound to attract the boy inside, only to meet in the confusion of a clumsy kiss.

From the deohri we climbed up the dark steps to the first floor. At the landing there was a niche in the wall in which in the old days, before the pump was fitted, the water-carrier poured water from his goatskin into a duct that led into the kitchen. From the landing the door opened into the verandah round the well. On the right there was a long room, our sitting-room, the baithak; opposite there were two rooms, one we used as a bedroom and one for storing blankets, quilts and other things that might be needed more often than the goods stored in the locked rooms on the ground floor. On the third side was another bedroom opposite the baithak and of the same size; the fourth side was the kitchen. The bedroom doors were blank wooden shutters but the baithak doors were panelled with coloured glass. The kitchen had no doors; it was an open alcove.

The second floor was similar to the first except that on the side facing the kitchen there were no rooms but an open space. This floor had more light, and with the small open terrace it looked more spacious. The terrace had an open air oven which was used on summer evenings for baking bread and keeping the food warm.

On the third floor were terraces with high wooden walls to give privacy. The stairs led into a closed landing beside which were the dry closets. Steps led from outside the landing room to the open roof above it from where we had a fine view of the city standing in a hump on the side of the citadel and sloping down to the green fertile country around. In the distance the first peaks of the Himalayas rose above the ground haze. In winter, after a rain, the mountains rose majestically above the green belt of the surrounding country, their peaks covered with snow, touched by pink in the mornings and mauve in the evenings. After sunset, before the cold early night descended, the mountains were a sombre dark blue, while the snow peaks still reflected light from the sun which had disappeared.

The walls in the verandah around the well on the first and second floors were ornately decorated with paintings in Persian style. The main motif was slender vases with large spreading branches and flowers painted in a formal style. The flowers were roses, pomegranate, narcissi and irises. I do not know when these walls were plastered and painted, but both plaster and paint had endured well. The plaster was nearly all intact, and the paintings had only slightly faded. The lines were exquisitely drawn in long, fine brush strokes.

We lived in a very informal style. There was little privacy, and we ate on the floor in the kitchen. If there were guests the servant brought the food into the baithak. If relations visited we received them in the lower baithak, but if strangers and formal visitors came the men were taken to the upstairs baithak while the women stayed below. The mode of living changed from one season to another. During the winter we spent the days in the sun on the open terrace of the second floor or on the roof, and in the evenings we moved downstairs to the snugness of the first floor rooms. During summer we spent the days in the dark cool rooms of the first floor, and in the evening we moved up to the second floor terrace and, as the weather became warmer, to the roof terrace.

There was still a great deal of self-containedness in our homes; we bought household commodities in bulk and stored wheat, rice and pulses from one crop to another, and till quite late times mother ground the wheat and maize herself on a stone mill. She bought raw cotton, ginned it on a small wooden gin in the house and had it carded by an itinerant carder, who came with his long bow which he suspended with a stout string from the ceiling. She spun the yarn on a wooden spinning wheel and gave it to the Julaha for weaving. She bought coconut oil and soda which she gave to the soap boiler for making washing soap; she made her own preserves, pickles and jams, while she gave the ingredients to the pansari for extracting essences and preparing sherbets. She embroidered, stitched and sewed, and had we had sisters she would have been steadily preparing and storing away their dowry. She minded or supervised the feed of the cow and the buffalo that we always kept by mixing oilcake, cottonseed, bran, salt, unrefined sugar and dried left-over wheat chappatis. She bought metal utensils by weight and had them tinned, and if they broke she sold the metal by weight. We even bought logs and had them chopped on the front thara by Kashmiri labourers who wandered about the Punjab during winter when their own land was frozen and unproductive. We also maintained a ritual contact with land by growing symbolically in a small pot a few plants of the grain in season.

Our mohalla was mixed, and in both its squares there were Hindu and Muslim homes. Except for the burqa, with which the Muslim women veiled themselves when they went outside the mohalla, there was very little difference in the dress. The Hindu ghagra, the voluminous ankle-length skirt, had practically gone out by my time and only a few old women wore it. The women always wore salwar kameez. There was no social stratification in our mohallas, and amongst our neighbours there was a Muslim lawyer, a Hindu confectioner, a Muslim clerk in the municipality, and a Brahmin family. Boys and girls played together, and in the afternoon the women would take out their low stools and embroidery and sit on their tharas, talking and gossiping.

People rose early in the morning. Many men had the village habit of going into the country for their morning ablutions. Some took a walk in the fields or on one of the roads leading out of town. On the way they cut a green neem or wattle twig and chewed one end which was made into a kind of brush to clean their teeth and thrown away after using it. They stopped at a well with a Persian wheel and had a bath. In winter well water is warm and in summer cool. There they met other men and exchanged news. Newspapers had barely reached Gujrat. On the way back through the town they passed through the open market square to buy fresh vegetables which had been plucked early the same morning and brought in from the market gardens surrounding Gujrat. After an early morning cooked meal men left for work by ten o'clock. Those who worked in offices returned home by five, but the shopkeepers, who began the day early, returned home at midday and then worked till late in the evening. Working hours varied from summer to winter. During the hot weather schools and offices opened at six in the morning and closed at midday; in the winter one worked from ten o'clock till four. In summer everyone slept in the afternoon, and in the evening the men went out for a walk or visiting friends. Sometimes after dinner husbands and wives went out together to visit relatives or friends, but without a specific purpose this was rare. Usually people retired early to sleep. Life thus ran on an even, slow tempo quickened occasionally by festivals, weddings and visits of relations from other towns. All such events were looked forward to long in advance.

The Hindu festivals were many, but those celebrated with enthusiasm were Lohri, Basant, Holi, Besakhi, Rakhri, Dusserah and Diwali. At Lohri, which came in January, large bonfires were lit in pits dug in the ground. There were special sweets of nougat covered with sesame seed and parched rice to eat, and there was always a special celebration for a baby who was having his first Lohri. We also exploded fire crackers. Little boys gathered firewood for days ahead. In the evening men, women and children gathered around the fires, which in the cold of a January night were most welcome. Late at night we went home to bed, tired and sleepy, with the sound of crackers still in our ears.

Basant came with spring and was the festival of the yellow colour of ripening crops, celebrated in the same way in towns as in villages. It marked the beginning of the kite flying season. Then came Holi, a festival of sheer rowdiness which every year seemed to grow worse. It was a day of complete licence when one splashed coloured water or threw powdered colours on each other and smeared colour on people's faces. Everybody put on old discarded clothes, for at the end of the day they would be a mess. The clothes were put aside for the next Holi, but it took a lot of scrubbing and washing to get the colours off faces, heads and hands. Some streets were notorious because the inhabitants would stand on their roofs and throw ashes, dust and contents of dust-bins, even night soil on passers-by in the street below. But no matter what one did nobody could complain or take it ill. Everything had to be treated in good humour. Even staying indoors was no protection, as friends came to your house and dragged you out into the street, and once you were drenched in colour you might as well go with them and take your revenge. Women played Holi in the mohalla while men ran berserk in the streets. Holi, it is said, shares its origin with April Fool's Day.

After Holi came Besahki in April. We used to celebrate it on the banks of the Chenab six miles away. It was, though in a quite different way, also full of noise and rough merriment; a pleasant combination of river picnic and festival.

Then came a long break in the hot summer months till the next festival in August, Rakhri or Raksha Bandhan, meaning the protection tie. Sisters tied rakhri, a coloured silk bracelet, round the wrist of their brothers and cousins. If a girl had no brother she would adopt one. The rakhris gradually became very ornate with little silk pompoms and glass pearls which we greatly admired round our wrists. To absent brothers the rakhris were sent by post in advance. Originally the custom meant a pledge of protection by brothers and male cousins, but now this meaning was more or less lost, and brothers had to pay some money to the sisters in return for the rakhri, something which we as young boys quite resented. We would be given silver rupees to pass on to our local adopted sisters, since we had no sisters of our own, and we used to protest that surely we boys could make a better use of the money than the girls who would only put it in their money boxes.

After Rakhri came the best festival season of all–Dusserah and Diwali. Both originated from the Ramayana; Dusserah enacting the battle between Ram and Ravan, at which the demon king of Ceylon was defeated, and Diwali in celebration of Ram's return home after fourteen years of exile. Well ahead of Dusserah a town committee was formed to collect money for a performance of the entire Ramayan. Local dramatic talent was selected for acting and production, and a stage was erected in the market square. The whole story of Ramayan was acted progressively each night for about a month. It was an entirely amateurish effort, all the actors were boys and men, and the performance was free to all. Some of the improvisations could be amusing and ingenious, and each year people wondered how the director would tackle a particular stage problem. Amongst the ticklish problems were the scene of Ram, Lakshman, Hanuman and their army crossing the water between India and Ceylon; Hanuman's flying to the Himalayas; and Lakshman ungallantly cutting Saroop Nakha's nose when he could stand her overtures no longer. Sometimes a difficult scene would be missed out and at other times they would use symbols, substituting words for action, or a combination of words and action. One director hinted the day before, that he was really going to make Ram and his army cross the sea, and we were all very curious about it, for no one had tackled this problem before. How could you run water on the small rickety stage? At the appropriate moment, anxiously awaited by all, two men appeared on the stage with a long half dry white dhoti, each holding two ends. They were swaying the dhoti as if to dry it, so that it billowed from side to side and heaved like a sea. Then Ram and his companions appeared on the stage and after some suitable words jumped over it to the other side to Ceylon. The whole thing was simply but effectively done and drew much applause. Living nearly a thousand miles from the sea it did not occur to us that the dhoti might have been blue.

We little boys used to hang around the Ram Leela hoping to be given a small part, usually that of a monkey in Hanuman's army. With a red mask of a monkey's face, red shirt and short pants and a tail sticking out at the back, holding gaily decorated red bows and arrows we pranced about and got in everybody's way. Hanuman would cuff us now and again and send a young monkey howling, while others jeered at the victim for being a fake warrior. Every evening after dinner we carried our own chairs to the Ram Leela if we did not want to sit on the ground. The performance went on till late at night, and next day people would minutely criticise the previous night's performance and compare it with the years before.

The performance varied in quality from day to day and from one year to another, but people were surprisingly charitable, not for want of local rivalries and jealousies but, I think, because the sight of a colourful stage with Ram, Sita and other characters of their Ramayan, whom people worshipped every day, alive and talking, moved them deeply. Dasarath's grief when Kaikeyi demanded her step-son Ram's exile so that her own son Bharat should ascend the throne; Bharat's loyal insistence on following Ram into exile; Sita's cries as Ravan carried her from her forest cottage; Lakshman's fainting after the wound in battle and Ram counting the night's hours waiting for Hanuman, who had flown to bring the sanjivani herb to save Lakshman's life from the Himalayas two thousand miles away, were some of the many poignant moments that brought tears to the eyes of the audience. These simple men and women, moved by the realism of the acting, wanted to go forward to worship the heroes of their life and thought. But there was much conscious and unconscious humour too, as when the Lakshman who was known to dislike the fellow playing Saroop Nakha acted with such realism that he nearly took his nose off. The very genuine howls of Saroop Nakha brought the house down. The little boys who stuck pins in their arrows to give painful jabs to the boys in Ravan's army also provided a realistic touch, much appreciated by the audience.

Night after night the Ram Leela continued to unfold the great epic till we reached the last scene of the defeat of Ravan. This was acted on an open field on the afternoon of the Dusserah day. An enormous, hideous effigy of Ravan surrounded by smaller effigies of his brother Kumbh Karan and his son Indrajit, made of paper and bamboo and stuffed with fire crackers, were erected. In bright new clothes we collected at the fair and spent recklessly the four or eight anna piece given to us, till the Ram Leela's moment of climax arrived. At dusk Ram, Lakshman and Sita drove up in an open horse carriage and amidst great applause Ram dramatically shot an arrow at Ravan, his coup de grace. Immediately Ravan and his companions burst into flames. Crackers exploded and rockets shot out of the effigies. There was great commotion and din when after a whole month's narration of our beloved epic, virtue at last triumphed over evil, and the wicked demon, Ravan, collapsed, his body racked and tortured by crackers and flames. We returned home with full stomachs, sad that the season of Ram Leela was over, but we would soon brighten up at the thought that the best of all festivals was yet to come, and so soon. In twenty-one days there will be Diwali.

Diwali has a touch of Christmas about it, particularly, as I was to discover later, the Scandinavian Christmas. It is a festival of the home when families unite. It was auspicious to be home on Diwali day to receive the blessings of the goddess Lakshmi. The preparations began many days ahead, and everyone in the home was given something to do. The women prepared sweets and made hattis on the wall. A portion of the wall was plastered with cowdung and painted white with red swastikas. Little projections, called hattis, of mud and straw, were fixed on the wall for placing the lamps. Earthenware cup-shaped lamps called diwas, which give Diwali its name, were first soaked in water. Little girls would roll wicks out of cottonwool and put them into the lamps which they filled with mustard oil. Later, coloured wax candles appeared on the scene. Father would have to have the house painted, bring some new silver rupee coins, and buy sweets from the bazaar. There were so many things to make and to buy–special sugar sweets in white, pink and yellow, moulded in the shape of horses; gaily painted clay figures of people and horses; coloured prints of Ram, Sita, Lakshman, Hanuman, Lakshmi and other gods, goddesses and scenes from mythology; paper and bamboo lanterns; candles and fireworks.

On Diwali day there was hectic activity, hanging the lanterns, placing the diwas and candles in rows, beginning with the steps before the house and going up all the way, on windows, wall parapets, inside the house and on the hattis. In the evening when everything was ready we would bathe again and put on new clothes. From then on we became impatient and urged the parents to begin the Diwali, only to be repeatedly told that we had to wait till it was dark; you cannot light lamps in daylight.

In November night falls early, and with our excitement pitched to frenzy we would rush to light the lamps. This was quite a task if it was breezy, for the flame on the wicks in the open earthenware diwas would flicker and go out and leave dark gaps in the lighted rows. Usually the evening was still, and row after row of little trembling flames would outline our house and the neighbouring houses until the whole mohalla was a mass of lights. We shouted to the children in the neighbouring houses, vying with each other who put up the better show. But we still could not eat the sweets until the family puja had been done. Our mother collected us all and we sat in front of the hattis for puja. On the floor, in front of the lighted lamps she placed a tray with silver rupees spread on it. The coins were smeared with saffron and covered with grains of rice as an offering to Lakshmi; it was called Lakshmi puja. There were trays of sweets lying on the floor, and when the puja finished we were given some prashad, an offering of sweets. As soon as the puja was over we rushed out to light the fire crackers. Our narrow mohalla became a fairyland with sparklers, rockets, coloured candles, and fireworks that delighted our simple tastes and were known by such beautiful names as moonlight, flower shedders and pomegranates, which threw cascades of sparkles like a fountain of fire.

A treat we always looked forward to was a visit to the bazaar to 'see the Diwali'. We were taken to the bazaar by the elders, holding their hands so as not to get lost in the crowd. It was a wonderful sight; rows of houses outlined with flickering lamps and candles, lanterns in different colours hanging from the balconies, and the confectioners' shops brilliantly lit with gas-lamps and with tiers of sweets sloping up to the ceiling. The sweets were made in all colours and arranged in decorative pyramids on shining trays. They were wrapped in very fine gold and silver foil. In the midst of this colourful mountain of temptation the halwai sat, fat and paunchy, weighing out sweets to his customers standing in the street, and giving an even shorter measure than usual. We returned home to find all the doors open, every room lit and the tray of saffron-covered silver rupees still at the puja altar. The rows of lamps and candles were still flickering but many of them had gone out. Tonight Lakshmi, the goddess of prosperity, visits every home, so all the doors must be left open and the lights burning to give her an open welcome. A curious custom had grown of propitiating Lakshmi by gambling. For days ahead people played games and gambled, and on the night of Diwali our parents let us also play, but with cowrie shells which were then still the lowest denomination of money.

Next morning we awoke with a feeling of anti-climax. Diwali was gone, and there would be no more festivals for over three months, till Lohri came again. We felt sad but tried to brighten the gloom with the thought that it was still a holiday. We busied ourselves with collecting wax from the bottom of the burned out candles. Then we melted the wax and made some half-hearted attempts at shaping candles, but real Diwali was over.

Festivals that we celebrated with great enthusiasm and eclat were in later years spoilt by the growing bitterness between Hindus and Muslims. The Hindus resented the Muslims slaughtering cows on their Bakri-Id, and the Muslims objected to the noise and music of our festivals, and would not let Dusserah, Diwali and Holi pass without trouble, sometimes leading to bloodshed. It reached such a pitch that for some years we did not celebrate our festivals for fear of provoking bloody riots. Even Ram Leela was dropped. On the other hand we began to add more festivals to our already sizeable list. Christmas is today celebrated in more clubs, restaurants, army messes and even homes in big towns than it was during the British days. Clubs hold children's Christmas parties and New Year dances. Republic Day and Independence Day are also acquiring the air of festivals; so while we acquire new festivals many of the old ones are losing their significance.

CHAPTER SEVEN

WE STAYED in Gujrat for about a year to complete our schooling, and seven years later I returned there to join college. As child and adolescent I got into tune with the spirit of the town, and a spirit it certainly had. It possessed a self-contained medieval unity of life in which people worked at their hereditary crafts and professions, and lived in their biradaris, friendly and tolerant of each other. In such a congested town, where everyone knew everyone else and his affairs, I suppose tolerance was essential. Yet underneath it there flowed currents, sometimes in complicated convolutions which caused embarrassment to the society, but usually without any tumult on the surface. The town had through the ages acquired a character and a reputation, unsavoury in parts, but of which its inhabitants were quite proud. Like its famous industry of forging weapons, swords and guns, it had a stored-up vitality which went ahead in a surge when opportunity came at the end of last century. There will be few successful professional families in the West Punjab who do not stem from this town and its district. Later, as the development spread, other districts like Sargodha, Shahpur, Sialkot and Gujranwala also made their contribution, when castes like the Puris of Ghartal, Sahnis of Bhera, and the Batras of Girot, all three from small places, unknown in the past, spread through the services and professions.

Though newcomers to Gujrat, through our grand-uncle we joined the local biradari and soon got to know most of the families. As a child I would sometimes accompany my mother when she went out visiting and shopping. Our progress was slow as she often stopped to talk. We would walk through the covered lane in front of our house into the second small square of our mohalla. She would be called by one of the Muslim women from her balcony. 'Bibi-ji, where are you going? You are taking your boy with you. By the grace of Allah, he has grown. I suppose he will be a big engineer like his father one day.' My mother would reply, invoking Parmatma, the Hindu name for God, in response to the neighbour's Allah. The neighbour's little girl, Fatima, would look at me curiously and ask if I would like to play hide and seek. The mother slapped her on her head and told her not to be so bold. Years later, when I came back to live in the same house, Fatima had grown into a lovely girl. She wore a burqa when she went out of the mohalla, but underneath the conventional demureness she was as bold as ever with a roving eye. On the other side of the square lived a Hindu confectioner whose wife used to come down and join my mother with a 'Behnji, how are you keeping?' And her little girl, Rupa, stood by her looking at me as if I was too good a boy to want to play with little girls. She also grew to be a beauty with flashing eyes. Both Rupa and Fatima were lively girls and there was talk that they were both in love with a Muslim boy of a wicked reputation. When Rupa's parents heard about it they immediately betrothed her and married her off inside a few months. The poor thing got married to a widower twice her age. When her doli left she cried bitterly, but in her case, as we in the mohalla knew, it was not for parting with her parents, who had dealt her hard, but for exchanging her flowering love against a dull old husband.

It was strange that in the narrow lanes of the confined city, under the strict watch of parents and neighbours, such affairs could develop at all, but secretly they did occur. Someone or the other always knew, because they had seen the girl disappearing into a dark deohri, or making signs from a balcony to someone passing below, or perhaps throwing a small tightly screwed-up ball of paper; a really daring one had climbed over a wall separating the terraces of two houses; another had thrown back the hood of her burqa in a lane far from home, where she thought no one would recognise her. Although such affairs sooner or later became known, people never talked too loudly. Somehow the city felt that everything must be contained within its walls, and it was practical to be discreet. It could always happen in your own family. Occasionally an affair would burst the bounds of propriety, but in such cases too it was somehow hushed and settled, though any time it might be raked up in a quarrel and thrown in someone's face.

My mother and I would walk on into the next lane which had only Hindu houses, and she would talk to some women sitting on a platform, gossiping, spinning but, like good Punjabis, always eating something, horse radishes with salt and pepper, sugar cane, parched gram and corn or whatever else the street vendors had to offer. The talk was usually about sickness in the house, especially of children; death, births and marriages; what they were cooking for the night. The profoundest discussion would be about some remedy which was known to have cured someone. And so we walked on, and though these conversations were dull to me there was always a chance of someone offering me a sweet or fruit. The next lane was a wholly Muslim one, known as Sheikhans' Gally. Sheikhs were Muslims who had been converted from Hinduism and given this high title as an immediate reward. Here also my mother knew many women but we felt strange because of a heavy garlic smell that emanated from their houses and the uneasy consciousness of their eating cow's meat. There was also a sense of strangeness in their invoking Allah and Khuda instead of Ishwar or Parmatma.

From here the lane opened into one of the main streets, and as soon as we entered it mother pulled her mantle over her face and held my hand. She crossed over into another lane to avoid walking in the street. This lane was inhabited by courtesans. It was like any other lane, but to me it had a mystery about it. I could not understand what these women were and why they seemed to have no menfolk and children. They looked like other Muslim women, for they were usually Muslims, and the odd Hindu girl strayed into their fold adopted their customs and manners; yet they had tired faces and bold, almost brazen, manners. They left their heads uncovered, for instance. In the mornings when other women looked fresh and clean after the bath these women looked haggard; and in the evenings when other women were tired and work-worn, they were all dressed and made up. Most of them were old, but some were young, mysteriously attractive, made up and decorated in a way that even our new brides did not dare; beautiful in a quite different way to our young women. These young ones did not seem to have the customary respect for the older women. Were they even related to them? They did not look like their daughters or nieces. And what were those curious strains of music that came from some room upstairs–a sitar, a tabla, the jingling ankle bells and a girlish voice endlessly repeating a refrain. I dared not ask my mother questions because I somehow felt that she would evade the explanation. I once saw some red colour coming out of a drain and trembled to think that they were doing some sacrifices inside the house.

An old courtesan sitting on a platform would talk to my mother who stopped to answer. She would make simple enquiries about our family. There was never any hesitation on my mother's part to talk to them, though I noticed that my young aunt or the men never did. But no one avoided that lane. These women were not pariahs or outcasts, they lived among us, and Gujrat contained them as a part of its life. Like other castes they served a purpose and were not scorned because they served it. They were not accepted or respected, but neither were they treated with contempt or prudery.

From the lane of the courtesans we would go through the Sonar Mohalla where all the gold and silversmiths lived together in a tight community. The Sonars were supposed never to give you full measure of gold and silver in ornaments. It was said that a Sonar who once made an ornament for his mother without keeping back part of the gold could not go to sleep for worrying over this deviation from a principle. He woke his mother in the middle of night and asked for the piece back, saying he had made a mistake and could not sleep till he had put it right. The Sonars married in their own biradari but without observing our rigid codes. We would usually stop at the house of the Sonar who made jewellery for us and talk to his wife. As usual, my mother treated her as an equal even though her husband would be very deferential in my father's presence. Somehow caste inequality in terms of social behaviour expressed itself more prominently in the case of men than women. It is interesting to think that while Khatris and Sonars had lived amicably in adjacent mohallas for generations there had never been any inter-marriage, inter-dining, or much social intercourse.

From the Sonar Mohalla we went through the Bheeri Galli, the narrowest lane in the city. We children loved sliding our shoulders against its lacquer-smooth walls. At the other end we entered a Khatri mohalla, and after exchanging some small talk with the women we met we passed on.

This mohalla had recently had a scandal. There was a head clerk in a government office and his wife, an elderly couple, living in this street. They had a daughter who at the age of nearly twenty was still unmarried. Many friends and people in their biradari had spoken to them about the inadvisability of leaving a daughter unmarried till such an age; it was risky and marred the chances of a good marriage because people became suspicious; and where would you find an eligible young man of twenty-five or more who was still unmarried? You would have to look for a widower. Yet the old man did not heed their advice. The girl was quite attractive and healthy, and everyone felt it would be understandable if she went wrong. One night there was great commotion, and the whole mohalla was awakened by the cries of 'Chor! chor!' It appeared that the old babu had got up in the night and found his daughter in the arms of a man. The moment she saw her father she cried out 'Thief! thief!' and pushed the man away as if in a struggle. The 'thief' disappeared quickly, but as he ran down the street he was recognised as the son of a prominent family with a mysterious reputation. He had already been suspected of various affairs, but burglary was something new. His family was affluent enough, and nobody really believed that he had tried to steal the girl's bangles; he was sure to be visiting the old babu's daughter with her consent. The scandal died down gradually, and the elders spoke to the old man seriously. The young man accepted the charge of attempted burglary and squared it up as best he could with the police.

It was the unwritten rule in such affairs that if the pair were caught the girl would immediately disclaim all acquaintance and accuse the man of assault, burglary or anything she could hastily think of. There was no question of sticking by her man, for such affairs were not supposed to lead anywhere, and the girl surrendered herself to the man on the traditional, tacit understanding that he took the entire risk. Somehow the society also helped the girl, presumably because it would be a very unpleasant task to take action against her. Instead, she was left to the mercy of parents or husband. Her partner could always fend for himself, so it did not matter too much if the blame were foisted on him. Actually, such affairs were not too many, and the society was almost puritanical in its morals and conventions, but it was pragmatic in its approach to the odd lapse and infraction. Gujrat probably had more such affairs than other towns and its boys and girls had a reputation for liveliness. The erring girl, married or unmarried, brought enough shame on her family to be sufficient punishment in itself. She put a black mark on their brow which was not easily washed off. People knew, even though they pretended not to notice. In new alliances and the biradari dealings it was visible for a long time.

Virginity was sacred. An unmarried girl was called a virgin. Pre-marital affairs were an exception, but not so rare were happenings within the family which never came to light. They were usually affairs between brother and sister-in-law, between a young aunt and nephew, and occasionally between a young stepmother and a stepson. There were many causes. One was the joint family system where people lived not in a single unit of husband, wife and children, but in a big crowd of relations all together in one house. Another cause was the arranged marriages which, though mostly happy, did occasionally bring together totally antipathetic personalities who, had the choice been theirs, would never have selected each other; for instance, a frigid husband and a passionate wife. Were it the other way round, the man could discreetly resort to the courtesans, but an unsatisfied woman had no such outlet and might therefore resort to a liaison within or without the family. Yet another cause was occasional disparity in age, again due to parents' choice. A mere girl would be married to a man as old as her father. A younger brother, son or nephew of the husband might attract her, where the husband repelled. Between a wife's younger sisters and the groom there is a tradition of bantering which begins at the wedding when they ask him tough and embarrassing questions, hide his shoes and play tricks. Such bantering sometimes led to a casual affair. Lastly, a young widow condemned to lifelong loneliness might have an affair with the late husband's brother, sometimes even his father. Being voiceless in the family, widows were easy victims.

Young widows were, in fact, a great problem, for while people would not accept remarriage at any cost, they did not know what to do with them. Whether a widow stayed with her own or her husband's parents or brothers she was a burden. Her misfortune was considered to be her fault; at least it was her fate. While her parents and brothers had sympathy, other relations showed none, particularly her mother-in-law who felt that she had brought evil luck and 'eaten up' her son. She was forbidden to dress and eat well, to share the family's festivities and joys, and often she was just an unpaid servant in the house, without the freedom to leave. The lot of the widows improved somewhat with the spread of the Arya Samaj which advocated remarriage, or education to befit them for a teaching job, but people were slow to react and continued to hold the old belief that God had so willed it. In our family, under the influence of father, two widows in fact managed to arrange their own marriages, but that came many years later.

From the Khatri mohalla we turned into the Mandi, Gujrat's market-place, which was a large square with wholesale and retail grocers and grain merchants' shops. The square was paved, and there were heaps of grain, pulses, gur, rice and other foodstuffs from which both retailers and consumers bought. In the centre of the square was a large banyan tree under which women sat on the ground selling vegetables which were grown outside the city wall and brought in fresh twice a day. The fresh and colourful vegetables were a very pleasant sight, arranged neatly in reed baskets. The vegetable sellers were always women and girls from the special Muslim caste of Arains. Unlike the ordinary Muslim farmers, they specialised in market gardening and never went in for cultivation of crops. The Arain men and boys worked at growing the vegetables and the women did the selling. My mother would stop and look at some vegetables, and the buying was always done after the same formula. 'How much are the brinjals, sister?' my mother would ask. 'Sister, what am I going to ask you, give whatever you like. They are half anna per seer,' was the vegetable woman's answer. There was a little bargaining, but as the low price left little scope for reducing it, the woman would weigh the quantity and give one or two brinjals extra as jhoonga. Jhoonga was a great institution: you were entitled by custom to receive a small quantity of what you bought in addition to the proper number or weight. As children we would always press the shopkeeper for more jhoonga, and the success of our buying was judged not so much by the bargain we drove but by the jhoonga we received.

I saw a fire for the first time in this market. It was a big fire, and next to the shop where it broke out was a kerosene store. Gujrat had never heard of a fire engine, so the whole town turned out to help. A long chain of buckets conveyed water from the nearest well, and for hours people fought a desperate battle. In a congested city like this, built of brick and timber, fires could be murderous, as a fire at one end of a narrow lane could seal off a large mohalla. Surprisingly, fires were a rare occurrence, and I do not recall another.

After buying our vegetables and exchanging enquiries about children my mother took her change, and we walked into the main street which led up the slope to the top of the city. This was a street of much interest to me. It began with a soda water shop with row upon row of coloured aerated drinks, of which there was a prodigious variety of synthetic flavours and colours. This shopkeeper boasted over fifty; and for one of his special customers, a local barrister who had been to England, he compounded an aerated mixture of beer and pink rose sherbet. After the drinks shop came a number of fruit shops, then cook shops which made Punjabi delicacies like potatoes and grams, nan, the Persian oven-baked bread, liver, kidneys and kababs and potato chops. As these delicacies sizzled on the coals, on a plate or a spit, their aroma rose tantalisingly to my nostrils. Next were the confectioners whose coloured sweets were an equal attraction to me and the flies. Then came the general merchants selling manufactured household articles, which in those days were mostly imported. The goods were usually British or German, and many of the brands had become household names. Japan had not quite entered the market. One could buy knives, scissors, buttons, cotton and silk thread, mirrors, soaps, bottled hair oils, razors, socks, woollen and cotton knitwear, etc. These imported things always held more glamour for us than the local ones. We preferred the imported combs to the hand-made wooden ones, the electroplated Sheffield and Solingen knives and scissors to the solid steel ones made by our local smiths, Pears and Vinolia soap to the home-boiled desi soap, and the shining coloured buttons to the simple cloth ones.

The street then began to rise towards the Chowk where the four main streets met. On the left was the Sonar bazaar, with the shops of gold and silversmiths; on the right the Pansaris, who sold herbal medicines, spices, rose petal jams used as a laxative, preserves, essences, rose and kewra waters, almonds, pistachio, assofoetida and many other interesting and exotic things. Nearby were shops where they made gold and silver leaf for spreading on sweets. Tiny particles of silver and gold were put between brown paper sheets about eight inches in length and five inches in width. A sheaf of such papers interleaved with the gold or silver particles was placed on a flat stone and beaten with a stone pestle until the gold and silver particles were beaten into the flimsiest leaves about four inches square. To spread these leaves on a sweet you pick it up still attached to the paper sheet and delicately let the leaf waft down. It looks decorative and is supposed to have tonic value. The sound from these shops as the leaves were beaten was like the tonk-tonk of the coppersmith bird.

Once passing this street I saw a strange and frightening sight that I could not understand. In a shop, completely empty of goods, there sat a man in a rigid pose of silent meditation in front of a tall brass lamp with a single wick in a bowl of oil. The man was dressed in plain white clothes and the lamp cast his shadow on the bare wall behind. As people passed in the street they stopped to look but no one talked to him, and he would not raise his eyes to look back at them. It was early in the morning and I could not understand why this man had to sit in broad daylight in front of a lamp and talk to no one. There was no wailing or crying in the house above and no sign of death. I did not dare to ask anyone till

I reached school, and there I learned that this shopkeeper was declaring himself bankrupt. The word for one who goes into bankruptcy is diwalia, meaning one who lights a lamp, the diwa. The act is called 'diwala nikalna', to take out the lamp. In due course the creditors will open discussions with the bankrupt, and his biradari or its panchayat may have to be called in, but this morning people merely watched the sad sight. This public confession, and the ritual of penance would not be forgotten for generations. 'Was not his father a diwalia; or was it his grandfather who took out the lamp?' someone will ask. And debts had to be honoured by sons and even grandsons.

The street continued to rise steeply from the square to the citadel, with narrow lanes on either side leading to other lanes and mohallas. Here the entrance to each mohalla was barred by a strong wooden gate with many stout erls at the back. It was the oldest part of the city and totally medieval. It had an old well, baoli, which was reached by a steep flight of steps and was supposed to be very deep, and so it must have been, as the citadel was high above the ground level. There was an old hamam, a steam bath, dating back into the Moghul or perhaps pre-Moghul times. We climbed up the main street till we turned into a lane to go into the house of some relations. In the citadel the houses were narrower than below, as the pressure on land must have been greater in the old days in this most secure part of the city. Some of these lanes and houses saw the sun for less than an hour in a day and were therefore dark and chilly in the winter, though cool in summer. We made some more calls, and while my mother talked to the women I watched other boys play in the lane. In this congested area there were hardly any open squares; only narrow twisting lanes, flanked by tall houses. One shuddered to think what happened here during invasions in the past. When the city was lost people retired into the citadel, barred the mohallas and houses and waited on housetops with cauldrons of boiling water and oil, while the invading soldiery ran about, mad with lust for loot and rape. When we read in our history books of Nadirshah's qatil-e-am in Delhi, the order for three days' general massacre which he gave his soldiers, it meant something to us living in a town like Gujrat.

Equal devastation was caused whenever plague broke out. In the dark lanes and houses, plague spread with the speed of dust-storms. It blew through every gali, mohalla and house picking victims at random. As it swept through a lane it would rush up the narrow steep stairs of a house and touch an inmate with its hot fingers, then jump over the terrace wall into the next house and through it down into the street below. Its victims would burn and writhe in pain for a day or two. The family and neighbours were scared when they helped, but help they did, although they knew that apart from the little comfort it gave, help was quite useless. The delirious victims hardly knew. Sometimes there were so many dead in a street that they had to wait for their turn to be taken out of town to the cremation grounds. When the mourners came back from the cremation, those next in order had been brought down, and as their funeral procession passed through the hushed streets people would ask who was it now. Sometimes it wiped out a whole family. Once when there was a mild outbreak of plague I myself lay in bed feeling hot and giddy. In my groins was a swollen gland which the old family doctor said was the dreaded sign. Everybody agreed except my uncle's wise munshi who said that though there was plague in one part of the town and the gland was good evidence, he somehow did not believe that I had it. He looked carefully down my leg till he saw a tiny, almost healed, cut under the ankle. This, he suggested, was the cause. And so it was.

From the citadel we returned to our house by a short-cut through the mohalla known as the Small Well with the Pipal Tree. I used to like returning this way because in the whole city, apart from the market, it had the only tree. It was a large, spreading pipal with a well underneath, always the coolest spot in the summer. Pipal is a lovely tree and rightly declared sacred by our ancestors. Its beautiful, bright green, perfectly formed and delicately-veined leaves are so fine and light that they tremble melodiously in the merest breath of wind, and each one of them acts like a fan. There is always a cool breeze under a pipal, and as it often has a well underneath, the spilled water adds to the coolness. The banyan tree has a severe majesty, while the pipal has a gentle friendliness about it. It is at its best when it has new leaves, smooth, pink and unbelievably soft and delicate, like the palms of a baby's hands. Under its maternal spread people sleep, worship and take vows, but we never went under it in dark because we were warned that it sheltered dains. We were told how to distinguish a dain. She is a beautiful woman, but her feet are turned backwards. And if you do not look out and get close to her she will take you away to eat you, for human flesh is her only food.

On the way we called at a Jhewar house, where my mother asked the wife to help with cooking and cleaning the utensils next week because we were expecting some guests.

By the First World War a ring of buildings had sprung up along the road which skirted the city wall. Among them were a number of institutions, a jail, a mission hospital and school. One or two enterprising shopkeepers had also ventured out. But there had long been a Civil Station, a kind of suburb of Government offices and bungalows. The early British officials built their bungalows in spacious surroundings outside the towns. In time these colonies grew into small self-contained townships of a standard pattern that was rather pleasant. In the residential part of the civil station there were large bungalows, each with its own fruit, vegetable and flower garden, cookhouse, servants quarters, stables and dhobi ghat. A long tree-lined drive led from the gate to the bungalow. They had rooms with high walls of sixteen feet or more, and deep verandahs all round, usually with well proportioned round columns. In the gardens they grew flowers, vegetables and trees imported from England, and that is how many of the flowers, and vegetables so familiar to us today were introduced to us. Many of these flowers which we looked upon as English, grew in their wild state in the Himalayas, but to our gardens they came via England.

In the non-residential area of the Civil Station there was a post office, a branch of the Imperial Bank which worked for the Government, a hospital, school, sometimes a college, Government offices, law courts, police headquarters and barracks, a parade ground, and the Company garden. These gardens were started in the days of the East India Company, and although most of them after 1857 were renamed Victoria Gardens, they continued nevertheless to be known as Company Gardens. There were usually in the larger towns a general store, run by a Parsi, selling European tinned and bottled provisions, liquors and general merchandise. In a part of the Company Gardens there was a club for the British residents. Later, as the number of Indians in the professions and services grew, they formed their own clubs. Ironically, the club named after the town was always exclusively British, presumably because it started as the first one. Each Civil Station, to round off its British origin, had a small Protestant Church and a few local Christians with biblical names like Daniel and Samuel. Roman Catholicism never made much headway in the Punjab. They were a small, sad community living around the church, in a no-man's casteland between the English and us; lost to us and never accepted by them.

My school, the Government High School of Gujrat, which my father, uncles, and before them my grand-uncle, had attended, was situated in the Civil Station, and it was typical of Government schools from the last century. It was a single storey brick building in the shape of an H. In front, facing the road, was a garden, at the back playgrounds, and on one side a hostel and some staff quarters. The English headmasters of my father's days had gone and were replaced by Indians. The school had ten grades and was divided into three sections: the first five years were known as the primary, the second three years were called the middle, and the last two years the high school. Teaching was in Urdu in the primary and the middle schools, and in English in the high school. We began by learning calligraphy and numerals on wooden boards, which we smeared with yellow clay every day. We wrote with reed pens which were sharpened every morning, and in small earthenware inkpots we soaked a rag in ink crystals made from lamp black. With this we learned to write on the clay surface Urdu lettering in the beautiful Persian script. At the end of school we washed off the clay and the writing and smeared on some fresh clay to prepare the surface for the following day.

Our curriculum was perhaps better than the one I came across in the more advanced schools in Bombay thirty years later. For example, we learned our geography in three stages; in the primary school we were taught the geography of our district and then of our province; in the middle school the geography of India and Asia, and in the high school the geography of the world. Similarly, our history teachings were divided into four sections: the Hindu, Muslim and British periods of Indian history and, as an optional subject in the high school, the history of England. I was therefore astounded to find that my daughter's first introduction to history and geography in a Bombay convent school was through the British Isles. She knew King Alfred and the towns and ports of England before she had heard of Ashoka and Calcutta. Despite the naïve dose of the blessings of the Angrezi Raj, the English Directors of Public Instruction in the Punjab had designed our studies well. The medium of instruction was first Urdu, but during the last five years of school we had to learn English and one of the classical languages, Sanskrit, Persian or Arabic. The whole curriculum was well balanced.

Events of interest at school were the annual cricket tournament, the visits of the school Inspector and the Governor of the Punjab, and fine days in the summer. Fine days were an institution that could only have been developed in the dry country of West Punjab. After a long succession of hot summer days, the monotony would one day be broken by a cloudy sky or, better still, a wet day when it rained heavily. Word would go round in the classrooms that it was a shame to be indoors working when it would be so much nicer to be out playing and getting wet. The luxurious feeling of running out into the rain and getting soaked is something only those who have lived in our dry climate can understand. Some bold ones among us would get together and write out an application to the headmaster. It ran something like this:

To: The Headmaster,
Government High School,
Gujrat, Punjab.

Gujrat,
Punjab.

Honoured Sir,

Today, by the grace of God, is a fine day. Therefore, we the students of the Government High School, Gujrat, Punjab, request that a holiday should be declared. For this act of kindness we shall for ever pray for your long life, happiness and prosperity.

Yours most obediently,
The Students
of the Government High School,
Gujrat, Punjab.

To make the best impression the application had to be written in English; it also had to invoke the grace of God, just in case God changed His mind and the sun came out. We would watch anxiously for the clouds to stay, and for some word from the headmaster. Suddenly, out of its hour, the school bell rang chaotically to say that the school was closed, and three hundred boys ran out with yells and whoops of joy. God and headmaster had both been kind, though now it did not matter even if God changed His mind.

Cricket was a popular game in the West Punjab, and Gujrat had a very fine team. The annual tournament was therefore a great event and caused a display of much enthusiasm. The days of the match were holidays, and we would relax in the winter sun, cheering and praying for our team, hoping the match would last its allotted span of four days. In the mornings and evenings we would hang round the hostel where the visiting team was accommodated. Whether we won or lost it was sad to see them depart, and to return to our classes. We also played the Indian games of gulli danda and kabodi, and football, volley ball, basket ball and hockey, but cricket interested us most.

The Schools Inspector came once in a year, and how we looked forward to it, for it was known that he came not to examine us but to inspect the work of the teachers, especially the headmaster. For days we would discuss with much bravado how we held the future of our masters in our hands; we could ruin them if we wished. By innocently giving ignorant answers we could make the Inspector think that the cause of our ignorance was bad teaching, and should the teacher try to explain that we were feigning ignorance, it would not look well for his discipline. If we wanted to we could convey in a few moments that we did not like our master. The masters knew all this and for days ahead were sweet and anxious. We enjoyed care and kindness unknown since the last visit of the Inspector. The brighter among us were carefully primed; the dull ones told to keep quiet, and if they were asked a question, the bright ones were to cut in enthusiastically so as not to give the dull ones a chance. But we knew too and the masters gently hinted at it, that scores could always be settled after the Inspector's visit; there was a limit to how far we could go. I can still remember the smile of blissful satisfaction on the master's face as I once stood in class reciting with great feeling and grand gesticulation:

Twinkle, twinkle, little star,
How I wonder what you are,
Up above the world so high,
Like a diamond in the sky.

The Inspector was so touched by my recitation that he gave me a two-anna piece as a prize. I could do no wrong for days afterwards in class. Throughout my school and college career that was not only the highest but the only distinction I ever achieved.

The visit of a Governor was a great event. It combined everything good in life–a holiday, sweets, fireworks and days of preparations when classes became a pleasure. We made streamers and buntings; mottoes of welcome and felicitation in letters of golden paper on red cloth; decorations of banana stems, mango leaves and marigolds; paper and cloth Union Jacks, and decorated pictures of the King Emperor and the Empress with loyal messages underneath. We learned to sing 'God Save the King' in both Urdu and English to different tunes. The day before the visit, dyers from town came to the school to dye our turbans at school expense, each class in a different colour, pink, saffron, blue, green and others.

The next morning, hours ahead of the time, we lined up in front of school on either side of the road, well scrubbed and washed clean, both the road and the boys. The two rows of brightly coloured turbans gave the effect of a rainbow in the decorated settings of foliage, flowers and coloured paper. In our hands we held the Union Jacks. The air was pleasantly scented by flowers, but our sensitive nostrils took in more keenly the odour of sweetmeats, usually yellow laddus, being prepared in the booths that the halwais had set up in the school. There was going to be a free distribution of sweetmeats, but we had to wait till the Governor had passed.

At last the procession came, led by the police band and marching policemen–we had no army in Gujrat. They were followed by a row of phaetons and victorias, belonging to the local gentry and specially painted and groomed for the occasion. There were then no motor-cars in Gujrat. In the phaeton in front sat the Governor and his Lady Sahiba, both dressed in quaint clothes, though even quainter was the A.D.C. who sat there in a high red-plumed helmet. The Governor kept doffing his grey top hat and his wife waved to us and smiled, somewhat immodestly we thought, as we waved our flags and shouted lusty hurras for the Governor, hurras for the King and Queen, hurras for the Empire, hurras for Great Britain. In the phaetons behind came the other Government servants, the local titled gentry of Rai Bahadurs and Khan Bahadurs, members of the Municipal Committee, and some leading zamindars of the district. As soon as the procession had passed, we broke ranks and ran to the school to claim our paper bags with five laddus each. In the evening there would be fireworks in the Company Gardens, and a visit to the railway station to look from a distance at the Governor's special train, painted in a beautiful ivory colour, guarded by soldiers.

There were other great events of this nature, the Victory Day in 1918, and the visit of the King's uncle, the Duke of Connaught. On Victory Day we were marched up to the parade ground where we were given special bronze medals, heard speeches and sang songs about the invincibility of Great Britain, the greatness of our King Emperor, the perfidy and never-in-doubt defeat of Germany. For the Duke of Connaught also medals were struck, sweets distributed and parades organised. We certainly enjoyed these events although they were not really meant for our enjoyment but, I suppose, to inculcate in us a sense of loyalty and attachment. We certainly learned to associate high British dignitaries with a holiday, bright turbans and sweetmeats, but the pomp and importance was of an impersonal kind. With their strange appearance and their distance, they meant very little to us except that they were great people for whom everybody was told to turn out. For the grown-ups it certainly meant more. To be invited to the parties in their honour was a mark of distinction that the important and the aspiring did not want to miss. It was an honour to be invited and proof of your insignificance if you were not. The crested ivory invitation cards to the Governor's party were treasured by some people and kept carefully wrapped in cloth to be displayed to some British official as a mark of acceptance. I wonder if the British felt it to be more than just a formality; they cannot have imagined that the loyal songs we sang and the naïve expressions of loyalty from our elders meant much in spite of the elation of the moment. Later, in England, when I saw an English crowd cheering the King and Queen I sensed at once the difference. A simple remark by someone, such as, 'He is looking well', conveyed a pride and affection that sprung from deeper sources. The Governor's face of purple-veined red hue, or his lady's powdered countenance, gave in any case no indication to us of their real feelings. Our earlier generations looked upon them with gratitude as symbols of justice and peace, but we were born to the 'blessings of the British Raj' and accepted them as the natural order of life. But even this order was soon to be disturbed, without much warning or build-up, and in the small town of Gujrat life was never to be quite the same until it ended in the cataclysm of 1947 which completely changed the pattern of centuries. For the second time a new idea reached the Punjab through a man from Kathiawar. First came Swami Dayanand's ideal of Arya Samaj, and now Gandhiji's new nationalism.

In Gujrat we felt the tremor only very slightly. Lately, some outsiders had given lectures on a subject that at first we found difficult to understand. The only public lectures we were used to hearing were the Kathas, religious discourses, and in more recent years, the Arya Samaj sermons, but political lectures were something quite new. These visitors spoke about the freedom of India, and this intrigued us; but when they talked in familiar analogies and idiom about the Kal Yug, we saw what they meant. Had it not been prophesied that there were seven eras in India's life and history: there had been a Sat Yug, the era of truth, justice and prosperity; and then there was to be a Kal Yug, an era of falsehood, of demoralisation, of slavery and poverty. This was Kal Yug, when man's word meant nothing, when he could swear falsely in these new courts of law and retain the fruits of falsehood. Man had lost respect for custom, for the guru, for the elders; he could defy his biradari and indulge in practices which yesterday would have forfeited caste and honour. 'An' (a great word meaning much more than just food) and milk and ghee were becoming scarce, where yesterday they flowed through Hindustan in rivers. This wealthy land was now a golden sparrow inside a cage, its feathers plucked one by one. These homely analogies, illustrated by legend and history, registered easily, but not so easily the conclusion to which they were linked, that it was all the fault of the Angrezi Sarkar. We could not readily see how the British were to blame for Kal Yug, which had been foretold so long ago.

Word reached us about the simple, small man from Kathiawar who spoke in the new idiom. Gandhi rechristened India Bharat Mata, a name that evoked nostalgic memories, and associated with Gao Mata, the mother cow. If this struck a chord in the Hindu mind, the Muslims soon responded to the Khilafat call, in support of the deposed Khalifa of Turkey, and the name of Madar-i-Hind, mother India. He preached the new language of national pride and spoke about the peace of the British as the peace of slavery. Gradually a new picture began to build in our minds, of India coming out of the Kal Yug into a new era of freedom and plenty, Ram Rajya.

When the news of Gandi's arrest came there was trouble also in our Gujrat. A young handsome cousin of ours, grandson of grand-uncle Thakur Das, led some young men to cut telegraph wires and march about the city, until they were picked up and put into the local jail. But in Lahore we heard that martial law was declared. Our mother happened to be in Lahore just at the time on a long-deferred visit to a cousin of our father, and suddenly she found herself cut off from home. She was not to be daunted and made several attempts at getting out but each time the soldiers sent her back to the city. I suppose she looked too simple and innocent a young woman to be suspected of breaking the martial law with any political intentions. Although no trains were running, she argued with the British soldiers that she must get to the station and sit there and wait. Knowing her, I think if she had got past them she would have walked home to Gujrat, eighty miles away.

All kinds of rumours floated out of Lahore of beatings and mass arrests, of people being made to crawl on their bellies on the roads, of students made to walk every day to Lahore Cantonment six miles away in the hot sun just to salute the flag. And then came the news of the Jallianwala Bagh at Amritsar. We heard that General Dyer took a position with his machine-guns at the only entrance of this densely packed sunken garden surrounded by tall old mansions, and fired and fired till his ammunition was exhausted. The crowd heaved in a blind mass, it climbed up the trees and over the short run of a low wall, but the guns kept gathering it back into a heap. At last, it was said, when there were no more bullets left to feed the over-heated guns, Dyer and his soldiers, tired, picked up their tools and went away, leaving the garden to wailing widows and orphans searching the heaps. Triumphantly Dyer declared that he had the whole rebellious city at his mercy and felt like reducing it to ashes, but then took pity on it and refrained. Truth and rumour spread like lightening.

People in Gujrat were stunned and fumbled back in their memory to Nadirshah. But Nadirshah was just an adventurer, a bandit who claimed he had an excuse: some of his soldiers had been murdered after Delhi had capitulated, and the order of general massacre was the punishment he prescribed for Delhi breaking its word. But this Sarkar was different; it had been kind and benign, it had ruled for sixty years without the traditional marks of power. Why this sudden change? After sixty years we in Gujrat had almost forgotten that we were ruled by the British. In the city you never saw an Englishman except some rare salesman throwing free cigarettes out of a tonga to promote the habit of smoking. You had to go out of the city gates into the Civil Station to see one of the three or four Englishmen posted in Gujrat, the Deputy Commissioner, the Superintendent of Police, sometimes the Executive Engineer, possibly the Sessions Judge, and perhaps the Padre Sahib. Indians were already becoming senior officials. In this atmosphere of calm acceptance the banging of the mailed fist seemed strange. Nobody had taken much notice of what the politicians had said, it was the sort of platitudes we were used to from our elders. They had always said: 'India was once the land of milk and ghee, look at this Kal Yug now.' And if some spoke about freedom and equality, was not that what our English books also taught?

There was now growing up a third generation of Punjabis, educated in English thought, who were beginning to think accordingly for themselves. My father's generation of professional men read the news and editorials in the Tribune and though they spoke discreetly, they began to think about politics for the first time. Everybody discussed; even we boys in school learned new names like Gandhi, Tilak, Lajpat Rai, Ali Brothers, Mother India and Azadi. Was a change under way? In their inevitable succession dynasties and kingdoms rose and fell like tides in a sea. The wise began to wag their heads again and utter old wisdom. When a Hakam, a ruler, is harsh out of proportion to the occasion, it can only be that he is afraid and unsure. If this does not work he will have to be harsher still the next time until he exhausts himself to no avail. Somehow these new Hakams did not look the kind who would relish harshness for very long. To the Punjab change was nothing new; it had been a recurring phenomenon for so long that the Punjabis had learnt to smell it like the distant rain on their parched and dusty soil.

In such simple terms we discussed and reasoned as the new movement spread in the Punjab, though the non-co-operation and satyagraha of the next few years somehow did not affect us much in Gujrat. There were occasional political meetings and hartals, some picketing of the one foreign liquor shop and the many cloth stores, but generally Gujrat took little interest in politics and continued its medieval tempo.

CHAPTER EIGHT

WHILE WE were living in Gujrat mother and father arranged the marriage of my uncle, who had now settled in a law practice.

Having taken his time over passing his degree he was now nearly twenty-four, an unusual age among us to remain unmarried. A lot of people were asking questions about the delay, and my mother felt that his marriage could not be postponed any longer. If the elders had had their way he would have been married long ago, while he was still studying, but times were changing and it was in accordance with father's own ideas that uncle preferred to wait for his marriage till he was settled in life. To the old way of thinking this was irrelevant. You married when you came of age and not when you began to earn. Marriage and earning were two separate things. Marriage was a social, familial and religious obligation, while earning was a matter of circumstance. To allow my uncle to remain unmarried till he was twenty-four was something that had never happened in our biradari. But now that uncle was earning, father agreed with mother that marriage was opportune, and this was made known.

In an arranged marriage there are many considerations which thoughtful parents take into account. The girl should of course be a Khatri, and a Bahri, and she should possess some education which in those days only meant that she should not be illiterate. As my uncle was well-built and tall, the girl should also be of good physique, but as he was of a pukka colour, a euphemism for being dark, the girl ought to be fair. Temperamentally she should be sober and serious, because my uncle had been wild in his college days. In short, what the parents were looking for was a girl who possessed his good points and compensated for his weaknesses. A new consideration that had developed in our class was that she should belong to a family that had taken to professions.

We began to receive many feelers from in and around Gujrat. Many of the girls my mother had seen herself or heard about from others, but as the boy was in her opinion accomplished, and as she was not worried about any other boys or girls of even near-marriageable age in our family, she could afford to be discriminating and finicky. Why should she not be, everyone agreed. The boy was good-looking, he was earning and had a well placed brother and uncle, even if he had no parents. If he had been wayward at college, a reputation that had reached Gujrat, it only meant he was experienced and knew the world. Nevertheless mother was advised not to wait too long, because too many refusals would make people talk. Just as my mother was beginning to relent, an offer came that interested her.

In Peroshah, a small town not far from Gujrat, in the direction of Bhimber and Kashmir, there was a Bahri Khatri family of the caste of Vohra. The father had recently retired from Government service as a revenue officer. From a small beginning he had risen high and had been awarded the title of Rai Bahadur. He was a personal friend and protege of the Governor of Punjab, O'Dwyer, whose munshi and companion he had been in his youth. Both had served and risen together. One of his sons had been to America for education. The girl was excellent in every way and the match most flattering to us. My mother spoke to father about it and suggested that we should call in the family barber, a Muslim, respectfully referred to by the title of Raja to open negotiations.

Raja heard the details carefully and offered to travel to Peroshah. When he reached there, he first approached some other family barbers, and then spent some time in the bazaar putting tactful questions about his mission. Having satisfied himself he repaired to Rai Bahadur's house, where he was received with courtesy when he declared that he was Raja to some of the respected families of Gujrat. His mission was obvious, though he was in no hurry to come to the subject. He fully savoured the importance attached to his errand and the consequent hospitality. He was treated with great respect because of his ability to make or mar the reputation of two families. As he smoked his hooka, he wisely discoursed on the subject of worldliness, bringing out carefully the satisfaction to parents of possessing good children. Such satisfaction of course was only really fulfilled when the children were suitably and happily married. Rai Bahadur and his visitors listened with suitable appreciative exclamations of agreement.

When the other visitors had left, Rai Bahadur asked Raja in confidence where he had come from. Raja gave only enough information to satisfy Rai Bahadur; he was not going to rush in with all details, for there was still the morning's hospitality to think of. In any case, both sides had to proceed delicately in such matters, with proper decorum and lack of curiosity. There must be no hasty or premature enquiries that might be taken for anxiety or eagerness. After that Rai Bahadur left him with instructions to his servants to make him comfortable for the night. Inside, he spoke to his wife who agreed that the proposal should be pursued.

In the morning when Raja had amply breakfasted on hot milk, parathas and sweets he belched appreciatively and pulled thoughtfully at his hooka. Instead of coming to the subject he launched on a well worded eulogy of Rai Bahadur, his name, his fame and his family. Having put his host at ease he began to talk about our own family, and eventually he landed on the exact spot, that is uncle. I think my uncle would have enjoyed listening; it would have appealed to his sense of humour. All his weaknesses were delicately turned into an individual kind of strength. He had spent many years at college, not just failing his examinations, but because the professors were so fond of him that they did not want him to go. He was an ornament of the college they could ill afford to lose. He had the skin of Lord Krishna, the blue of dusk. God had taken away his parents but amply compensated him with a brother and sister-in-law who had brought him up as their first child. His brother was a great engineer who had built the Bullokee Dam single-handed, and to the farmers in the new canal areas he was God.

In the afternoon, after further consultations inside, Rai Bahadur told Raja in simple words with emotion behind them, that they were very flattered at the proposition, and he was willing to give his youngest child, his favourite in old age, to us. He was sure she would be happy in her future home. He thanked Raja and praised him much, genuinely and feelingly.

Raja returned to Gujrat in a tonga the same evening, a journey that he would ordinarily have done on foot. He was much satisfied with himself and his delicate handling of the mission, and sent word to us that he had much to tell and would present himself in the morning. Again, Raja was not the indelicate man to hurry; but the message said enough to satisfy us. In the morning he came to see father and gave a detailed account of his mission. Suitably rewarded, he went away blessing both families and setting great expectations on such a union, and no doubt including the hope of richer rewards for himself at the time of the wedding.

After sounding uncle, who agreed with due modesty and said that he would be guided by their wishes, our mother decided to visit Peroshah herself. Accompanied by an elderly aunt she travelled up a few days later and arrived at the house of Rai Bahadur where they were already expected. My mother slowly came to the subject. Young and inexperienced she proceeded without the sureness of Raja, but being in loco parentis gave her the natural dignity of her role. Mother praised uncle and Rai Bahadur's wife likewise praised her daughter. In fact, the very sweets my mother had eaten were prepared by the girl, and the cushion on which she was sitting had been embroidered by her. She was a talented, educated girl. Nowadays boys demanded education, and so girls had to be given some schooling; not too much, for that made them too forward and interfered with their domesticity. On the cushion not only had the girl embroidered the word welcome in Hindi but, it might be noticed, in English as well. They believed in bringing up their children well. It was so necessary nowadays. And so the girl's mother went on, not knowing how to stop, till my mother delicately suggested a desire to see the girl. This was the crucial moment.

All mothers have their natural pride, however anxious they may be to find a suitable boy for their daughter, to discharge their debt in life, to send her to a good home where one day she will be Grihalakshmi, goddess of the house. Though mothers like to think their daughters perfect, there is always the lurking fear that the stranger, a mother herself, may be so proud of her son, that her own jewel of a girl may not appear good enough. There will be other offers, if God wishes, just as good and possibly even better, but each refusal hurts the mother's pride.

The daughter had been sent away the moment these strangers entered the house. She had guessed the purpose of their call and was nervously trying to do some work in another room while her future was being decided. A hundred questions darted anxiously through her innocent mind, and as she was agitatedly trying to piece together her thoughts, her mother called. 'Prepare some sherbet and bring it out here for the guests, my son.' Fond parents in affectionate moments referred to their daughters as son, putra. Shyly, with the mantle half hiding her childish face, the girl walked up to my mother with a shining bronze jug full of sugared water. My mother had been carefully watching her as she walked across the courtyard to see if she limped or had any other physical defect. And now she scrutinised her from her feet upward to make sure that she was sound of limb. The girl bowed before my mother. She was simply dressed, without any jewellery, as became a virgin. She wore a plain white salwar, a red kameez of a subdued pattern, a home-dyed green dupatta. On her slender wrists she had coloured glass bangles and in her ears thin gold rings, more to keep the pierced lobes open than as ornament. Her black hair was parted in the middle and tied into a single plait woven with a black cord. Her figure was childish, her breasts immature, and although she was seventeen mother thought she looked less. She had the demure simplicity of a well-bred girl. Her face, my mother thought, was beautiful, and flushed in shyness.

'What is her name?' asked mother.

'We call her Savitri,' her mother answered.

My mother deliberated for a moment and then said, 'It is a beautiful name and suits her well. We haven't got a Savitri in our home.' That settled the matter.

In due course the horoscopes of uncle and Savitri were shown to the pandits to make sure of their compatibility. We were assured that the gods agreed to the match. Here was a youth whom the sun had blessed with power, and Venus, with us a male, with manliness and vigour; a girl who would run her home wisely, blessed by Jupiter. On an appointed day Rai Bahadur's family came to Gujrat to offer shagan, the ceremonial earnest of betrothal. From the girl's side only the male relations came. They brought with them a procession of men carrying large trays containing sweets, fresh and dried fruits, which must include coconuts, almonds and dried dates. They also gave one hundred and one silver rupees in cash. One gave cash according to one's capacity, but the amount given on all auspicious occasions was in odd sums of eleven, twenty-one, thirty-one, fifty-one or one hundred and one rupees, the only exception to this rule being twenty-five rupees. If the engagement was broken the cash was returned to the girl's parents. We received the guests with grave courtesy, and my uncle bowed and touched the feet of Rai Bahadur who put a saffron tilak mark on his future son-in-law's forehead. Other relations from both sides exchanged tilak, and Rai Bahadur gave token amounts of a few rupees to each of our relations present. With further exchange of courtesies the guests departed. The sweets were later distributed by us among our relations and biradari in proportion to closeness of relationship, and to the biradari according to the adopted practice. The horoscopes were again consulted to fix an auspicious date for the wedding.

In the old days girls were betrothed at an early age, though the wedding took place when they reached puberty. In fact girls were sometimes promised by their parents as babies in arms to a family with whom they were on close terms. An elderly lady once told me that she was engaged even before she was born, and the reason was quite accidental. Her mother had once gone to some good family friends with her baby girl of two. She was a pretty child, and as she played with the four year old boy of the other family, both mothers looked at them proudly. The boy's mother said that she must have this little girl as her future daughter-in-law. The girl's mother agreed to the proposal in principle, but as she felt that a difference of only two years in age was too small she promised that she would give them her next daughter instead. A couple of years later she produced another daughter, the said lady.

The difference of four years between her and the boy was considered suitable, and so they were engaged.

Like all mothers, almost from the day Savitri was born her mother had begun to collect her dowry, but about a month before the wedding preparations started in real earnest. Tailors, embroiderers, furniture makers, coppersmiths and goldsmiths arrived. The confectioners came with their enormous vessels and lit big fires to make maunds of sweets for the wedding feast and for distributing. Arrangements had to be made for receiving the wedding party, putting them up for three nights and feeding and entertaining them. Rai Bahadur was the leading man of Peroshah, and as this was the last wedding in the family everything had to be done in great style. Weddings were exhausting affairs for the girl's family in more ways than one.

The first ceremony after the shagan was to send bhocha to our mother. They sent her some money, and a set of clothes, some ornaments, copra, dried dates, rice and sugar. Some days later they sent another set of gifts known as gad, consisting of a heavy mantle with gold border, some lighter clothes and dried fruits, rice and sugar. In fact, from the day of shagan this interminable traffic of gifts in cash and kind from the girl's people had begun. All through her married life a girl will receive gifts from her parents, brothers and uncles–when her children are born, at the various ceremonies for the children, and when they get married.

As the day of the wedding drew near relations began to arrive. First came the women and children, later the men. The local invitations were sent through their Raja who called on each home and left two tablets of soap. This was an old custom to enable people to wash their clothes for coming to the wedding. The whole house was full of guests, and there was much confusion. The elderly women used to relish the opportunity to ventilate old grievances, real or imagined. All relations were assembled and it was a chance too good to be missed. A grand family row sent away everybody pleased and satisfied.

At nights, women and girls used to gather in the large courtyard and sing to the accompaniment of a small, oblong, two-sided drum, called dholki. The songs were traditional, handed down the generations, and were known as suhag de geet, to wish the girl a happy married life. They were in dialogue form.

Father: *My daughter, why are you standing behind the sandalwood tree?*
Daughter: *I am standing here, father, because I want a good marriage.*
Father: *My daughter, what kind of a husband do you want?*
Daughter: *Father, among the stars as the moon stands bright;*
Beside the moon as Krishna stands bright;
I want a match like him.

The girl then turns to her brothers, and to her uncles in similar refrain.

Till late in the night the beat of the dholki and the singing continued while the girl sat quietly in one corner in a reverie. She had not seen her betrothed, but these songs seemed to reassure her.

There was a series of ceremonies to perform during the last two days: the gana, mayan, shanti path, choora and the wedding proper. Savitri was dressed in simple old clothes, wrapped in an old blanket and made to sit in a back room while excitement and confusion mounted in the house. Raw sugar and salted cakes were placed in her lap. Mouli, the auspicious thread, was tied round her wrist and she was told by her girl friends, who were now in constant attendance, to tie the so called gana really tight because it would have to be opened by her husband when he took her home. The girls smeared her hands and feet with henna, and put the paste on their own hands and feet too. They also made tears in Savitri's old clothes. These two last days were called mayan, and special songs were sung:

Blessed be the mother who bore such a daughter,
'In old and soiled' clothes in mayan she put her.

Early on the wedding morning, before the stars had faded in the sky, men came into the ladies' courtyard to make the vedi, a pavilion of leaves and flowers, in which the wedding ceremony would take place that night. They brought four big banana plants and a lot of foliage. The banana plants were put as pillars, and a top covering was made of twigs and mango foliage. Inside the pavilion were placed two new square reed baskets, of the kind that vegetable-sellers used, upside down to serve as stools. The vedi had to be completed before sunrise. During the day women and children continued to decorate it with flowers and garlands, sprinkle it with red powder and hang coconuts on it.

After sunrise there was the ceremony of shanti path, the way of peace, at which prayers were said so that all might go well at the wedding. Savitri came out of the house and sat in the vedi, still in her old clothes. Garlands of cowrie shells and copra were tied to her wrists. Her mother's brother and his wife brought the choora, a set of red ivory bangles reaching from wrist to elbow. They were to remain on her arms as a sign of her newly-wed status for a whole year, so that wherever she went people would know she was a new bride. After a year the choora would be taken off ceremoniously, but should the husband die before the year was out she would break the bangles herself on her arms. She was anointed with oil, and a dried date was put into her mouth. After this ceremony Savitri got up and returned to her room. Since the previous night everyone in the house had been fasting. Now the fast was broken by all except by Savitri and her parents who would continue to abstain from food until the wedding ceremony was over.

Savitri never took off her choora!

The evening came, the time to prepare her for marriage. Savitri had not bathed or changed clothes for two days. A young married couple were chosen to go to a well with the pandit. There they did puja and drew a pitcher of water. In this blessed water Savitri was bathed. After that the women busied themselves with the pleasant task of making-up and dressing the bride. She was anointed with sandalwood oil, and her hair was dressed into long plaits; her hands and feet had already been dyed red with henna; her lips were stained with red juice of wattle bark; her eye lashes darkened with kohl. She was now dressed in red clothes, rich and beautiful, for red is a bride's colour in the Punjab. She was bedecked with gold jewellery from head to foot, one special piece for each part of the body. On her head was a round cup-shaped ornament, chownk, which lifted her dupatta gracefully. There were two smaller pieces, called phool, flowers, on either side. All three were delicately worked and each had a blue stone studded on top. On each side of the hair parting were flat, broad pieces, twitarian, with rows of little pendants, joined over the parting with a fine gold chain. Suspended from the hair with another gold chain was shingar patti that rested on her forehead like an inverted new moon. In her ears were heavy rings in the shape of inverted cups with pendants, called jhumke, and in one of the nostrils a clove-shaped pin, called by that name, laong. Around her neck was a flat ornament, known as gulu band, and a long garland of old English sovereigns alternating with small round buds of gold. She had five rings, one on each finger, each ring connected with delicate gold chains converging to bracelets round the wrists. On her arms was the new bright red choora, and round the wrists she had gold bangles and bracelets. Above the elbow she wore a single heavy bangle with the ends in the shape of a tiger's head. She also wore flat anklets called paonchies, which rested gracefully over her feet; on her toes she wore little bells which tinkled as she walked. She wore a red velvet salwar and kameez with heavy gold embroidery round the collar and the cuffs, the hem of the shirt and on the edges of the salwar. Her dupatta, the mantle, was also red with a gold border. She was wrapped in a red phulkari of the bagh design. Tall though Savitri was, she was weighed down by the heavy clothes and jewellery. Tired by the strain of the last two mayan days and the fasting, nervous at the ordeal of the long wedding ceremony and of the departure and all that lay in store for her, unknown and unfamiliar, her knees turned to water as she tried to rise on her feet. She was supported and led into her room. Women looked at her in admiration; her girl friends in envy. After the two days in old clothes, without a bath, she now blossomed out like a flower. The old women said that mayan was a good custom; it helped to produce a contrast and it also rested the girl.

Back in her room, Savitri waited through the long tedious hours till midnight, which the pandit had declared as the auspicious moment for the wedding ceremony.

While all this was going on in Peroshah, we were also busy in Gujrat. A month before father had sent out invitations. The

English custom of printed invitation cards had already reached our town, and we asked the small local press to print the cards. The text was in Urdu and invited you to collect at our house on the afternoon of the wedding day and proceed with the party to Peroshah where there would be sehra bandi in the evening; milni later at the bride's house, followed by dinner; and the wedding ceremony at midnight. The barat would stay in Peroshah for three nights and return on the morning of the fourth day. In the bottom left-hand corner was a pompous though cryptic R.S.V.P. which was the latest superfluous imported refinement. It was superfluous for no one ever refused a wedding invitation. Each card was sprinkled with saffron and stained red to mark the auspiciousness of the occasion. Lists were carefully made of all those attending and the total number was discussed, almost negotiated, with the Rai Bahadur's family. We had over two hundred persons to invite. Raja went to see Rai Bahadur who, though welcoming such a large number, protested that Peroshah was after all a small place and it would be difficult to put up so many guests for three nights and to do their very best. Eventually, a number was agreed upon. The girl's side nevertheless allowed for more, knowing full well that there would be last-minute invitations, and people would bring along their own guests.

Guests from outside Gujrat had to be put up at our house and the houses of our relations and friends. The near-relations arrived with their families days ahead, and our house was as full as the bride's. On the bride's side they prepared a dowry, daj; on our side we were busy preparing clothes and jewellery for the bride, called vari. In addition, sets of clothes had to be made for presenting to the bridegroom's sisters. We also performed ceremonies of shant, gana and mayan; and of course we had gifts to send to Peroshah needed for the ceremonies in the bride's house.

On the wedding day all the men assembled, dressed in new clothes, happy and eager, at the tonga stand by my grand-uncle's house outside the town, to set out for Peroshah. All the tongas in town and from the neighbouring places had been hired to take the barat. This was before the convenient motor-buses had arrived. The barat was accompanied by a brass band, the fireworks people carrying their stock of crackers and contraptions of bamboos with spiral fireworks, and people carrying gas-lamps. But the most colourful sight of all was the horse on which my uncle was to ride that night to his bride's house. They had decorated the horse in advance, always a mare for this purpose. She had been specially washed and groomed till her skin shone when her owner brought her to our house. She was caparisoned and saddled magnificently, and auspicious coloured threads were tied to her mane and to the reins. When the mare stood in front of our house, she was fussed and decorated, and our aunts, the bridegroom's sisters, brought a large tray full of grams covered with silver leaf and fed her. The horse was having its day too, for it was carrying a bridegroom, who has the status of a king, and a king's mount has its own importance. Before leaving the house, the last ceremony was the bag pharai, when our uncle was handed the reins of the horse by his sisters. He had to give them some money for that and they sang the song of bag pharai:

Brother, what will you give for holding your reins
What are you going to give your sisters.

And with blades of grass dipped in saffron the sisters sprinkled him before he left the house.

The barat arrived in Peroshah in the afternoon and was met by relations and friends of Savitri's family and escorted to the dharamshala, the temple inn. Here they rested and were given sweet drinks and light refreshments. Many of them were going to stay at the dharamsala, others were taken to the janj ghar, a hall built by the community for the reception of barats. Important guests like my uncle and our family were put up at one of Rai Bahadur's own houses. The whole village had turned up to see the barat and to make critical comments on the groom and his party. After all, the Rai Bahadur was somebody in Peroshah and they wanted to satisfy themselves that his Savitri was going to a house of equivalent status. They took the customary privilege of making caustic comments just sufficiently loud for us to hear. Some wags in the barat matched their wit with the locals, and there was much amusement all round. 'If you have any other girls bring them out;

it is not often that you in Peroshah have the honour of getting grooms from Gujrat,' shouted one of the baratis. To this one of the locals retorted, 'Go away, we have heard the reputation of Gujrati goondas; what surprises us is that Rai Bahadur agreed.' This boy looks all right, but as for the rest of them, they look as if there is going to be a famine in Peroshah after they leave.' And so the bantering went on.

Tall, trim and upstanding, uncle Dwarka Prashad looked a striking figure dressed in the classical robes of a khatri warrior king. The old custom is that if a king meets a wedding party on its way, it is he who dismounts as a mark of deference. On his head he wore a silver crown over his turban, on which was tied gold braid and then another garland of roses, jasmines and marigolds that fell over his face in a cascade of gold threads and flowers. It was called sehra. It was blessed first by the pandit and then by grand-uncle, followed by all the baratis as they came forward to touch it and wish him well. He wore a long red, buttonless cloak, tied with tabs and trimmed on the edges with gold; on his legs a pair of tight trousers; on his feet gold-embroidered Punjabi Pothowari shoes with turned up spurs in front; and around his waist a sword in a red velvet scabbard with silver mountings. Behind him in the saddle sat my elder brother, for according to custom the groom rode to the bride's house accompanied by his best man, always a young brother, cousin or nephew.

Through the streets of Peroshah, headed by the brass band and men holding gas-lamps over their heads, while fire crackers were exploding, the colourful procession with our uncle sitting on his horse wended its way by a circuitous route to cover the main streets. Some people carrying silver carafes were sprinkling rose water. On the way we stopped by a jandi tree, where uncle alighted from his horse and with his sword made a ceremonial cut in the gnarled hard wood, a custom meant to test the khatri groom's prowess and the sharpness of his sword. In the old days he was supposed to slice the stem or a thick branch of the tree with one blow. However great our hero-worship for our athletic uncle, his khatri skill with the sword was small, and he made the merest scratch. The procession continued midst much noise and music. As we reached the Rai Bahadur's house the procession solemnly came to a halt. Awaiting us, under an archway of leaves and flowers, stood the male members of Rai Bahadur's family, headed by the old man himself, a handsome figure dressed in the pink turban customary for the bride's father, a white cloak-like double-breasted long coat, which bore an influence of the English frock-coat, white salwar and Punjabi shoes. Deferentially behind him stood his brothers, brothers-in-law, sons and other relations in that order. We also formed in similar order. In the absence of a grandfather, we had grand-uncle at our head. There was a short ceremony of anointing the groom with oil, as the two processions stood facing each other in silence, and then followed milni, the ceremony of a formal introduction of the two families.

Rai Bahadur moved forward from the bride's side; from ours our grand-uncle stepped forward. They embraced each other, and Rai Bahadur put a garland round grand-uncle's neck, and then took out a saffron-stained envelope containing some money, which after passing twice round grand-uncle's head he presented to him. They were followed by Rai Bahadur's brothers, in order of seniority, meeting our father and his brothers. According to prior agreement a selected list of relations did milni with each other, and in proportion to their importance our side received money from their opposite numbers. At this stage, while the two groups stood facing each other and uncle still sat on the horse, a sehra was recited. A friend of the family with poetic pretensions had composed a poem, also known as the sehra, in which he eulogised uncle, felicitated the company, and wished him on everybody's behalf a long and happy married life. The poem, written in illuminated letters and framed in a colourful Persian border, was presented to uncle.

After milni the groom alighted from his horse, which in all its splendour was taken away. Led by womenfolk Savitri, with her head bent and veiled, came forward to receive the groom and put a garland round his neck. She was then led back. The groom was taken inside the house and surrounded by the women and girls who put him through a quiz-ceremony of teasing him and testing his wit. The mother-in-law, sisters-in-law and others put him questions which he had to answer in verse. Usually the grooms were coached by the womenfolk at home. Some were very bold and improvised answers which made the girls giggle and then go into peals of laughter. Such grooms were very popular. News would soon reach the bride how the groom was faring: girls would run in and give exaggerated accounts of what he looked like, his wit and intelligence. The women pressed money into his hand, and the ordeal over, he was allowed to leave.

In the courtyard the barat was being fed, and how the wedding guests used to eat! They would sit in long rows on the ground and in front of them metal trays and cups were placed. The food was cooked by professional cooks of Jhewar caste, but never served by them, for in those days it would have been a mark of disrespect to have the guests served by hired men. Members of the family and biradari would personally wait upon them. Nor did the girl's side sit down with the guests; they always had their meal afterwards. It was also a custom to serve sweets on the first or the second afternoon, sometimes in a khurli, which literally meant a manger. White sheets would be spread in front of the guests, and the sweets piled from one end to the other, like filling a manger. There was naturally many times more than they could consume, and the guests were therefore given coloured silk handkerchiefs in which they could take away what they could not finish. The khurli was very expensive and few could afford it. It therefore created a sensation which was remembered for years.

After dinner most of the guests left, and preparations began for the wedding ceremony which was due to start after midnight. The pandit came with trays of incense rubbed in ghee, holy water from the Ganges, puffed rice, wheat flour, honey and sacred thread. He sat in front of the hawab kund, an iron receptacle in which the sacrificial fire was burning. In the four corners around the fire he arranged piles of fruit and burning incense. The time was now drawing near, and close relations sat down on the carpets spread on the floor. The pandit was seated in front of the fire, and on the other side the bride and groom were led up. Swathed in the red phulkari, with her red mantle drawn low over the face, Savitri was barely visible. Demureness combined with nerves and fatigue made her look like the victim of a sacrifice as she was escorted to the fire, affectionately supported, according to custom, by her maternal uncle. Our uncle walked up with not a great deal more confidence. They both sat down on the upturned reed baskets facing east, she on his left, with the side of her phulkari tied to his sword, a symbolic tying together of their fates, her honour represented by her head covering and his protection by the sword.

Savitri had still not seen her bridegroom and was anxious to know what he looked like, yet she dared not raise her mantle or look up. She could only see his knees and calves covered in tight trousers. They looked sturdy. She could tell that he was tall, but was he good-looking? Was he going to make a good husband like her father, who still affectionately called her mother rani? She was already tied to him and his for ever. Many years lay ahead, happy years probably, as most marriages were happy. Her mind became bolder as her thoughts ran on. Would she bear him many children? At this she felt shy and guilty and was awakened from her reverie by the fire which rose into a flame as the pandit finished the first mantra with a long intoned 'om swaha', and we all picked up a handful of incense and threw it into the fire.

The pandit went on chanting the mantras, and the fire would flare up each time he finished one. The ceremony, which lasted for many hours, seemed to consist of three parts: the worship of the fire by the bride and the groom, the vows, and ritual symbolising the union. The vows ran like this:

Savitri's father to the bridegroom:

> *I give you my daughter, whom I have brought up with great love and affection, as a gift to you. Look after her; that is your duty.*

Uncle:

> *I accept her. She is half of my body. I will look after her.*

Savitri to her bridegroom:

> *I offer you my body, my mind and my possessions. I will serve you; you are my master; you are everything to me, after God. I will never look at another man. Apart from you, all other men will be like father, brother or son to me.*

After the vows they both got up, stiff and tired, having sat rigidly and self-consciously for long hours. Tied to each other, now man and wife, they walked twice round the fire, he in front and she behind him in an anti clock-wise direction. They then walked twice round the fire again, now she in front and he following. This ceremony seemed to establish their equality, each leading the other twice round the sacred fire. They then embarked on the symbolic journey of life, the yatra of seven steps; one step for health, another for prosperity; a third for children, and so on.

Dawn was breaking as the long vedic marriage came to an end. By now a number of baratis had joined, having rested a few hours after the sumptuous meal. As the ceremony finished, Savitri's brother gave her parched rice; she gave it to her husband, who threw it into the fire. It now remained for the two family priests verbally to witness the marriage. Each purohit on behalf of his family recited its lineage: Dwarka Prasad, son of Maya Das, son of Suhawa Mal. . . .

Savitri and Dwarka Prashad, total strangers still, were now man and wife, married in ancient verdic rites, without any written word. They sat again on the reed stools while people showered rose petals on them. Everybody got up and one by one walked up to them to give them blessings, ashirvad. They both thanked with joined hands. As they got up rose petals scattered on the floor. Savitri was led away into the house, and my uncle walked back to where we were staying. They were man and wife, but they would not be together till she reached our home in Gujrat. The ordeal of ceremonies was not over yet; her worst trial, leaving her ancestral home, was yet to come.

When the guests left Savitri's father and mother, who had not eaten for over a day, broke their fast. Having completed the kanya dan, the gift of his daughter, the father was now given some milk. The others complimented the father on having performed his duty well, and the daughter thanked him for what he had done for her.

Others: *The father drinks milk out of a bowl, and the brother bathes in Ganga.*

Daughter: *Bless, you, father, for spending your earnings on me.*
Bless you, mother, who give birth to me.

In this refrain the songs continued.

On the last day, Savitri's dowry was displayed. In the courtyard charpoys were covered with durries and on these were arrayed the clothes, jewellery, linen, household utensils and cash. There was furniture, a big bed, a low chair and some modern pieces for her new home. The dowry also contained phulkaris which went down from mother to daughter, and some inherited clothes, but these had become merely symbolic because no one wore them any longer. The bride's friends and relations and nearly half Peroshah came to look at the daj. The elder women examined it with critical eyes and stored every article in their memories: the number of suits of clothes for Savitri and her husband, their quality and value; the workmanship and the weight and value of the gold in the jewellery; the number of utensils, their metal and weight. Later they would discuss it and compare it with other dowries. The most important points to note were the gold and the cash.

As people walked around and praised the dowry, Savitri's mother and father accepted the compliments with the simple and modest answer: 'This is nothing.' Our grand-uncle on our behalf thanked the Rai Bahadur in well-chosen words and said, 'How can we take all this; you have given us so much'. Savitri's mother gave him some money as daj dekhai, dowry showing. The women sang a song to express the thanks of the groom's father:

You have filled our house inside, outside, in front and behind;
And the beautiful daughter you have given us will be its ornament.

Later in the day a procession came from our side carrying vari, gifts of clothes and jewellery for the bride and the groom. It was taken indoors and examined carefully by the womenfolk who selected one suit of clothes and jewellery for the bride to wear at the time of her departure. After that one of our uncles took charge of both the vari and the daj, made a list of all the articles in the daj and had them packed, ready for leaving the next day. The departure was set for ten o'clock in the morning.

The packing and carting away of Savitri's daj was a sign to her parents and family that the time for parting had come at last. For days her father and mother had been too busy to think of anything but the needs of the moment. Now the wedding was over, the daj on which they had worked for months was packed and gone. Tomorrow Savitri would also leave, and with her all the guests. The house that had been full of people, noise, music and happiness would suddenly be quiet. Rai Bahadur had not kept good health of late, but the hustle and bustle had kept him active and busy. With this sudden sense of anti-climax he felt old and tired; life would be empty without any children in the house, and Savitri who had come much later than the others was his favourite.

That night the barat had an early dinner, without the usual liveliness. Back in their room for their first early night's rest, Savitri's mother and father tried to console each other with the satisfaction of a job done, of a debt discharged. The thought of the parting in the morning left them both with a hollow feeling. Savitri's mother pulled herself up and with a mother's fortitude began to talk of the future. Savitri is lucky, Dwarka Prashad is a fine young man, handsome, healthy; a man who will take good care of our girl. She will have children, and living so close she will come and visit us often. The house will have children's laughter again and they themselves will go to Gujrat frequently to see her. And with these thoughts, combining sadness with courage, they went into a fitful sleep.

Savitri lay huddled in her bed, with many other women in the room. They were all tired and slept soundly, but her confused thoughts kept her awake. A girl of barely eighteen, brought up in simple surroundings, she knew no more about life than a child. She had always been close to her mother, as the only child in the home for many years. She had played with other girls and had hardly been conscious of growing, till the other day when two women arrived from Gujrat and she was told in advance by her mother that they were coming to look at her. Her mother had explained that she was now a grown-up girl and could not expect to stay with her parents much longer, however hard it would be for them to lose her. And now she was the wife of this stranger whose face she still had not seen. Tomorrow she would leave her home for good, to return to it only occasionally as a visitor. She lay wide awake, half afraid and half curious, with sadness sweeping her as the night grew shorter and the hour of parting came nearer. She tried to console herself with the thought of returning home next week with her husband; the joy of meeting again her parents and friends; the importance of coming home as a married woman, an object of curiosity and admiration. But fear and sadness soon returned.

The household was up very early. Last evening's sadness had given way to the excitement of the biggest moment of the wedding, the departure of the doli, the bride's palanquin. Friends and neighbours were collecting to see the bride leaving. The village dai, the midwife who had brought her into the world, was present to accompany her, as the custom was, on her first venture into a new world. Savitri felt consoled by this thoughtful custom. Till she returned home next week the dai would be close to her. 'My child, do not be afraid, I will be with you the whole time; you will talk to me about everything; I will be your mother.' With these words the dai encouraged Savitri. 'I brought you into the world and I will now launch you on your new life.'

The palanquin bearers arrived with the doli. Covered with a red cloth with white trimmings, it was placed near the front door. Inside Savitri surrounded by her parents and relations was waiting for the final moment. They all blessed her, and her father and mother gave her their last words of advice. 'Beta, you have to go now. You are going to your new home, and though you will not forget us, you must think of your husband and your new home first. You should make a dutiful wife.' These were Rai Bahadur's last words. Her mother held her close to her breast, loath to leave. She put some money into her lap, and one by one her sisters and aunts came up and hugged her and gave money. At last her maternal uncle gathered her in his arms and with faltering steps Savitri walked up to the doli. Her mother and other women moved forward to take a last look, before the flap of the doli was lowered. Savitri cried as if her heart would break. Her mother could not contain herself any longer, and sobbed. The women chanted the farewell song of the doli:

Father you have put your daughter in the doli;
People shower blessings on you.
Bless you father for all you have showered on me;
Bless you mother who bore me.
They are taking me away, father, in the doli.

We on our side stood silently gazing at Savitri's parents. All eyes were wet, even ours. Grand-uncle, erect and venerable with his white beard, stepped forward and made a short valediction. 'Rai Bahadur, you must not be sad; this is not the moment for sadness. You have discharged your duty well; you should be proud. We are happy to take your daughter away; she will be the light of our home. Your loss is our gain.' Rai Bahadur bowed his head in gratitude at these words. They embraced each other.

'Let us go, it is getting late,' said grand-uncle, and at that the bearers lifted the ḍoli by its poles and the procession moved on. Savitri's people walked behind the doli, the women singing, the men silent, till they came to the end of the street. We moved on towards Gujrat.

We reached Gujrat by midday, but the doli could not be taken into the house until it was ḍark and the bride had been shown the evening star. In the evening the doli was taken through the streets and lanes of Gujrat to our house and placed on the platform in front. Our lane was full of our biradari and neighbours waiting to receive the doli. Our grand-aunt, in the position of mother-in-law, received Savitri, passed a bowl of water round her head and drank it. The bride was then taken into the deohri where the ceremony of showing the bride's face took place. The women came up and lifted Savitri's veil, blessed her and gave her money. Savitri bowed deeply and touched our grand-uncle's feet. She was then taken upstairs into her new home and given some food, which she barely touched. It was now late in the night and she was led to her bridal chamber. The last one to leave her, with affectionate words of encouragement, was the dai.

Today, Punjabi weddings are different. Gone are the horoscopes, the barbers, the songs, many of the symbol-rich ceremonies; the noisy pleasures which for simple people were the only entertainment in life; gone are the phulkaris and the heavy classical jewellery. Gone too is the bride's fear of an unknown future; gone the sadness of the parting.

CHAPTER NINE

CHILDBIRTH WAS held in terror in those days, especially the first one, when a girl was said to come back to her husband's house for the second time as a gift from God, provided things went well; and so often they did not. Childbirth always took place at home and was entrusted to the care of the family dai. Dais were usually old Muslim women who had earned a reputation for midwifery. Like the family barber, there were family dais who over years delivered succeeding generations. Savitri was therefore greatly encouraged when after the first confused realisation that she was going to have a baby my mother told her that they would send for her old dai. Raja was once again called in and told to go to Peroshah to break the good news. To our relations in Gujrat the news was delivered through the family priest, the Purohit, but to the biradaris and friends through Raja. In a few days Savitri's people sent some gifts and a new set of clothes in honour of the coming event, and her mother came over herself, proud and happy, and asked us if she could take Savitri to Peroshah for a few days to show off her expectant daughter. This was a custom largely meant to reassure the young bride, because back in familiar surroundings and among her friends and relatives who fussed and congratulated her, she lost the initial fear and began to feel important.

Back in Gujrat, Savitri led a relaxed life and filled her leisure with dreams. With her red ivory choora still on her arms, wearing her bridal clothes of velvet and brocade, she would go out visiting with my mother in the afternoons, on display as a happy bride whose fulfilment was coming in such auspicious time, in less than a year of her wedding. She was congratulated and blessed wherever she went, and given much advice. A bride so young and pretty, fruitful already, with the double bloom on her face of bridal happiness and the coming motherhood, must indeed have been blessed by the gods. And whom the gods blessed, everyone else also was eager to bless. 'May you have a son like four moons.' Passing through the street of the courtesans, mother would stop to talk to the women as they looked enviously at Savitri. With their own bodies overfulfilled, yet never loved, with occasional maternity whose only purpose was to bring forth a nameless daughter to provide for their old age, they looked at Savitri, demure and happy, with a far-away look of sadness. Her joy was never to be theirs. They blessed her too. Mother took Savitri to the Arya Samaj, and had the havan done at home, for the sacred fire to purify it. For luck she took her to the temple too to be blessed by the immortal pair, Shiva and Parvati.

Some time before Savitri was due, the dai arrived. She took charge of everything and bustled about. She checked what preparations had been made. She hoped that her husband as a good Khatri had done his duty and told her the appropriate heroic tales to make the boy brave. She must not go near maimed or ugly beggars. Mother dutifully accepted the role of taking instructions from the dai and did as she was told. She remembered her own dai.

When the time came, we children were sent away to a neighbouring mohalla to father's maternal uncle's house, but we kept dropping in to find out what was happening. One morning we were awakened early to be told that Savitri had given birth to a son at night. We rushed to our house, but as we climbed upstairs we felt there was something wrong. There was hushed silence, not the happy chaos usually prevailing at the birth of a son. Mother took us aside and told us that the baby was not well and Savitri had fever. After that we were ignored and nobody seemed to mind if we hung around.

Later in the day Savitri's mother and father arrived because Raja had been sent immediately to Peroshah to give the news cautiously. The dai had recognised the danger, and her inability to meet it, and had suggested that the big doctor from the hospital should be sent for. Uncle Dwarka Prashad rushed out, and as he went through the mohalla the anxious neighbours guessed. Some hours later when the doctor came out of our house and walked back through the mohalla, alone, followed only by the peon carrying his bag, they all knew.

When the doctor realised that further effort was no use, he whispered to my mother the dreaded Hindu formula, 'I think the girl should now be lowered on to the floor.' Helped by others, she lifted Savitri from the bed and put her on the floor, which had been hastily plastered with water and some cowdung. She was laid with her head to the north and the feet pointing south, as countless generations of Aryans had been laid over the axis of mother earth. From the top of the head the soul was supposed to leave the body towards the ancient home of the Aryan ancestors near the North Pole. A few drops of water from the sacred Mother Ganga were put into her mouth, and the aromatic leaf of the holy Tulsi plant, which is grown in a pot in every Hindu home, was placed between her lips. Slowly life was leaving Savitri's body, burning with the heat of the fever, her baby lying already lifeless near her. A small lamp made out of dough, with melted ghee and a cotton wick, was put near her. As life would stop flickering in one body it would symbolically rise in a tiny flame in another. The soul would soar up and perhaps somewhere enter another body, till purified of all sin it would rise and merge into Nirvan, to be reborn no more. Who knows, my mother thought, where Savitri's soul was first born, and whether she was its last home. Had it finished its eternal quest, or would it continue the search for peace? Whatever its past or future, whether it stopped here or continued, in its sojourn, through Savitri's body, innocent and sinless, it could only have gone upward to a higher existence. It could only have gained a step nearer to Nirvan. Under the first impact of the shock her thoughts raced on, but she awakened herself from her reverie as she heard the sobs of Savitri's mother and father. She rushed out of the room to busy herself with all that had to be done. Outside she told uncle Dwarka Prashad to go in. She whispered into his ear, 'The boy looked just like you.' She then went down to the deohri, where Raja was waiting. She told him to go immediately to the family Brahmin and on the way to warn the acharyas to be ready.

The pandit came and performed the shanti path, bidding peace to the soul on its onward journey, as shanti path had been performed on the morning of Savitri's wedding to bid her well on her journey into her new life. The pandit suggested that some wheat and rice should be given in charity. Some wheat and rice were symbolically brought on a plate and the pandit made Sivitri touch the grains. He coaxed her to utter the Gaytri Mantra as her last invocation. She whispered OM, and as she could whisper no more, her eyes were closed, her mouth gently shut and her arms folded across the breast. The pandit announced that the soul had departed. His task over, he left the room and sent for the acharyas, the Brahmins who take over when death sets in.

As the acharya came into the room he offered condolences and said a few formal words in praise of the departed. As Savitri had no sons, my elder brother was chosen to perform certain ceremonies. He was bathed, Raja shaved his head, and he was put into a new, unwashed raw silk dhoti and had to sit by the oil lamp, in a corner of the room. The lamp had to be kept filled with mustard oil to keep it burning for ten days until all the ceremonies were over. Food would be served to him first and brought to him to eat near the lamp. As a mere boy, my brother was somewhat frightened by the role he was called upon to play. He must have thought of the happier role he had played as uncle's sarbhala when he rode behind him on the horse on our way to Savitri's house for the wedding.

An elder in the family was given the duty of writing post-cards to relatives and friends announcing the death. Each card bore a simple message that at this time, on this day of the month and year, Savitri had gone heavenward and taken the new-born child with her. The card was torn at one edge to indicate, even before it was read, that it brought a message of death. Telegrams were sent to those relatives who were near enough to reach in time for the funeral.

As the news spread members of our biradari began to drop in. As they passed through the street our neighbours joined them. Durries and mats were spread on the thara in front of our house and in the mohalla square for the callers to sit on. Our elders stood at the door, and as visitors came with folded hands and said, 'Very much grieved, how much we cannot say', they replied with their hands stretched out in a gesture of infinity, 'God's will.' The elderly callers touched Dwarka Prashad on the shoulder and said, 'Son, have patience, there is no alternative but to accept God's will with fortitude. Bear the loss like a man, it will give courage to everyone else, especially to her mother and father.'

One member of the biradari always came forward on these occasions and offered to make all the arrangements for the funeral rites. Others, who were good at helping at weddings and funerals, came up behind him and asked to be told whatever tasks they were considered fit to undertake. These were the moments when the biradari came into its own. Everything would be taken off the hands of the bereaved family, and without fuss, very quietly, everything would be taken care of. It was a great feeling for the family, a feeling of importance, of belonging and affection, to be waited upon in their grief. With smooth and experienced efficiency the men and women divided up their tasks, and someone took overall direction. One person ran to the post office to send the letters and telegrams; another went to buy materials for the ceremonies–incense, ghee, mouli and rice; another went to buy new unstitched cloth for the shroud, and handwoven red, purple or magenta cotton or silk for covering; another to buy flowers; another to buy bamboo sticks, some fagots of sandalwood, a mat woven from date-palm fronds, some string, an earthenware pitcher and bowl. A large variety of materials was needed for the coffin and the cremation. In villages a handcart would go round and the biradari members would each give an unsplit log of wood as their contribution for the funeral pyre.

Inside, four women washed Savitri. Her body was first smeared from head to foot with milk curds and then washed with water. Her mother wished her to be dressed in her wedding clothes, her hair oiled and dressed and a red mark placed on her forehead and in the parting of her hair. The choora was taken off because it was inauspicious to burn it. She was then wrapped in a scarlet silk shawl and garlanded round her neck, and flowers were heaped on her breast. So dressed, she looked the bride she was not so long ago. And like the bride she was taken down to the deohri, where she was placed on the bamboo and mat stretcher and tied to it. Now that she was ready to leave, just as when she had arrived, the women came forward to lift the covering and look at her face. While the men stood at the back sobbing silently, the women gave unrestrained vent to their grief, and suddenly one coalesced wail rose through the well of the house. Grand-uncle stepped forward and gently pushed the women, who were smothering Savitri's face with kisses. 'It is getting late,' he said. 'It is time to start.' He had said just those words standing by Savitri's palanquin.

Men came forward and lifted the bier and moved on. While passing through our mohalla they held it low so that the neighbours and others waiting in the street could take a last look. At the end of the street they covered her face and lifted the bier on their shoulders and started at a brisk pace. Every few steps another mourner would join the carriers out of duty and piety. It was considered a blessing to carry it. To the monotonous chant of 'Ram Nam Sat hai', God's name is truth, sprinkling water with a tuft of kusha grass, throwing coins in the air over the body for the poor to pick up, the procession moved on through the streets till it reached the cremation grounds. They lowered the bier to the ground at the entrance, and the acharya performed the symbolic ceremony of breaking the earthenware pitcher full of water. The pitcher had to be dropped in such a way that its neck also broke, to prevent death visiting the family again too soon. The women were persuaded to return, and reluctantly they started back, stopping on the way to bathe at a well.

The acharya performed the last rites, the ceremony of prayer for eternal peace to the departed soul and for the welfare of the family. Some people had arrived earlier to arrange the funeral pyre. The big and heavy logs were placed at the bottom, then the smaller ones; the still smaller logs formed rests for head and feet. Three iron bars were stuck in the ground on each side to prevent the logs from rolling off the pyre. The body was placed on the logs and covered with a few pieces of sandalwood and then smaller logs with some big ones on top again. A bundle of dried twigs and reeds was made into a small pillow and pushed between the logs under her head. Incense and ghee were then poured all over the pyre.

When everything was ready, some elders led Dwarka Prashad to the final and the most painful act. Everyone fell back and left him and the acharya sitting near the pyre. The acharya recited some last mantras and lit a torch of dried reeds which he handed over to Dwarka Prashad, and then walked away.

Dwarka Prashad stood alone, staring vacantly at the pyre. Between the logs he could see the still form of Savitri which he had learned to know so well. He saw the shape of her head, the curve of her breasts and her thighs, and her feet pointing up. In deep youthful sleep he had sometimes seen her lying on her back covered under a bedsheet, as still as she was now. As intimacy grew he had seen her whole body lying expectantly vibrant, but now she looked so relaxed. He felt the growing heat of the torch but he stood still. His feet would not move. As the torch burst into a fierce flame and he still would not move, grand-uncle came forward and put his hand under his elbow and led him close to the pyre. 'Dwarka Prashad,' he whispered hoarsely, 'this is something which only you must do.'

There was a little smoke from the pillow of dry grass, a crackle and then a small tongue of flame leapt and licked the red silk shawl. It grew into a fire which spread to the dry logs. Fed by incense and ghee, as it rushed through the pyre, the fire raged and flames leaped high. The mourners fell back as the intense flames consumed everything in their way. 'Let us now go,' said grand-uncle.

Some other mourners had taken the baby to the river Chenab, a few miles away. There they made a small stretcher from bamboos and reeds, and covered it with soft rushes and leaves. On it they laid the baby wrapped in a piece of red silk and covered with marigolds. The little bier then floated gently downstream. Babies and children were floated on the rivers, or if the river was far away, buried, but they were never cremated.

On their way home the mourners stopped at a well to bathe. The acharya again performed the prayer of peace. As the last prayer was said, the mourners, sitting behind the acharya, all facing in the direction of the town, picked up a straw which each person threw behind over his shoulder. They all got up and walked back to Gujrat.

Back in our mohalla, people sat on the mats in front of the house and planned the future ceremonies, the one for the fourth day, the Choutha; the Daswan of the tenth day; and the Kirya on the thirteenth day. These decided, the men of our family stood up and with folded hands said, 'Please come.' So soon after the going away of a dear one, it is not appropriate to say 'Please go.' The mourners folded their hands, bowed and departed.

No fire was lit in the house but the neighbours and the biradari had thoughtfully prepared a simple meal and sent it to our house in the evening. They coaxed us to eat at least a few morsels with the formal words, 'By giving up food you cannot bring back the dead. Your loss is irreparable, your grief so deep, but you must keep body and soul together because in this world life and death go side by side.' Such words of condolence and encouragement were traditionally uttered.

On the fourth day the biradari gathered at our house in the morning to go and collect 'the flowers', as the bones were called because of the way they burst at the ends. A bone from each limb of the body was placed on a tray and washed with milk. They were then put into a new earthenware pitcher which was tied in a red cloth and marked with Savitri's name. The jar was handed over to the sadhu who lived at the cremation ghat. The ashes were collected in a bag to be immersed in the nearest stream of flowing water.

The Daswan and the Kirya ceremonies over, the acharyas were sent away with a complete set of new clothes, bed linen and utensils, for it was believed that the gifts reached the dead. At the last ceremony Savitri's parents sent Dwarka Prashad a turban to signify their continued relationship. The acharya blessed the family and prayed for peace to all. This marked the end of mourning. Next morning everything in the house was washed or put in the sun, and after this we began usual social life again. On the seventeenth day some Brahmins were called in and fed and given a dakshina of cash, fruit and food, which is also believed to reach the dead. Members of the family will not partake of this food.

The very last rites for Savitri took place at Hardwar where uncle went later. He took the 'flowers', and on the steps of the ghat on the Ganga, where the river leaves the Himalayas and enters the plains, he sat with the family panda and performed the last rites. The 'flowers' were then taken in a boat into the mid-stream and scattered on the fast-flowing river. This broke his last link with Savitri, and from then on she was only a memory. In the evening, as dusk fell over the hills and the river, he went to the ghat again. In a cup-shaped boat made from the thick, waxy leaf of the dhak tree, the flame of the forest, he filled roses and jasmines and placed on them a little earthenware lamp. His little boat, with many others like it, with their lamps lit, floated gently downstream. On still nights hundreds of these boats with their flickering lights floating on the silvery breast of Mother Ganga is a sight so delicately symbolical of life itself.

After making a sad entry of his visit in the family book, uncle left Hardwar to return home.

We had finished our school examinations and had been staying on in Gujrat, waiting for aunt Savitri's baby. But now there was nothing to do, and mother was glad that uncle Dwarka Prashad declined her offer to stay on for a while to look after him. He said he preferred to be alone, and my mother felt that he did not want us around. She was relieved to leave the house where she could still hear Savitri's ebbing moans. Father had put his foot down that there was to be no mourning in the traditional style. He felt that it insulted the grief of the bereaved. Rai Bahadur and his wife were completely broken and did not care. They withdrew to Peroshah and we never saw them again. First the Rai Bahadur, and then Savitri's mother died within the year.

If engagements and weddings were complex and prolonged, so were funerals and mourning. If we enjoyed long and heartily at weddings we paid back dearly at mourning. The Punjabis never did anything in half measures, especially our women, with whom mourning had become an art and a test of both skill and stamina. Often the grief was borne with great courage, but the spirit and flesh broke down under the strain of mourning. The original, symbol-rich ritual had become mixed with some very ugly mourning customs. Curiously, while the prolonged mourning, with its ugly passages, was entirely on the women's side, when men congregated to condole there was calm, dignified silence, broken by words of philosophical wisdom. 'What God gives He takes back; who are we to protest', was the general theme. They sat silently, with covered heads, and with occasional sighs praised God and the departed.

The women seemed to find in death some physical and mental catharsis. They cried, they wailed, they beat their breasts, in rhythm and in rhyme. They did it to traditional pattern, with improvisations. They would sit in a group, with their faces covered with their mantles, holding one end of it, the pala, which gave this form of mourning its name. With the pala they dabbed their eyes and blew their noses as they cried in a song. The leader improvised the dirge as she went along, and the others followed. To express their sympathy, each would in turn come up to the bereaved, put her hands on her shoulder and cry in an intimate language and tone, occasionally hugging her. As further evidence of her grief she would blow her nose often and profusely into the pala of her mantle. They never gave relief to the poor woman, already in deep distress.

The most gruesome spectacle of all was the siyapa, which used to scare us children. The women would form a mourning squad in the deohri and one of them, the most experienced of them all, who had perhaps led at a number of deaths, would lead the siyapa. She would select the squad and then stand in the middle with the rest, twenty-five or more, in several rings around her. They would all bare their breasts and gird up their garments to bare their thighs, and at a word from her begin to beat their breasts, their cheeks, their foreheads and thighs rhythmically in that order, keeping time with the mourning song, sung in a quick tempo. The leader usually sang the song she had improvised at the death of her son or husband; others followed her. While directing the siyapa she kept a stern eye on the performers and sent away anyone who could not keep pace or made an awkward movement. The women turned out would sit crestfallen with the others on the floor and join the pala. The noise of the beaten flesh and the quick song, with an occasional fainting, made the whole thing so horrible that in our days the biradaris finally said no and the custom died rapidly.

CHAPTER TEN

SARGODHA, where we joined father at his new posting, was a town barely twenty years old and part of the new phenomenon of development in the old Punjab. The land between the rivers had been covered by the new canal system, whose special contribution was the irrigation of the desert area in the west and southwest Punjab. Till the end of the last century this was just scrub and waste, inhabited very sparsely by some wandering herdsmen, who were called junglis. They kept sheep, goat and buffalo, and raised a little grain.

The new canals brought water to the land which had always lain fallow because of a scant and uncertain rainfall. But it was fertile because since time these rivers had broken their banks in flood, continuously altering their course and adding fresh layers of rich alluvial top soil. And now these canals brought a perennial supply of water, and in their wake communications, roads and railways. Having dug the canals, the task before the Government was to people this land. They raised a cadre of energetic men called Land Settlement Officers, who set about attracting people from the populated Punjab to this land of opportunity. People were at first hesitant to go into the jungle, whose main inhabitants were jackals, hyenas, foxes and deer. But those who did sent back enthusiastic reports. The virgin soil, with its energy stored for millenia, seemed to hunger for the thrust of man's plough, and the seed he scattered brought forth crops that astounded him. And a man could ask for as much land as he wanted; the more he asked the better it pleased the sahibs, who happily filled in the squares on their maps. One enterprising man, the story went, got on his horse and rode beside the sahib, first in one direction and then in another. They rode all day till they arrived back in the evening to where they had started, and that, said this young stalwart, was all his land, if the sahib agreed. The sahib was only too happy to agree; he would work all night to fill so many more squares in his settlement plans. This was the first of the famous Tiwanas of Shahpur, near Sargodha. The man in charge of the colonisation of the Sargodha area, to whose energy and drive the scheme owed much, was Malcolm Hailey, later governor of the Punjab. It was ironical that having done so much for the province, when he came to govern it the rise of political consciousness made him quite unpopular.

Wherever a few families settled together they made a village, but Government were anxious to found new towns to provide outlets for the produce from the villages and serve as centres of administration and education. Sargodha was such a town. There were others, Lyallpur and Montgomery, entirely new, while many small hamlets soon became tehsils and district towns. The untiring Settlement Officers literally dragged people to these new towns. 'Take some land in this town,' they would press a farmer while he was receiving his arable squares. 'All right, Sahib, give me a "peg of land" enough to tether a horse. It may be useful when I come into the new town to pay my revenue dues.' 'No, no,' the sahib would urge, 'take an acre, two acres, more if you like.'

Starting from scratch, these towns were made in the image of the Settlement Officers, practical, orderly and colourless. Methodically planned, Sargodha was so different from the medieval Gujrat. It was built in a square, bounded by the new canal on one side and by the new railway line that went across the canal at a right angle on another; on the third side it had a belt of gardens, fruit orchards and vegetable patches through which ran a water distributory; and on the fourth, set apart from the city, there was a mandi, the wholesale produce market next to the railway station. The town was divided into two parts, the city and the mandi on one side of the railway line, and the civil station on the other. On the outskirts there were three more innovations, the waterworks, a seed farm, and an area set apart for factories, mainly cotton gins, flour and oil mills and a new luxury, an ice factory.

The mandi was a big square with ground floor shops on all sides. Here the produce of the surrounding country, wheat cotton, millets and oilseeds, came in. The farmers brought the commodities in large carts drawn by pairs of bullocks or male buffaloes, or on camel back, and unloaded them in the square in mounds. Most picturesque were the heaps of cotton, pure white and fluffy, like fresh piles of snowdrift. The farmers, the wholesale buyers and commission agents, among them the representatives of the large European produce firms of Ralli Brothers, Louis Drayfus, Volkart Brothers, and their Japanese counterparts, Toyo Menka Kaisha, Mitsu Bishi and others, and the professional auctioneers would move from one pile to another. Men would pick up a handful of wheat, look at it casually and let it drop through their fingers, as the auctioneer sang the bids in a soft voice. No one spoke, but at a nod from someone the auctioneer varied the pitch of his monotonous, sing-song four rupees two annas, four rupees two annas, four rupees two annas, to four rupees three annas. At another nod he changed from the three annas to four annas, and suddenly without a word he stopped and moved away to another heap followed by the silent crowd, while a munshi entered the completed transaction in a notebook. In another system of auctioning, the broker and the bidder stretched their hands under a towel and the bidder made his offer by holding the auctioneer's fingers. This was a cumbersome method and gave way to the open bidding. Months' toil, hopes and fears were settled in a few minutes. The farmer would walk back to the shop of his arhti, the man who advanced him money and sold him his seed, to settle his account before harnessing his bullocks. From the railway station next door the produce packed in gunny bags would be sent to destinations all over the Punjab, India, and it was said, even across the sea.

The Civil Station was built in a large rectangle along the railway lines. The bungalows varied in size with the importance of the official, and there were also some private bungalows belonging to some big zamindars. British social life centred round the church, the club and the polo ground. In Sargodha their wine and provision store rejoiced in the name of London House. In 1918 the senior district officers were mostly British, but Indians had already begun to arrive on the scene, and the first problem of social adjustment had begun. When the deputy commissioner was an Indian, as the head of the district he could not be kept out of the club, unless he solved the problem by being of the older type, and therefore glad to be spared the onerous honour of mixing with the

Sahibs. But if he belonged to the I.C.S., educated at Oxford or Cambridge, there was a problem; at least the Service had to be honoured. Within the British membership there were also problems. The I.C.S. deputy commissioner, his assistant commissioner and the sessions judge formed one natural group in which the police superintendent fitted in if he was an ex-army man, and for reasons of practical courtesy the civil surgeon also, because it was always well to make the doctor feel your equal, and in any case he was usually also from the army and had university education. The status of the engineers depended upon their background. If they came of the right background, they were accepted, otherwise, like the bank manager and the police officer they were just tolerated. It helped too if you were a Scot and had retained the accent, because then like the parson and the doctor you acquired a certain social neutralness and a fairly high minimum level of acceptance. This concession did not however automatically apply to the Irishman, who along with the Scot was the backbone of the earlier services. And a complicating factor in the Sargodha British community was the neighbouring army remount depot, where the service corps had a stud farm for raising horses and mules. It had a number of British officers of an inferior social grade. Fortunately the depot was a few miles away, and as motor-cars had not yet arrived in Sargodha the remount officers could not come to the club every evening, but at week-ends they came in strength. At Christmas, New Year, and when the Governor visited Sargodha, the club was one well-knit community; at other times, while it offered a solid façade to us it had its own layers inside.

On the other side of the railway lines were the Company gardens and the hospital. After that began the city, which extended up to the fruit and vegetable gardens. The city was planned in square blocks, of which by our time there were sixteen. It could only expand in one direction and there already a seventeenth block was going up. There were two main roads with shops running laterally, and two vertically with the residential areas behind them. A residential block had two entrances from opposite sides and enclosed a spacious square, with a wide lane running behind containing another two rows of houses. Provision had been made for a high school, a market place, an orthodox Hindu temple, an Arya Samaj, a Muslim Mosque and a Sikh Gurdwara. There was a waterworks and piped water supply system. The blocks were numbered, and while some were exclusively Hindu, Sikh or Muslim, others were mixed. An area had been set apart for the prostitutes, singing and dancing girls.

Sargodha, as can be imagined, was a much cleaner and healthier city than Gujrat. It was planned, well laid out and had plenty of light and air. Its streets and lanes were wide and straight. Somehow the clean, hygenic, impersonal layout seemed to mould the population into the pattern that the settlement officer of the late Victorian period must have had in mind. There was more social and political awakening in Sargodha; its municipal affairs were better run; its communities had started new schools. The singing and dancing girls were moved out of the city, first near the canal bank, and then still further away. It was typical of the new spirit of Sargodha that its biradaris tried to stop wasteful expenditure at weddings by banning fireworks, and had they got away with this they would probably have stopped music and entertainment as well. But with all this Sargodha was drab and had none of the colour of Gujrat, neither the city nor its people.

To Sargodha people came to settle from all over the West Punjab, professionals, traders and businessmen, artisans of all castes. Old ties were severed, and new ones were formed. The block we lived in contained mostly professional families, both Khatris and Aroras, and a new affinity sprang up between them. It began with the men, thrown together in work, and spread to the women. In Sargodha our mother hardly visited any but professional homes, Khatri or Arora. In fact the bonds of education and work supplanted the old caste bonds, and a new society emerged with four castes whose membership was cutting across the traditional pattern. They were the professionals drawn from all castes; the traders, who were Aroras, but with an odd Khatri amongst them; the artisans; and in the surrounding villages, the zamindars, often very wealthy. This re-grouping had not yet started to affect the marriage customs. Khatris still married only Khatris, and Aroras other Aroras, but they were not any longer so strict about the right sub-castes. Instead, professional families married into families of the same social standing and education, and traders among traders, zamindars into other farming families. The old, tightly knit biradari system was going, and there was a new more broad based sense of relationship. Among us the Arya Samaj took the place of the old biradari.

While we were in Sargodha the influenza hit the Punjab. Post-cards with edges torn began to arrive almost every week. Father went down also and lay hovering between life and death for days. Perhaps his iron constitution, the result of years of hard outdoor life, saved him. Two of his nephews and both his sisters died within a week. We wondered what this plague was, though we had heard that it came from Europe, from its battlefields. Slowly he recovered from his illness, and when he was able to move about the house mother arranged a havan ceremony to cleanse the home of the illness. She distributed sweets and hoped that this strange foreign affliction would not come our way again. Yam-doot, the messenger of the god of death, had visited our family too often in the past year.

Perhaps in celebration of father's recovery, or because time was ripe otherwise, the first mechanical contraption arrived in our house. It was a Singer sewing machine, shining black and chromium-plated, with a highly polished case in wood. Few homes as yet possessed one. With it came a colourful calendar showing Singer's popularity in different countries of the world. This was my first introduction to people of other races, if only in pictures. Father now regaining strength and interest in life, at once converted to advantage the slogan on this calendar, 'Singer preferred in every country.' He exhorted us to learn singing in addition to studies. Even if we had no special talent for it, we must work hard because singing was a great accomplishment. He was convinced in his humourless way that the Singer people were using to good advantage the international love of singing.

After two years at Sargodha father was transferred to Muzaffargarh, the last town in the south-west corner of the Punjab, near the river Indus. There was still another town, Dera Ghazi Khan, further west, but that was on the other side of the Indus and was considered out of the Punjab. All these towns on the Indus, like Dera Ghazi Khan, Dera Ismail Khan, Issa Khail, Moosa Khail, Miram Shah, Shalozan, Parachinar, with their sonorous names, were considered Pathan and not Punjabi. Though the Hindus there were Punjabis, mostly merchants, and spoke Punjabi and frequently married in the Punjab proper, somehow because of their Pathan looks, often with fair skins and grey eyes, their clothes and manners, we never regarded them as quite our kind. But marriages into these frontier families were popular, I think because of an atavistic preference for the race and colour type derived from our Aryan ancestors.

The admiration of a fair colour probably stemmed from the time of the Aryans. It was almost an obsession with our society in a way that I never came across even among the British whom we believed to be very colour and race conscious, judging by their racial aloofness in India. From the time a baby is born its complexion is all important. The second question asked about the newborn is always, 'Is it fair or dark?' Mothers put a black mark every morning on a fair-skinned child's forehead, and a black cord round its waist to ward off the evil eye. A little girl with dark complexion is a mild source of worry to the parents from the beginning: 'How shall we find a suitable match; who will have her? We shall not be able to find a handsome fair boy; we shall have to raise a big dowry.' When it came to marriage, the first question is, 'Is he fair; is she fair.' Fairness could cover many defects and sins. Whether the proposed match was tall or short, plain or handsome, clever or dull, fairness offset everything. The face of a moon, the skin of jasmine, the complexion of rose; who cared if she could not cook and sew. Later, in the Tribune, the paper of educated middle class Punjabis, matrimonial advertisements would always begin by asking for a fair bride. But dark boys and girls also had to be married, and if the fair only married the fair, we would in time have had two unrelated colour castes. To avoid this the society instinctively developed an excuse. It appears to have been discovered that Lord Krishna was dark, the colour of dusk.

The Muslim invaders of Turkish and Moghul blood must have strengthened our colour consciousness. With their poetry of 'saman araz' and 'gul araz', the jasmine and rose hues, they re-emphasised our traditional preferences. There was however a limit to fairness. When the British came, their very fair hair and pink skins fell outside our acceptable scale. They were too fair. With us the hair must always be dark, the skin pale but not white, and the cheeks have only a touch of rose in the cold winter. European fairness was too extreme for us to appreciate and, besides, it reddened in our sun. Similarly, the eyes were best dark, though a wine colour could be attractive; but light coloured eyes, grey or blue, were signs of faithlessness and untrustworthiness, as also light colour of hair. The ideal of beauty was summed up in these similes: hair dark and thick as billowing rain clouds, eyes soft and black as a gazelle's, and skin the colour of wheat.

Muzaffargarh was barely Punjab as we knew it. Far from the mountains, it had a landscape of date groves and soil covered with patches of saltpetre, looking like a fresh fall of snow; the houses were built of mud and straw instead of baked brick, the people were smaller and sharp featured, seldom Khatri and mostly Aroras, usually poor and humble before the Muslims, calling themselves in self-disparagement poor Kirars. Even the animals were different, for here donkeys were used instead of horses and the camel instead of the bullock. We found the people and the land very strange at first. We had already felt some change in the Sargodha people, in their accent and slightly un-Punjabi ways, but these people were almost incomprehensible. But soon we began to recognise the Punjabi Hindu society in its familiar framework, the castes and sub-castes, the customs, rituals, fasts, fairs and festivals; and the newly-started Arya Samaj immediately offered us a kind of biradari.

The land was in part sour with the saltpetre, kullar, which seemed to rise out of the ground in patches of soft, powdery white. It would rise on walls of buildings and eat up the plaster and then the bricks. Nothing seemed to stop it. The more you removed it out of the ground the more it came up. It sometimes covered a whole field, or it came up in small patches. Nothing would grow in it and nothing seemed to kill it. People accepted it as a white scourge. They made no use of it. There were some non-perennial canals which brought water during the summer months. Rainfall was scanty. The summer monsoon barely reached here, but there were some showers from the winter monsoon off the Arabian sea. Whatever water the canals brought was therefore most welcome. In this dry rainless climate the only thing that grew in abundance was the date palm. It was almost a date economy. The flesh of the dates was eaten fresh or dried; the stones were ground into a flour; the fronds were used for thatch, while the young shoots were dyed into bright colours for basket weaving; the stalks which bore fruit were used as brooms; its bark made fuel; and when the tree died the long stem was made into a channel for use on a persian wheel, while out of the root came a succulent, white porous vegetable matter which was a delicacy eaten raw or pickled. Date was their wealth and the kullar seemed not to bother it. But we boys bore a grudge against the date palm, for our school masters loved to whittle the stems of its fronds to make steeped and supple canes which cut viciously into the palms of our hands, where the Punjabi boys traditionally received their punishment. On cold frosty mornings, when our fingers refused to move in the open draughty classrooms, a sadistic teacher would use such a stick to 'thaw' our hands.

Muzaffargarh as a town was already unlike other Punjabi towns, for it had a touch of the trans-Indus Baluch country and the Persia beyond. Its square mud brick houses were in the Muslim style of a high blank wall with inner and outer courtyards. We did not live in the canal colony as there was no accommodation, and we took a house on the outskirts. It had high blank walls on four sides, with a shuttered gate in the front wall. The outer courtyard, as you entered, was shaped like a reversed L. On the left there was the reception room used for my father's office and two living-rooms for men visitors. At the top of the right-hand side of this courtyard were servants quarters, stables and tonga and cattle sheds. Through a door protected by a purda wall you entered the inner courtyard, with the residential quarters built on the left, and a wing facing the entrance containing the kitchen and pantries.

Through one of the living-rooms you entered father's office and came out into the outer courtyard. As we did not observe purda we did not use the two courtyards for their different purposes, but among Muslims life flowed in two separate streams, in the outer courtyard of the men and in the inner courtyard of the women. Only members of the family, close relations, women, and maid-servants entered inside. In this town we had our first experience of strict purda. Among us, in the upper Punjab, women pulled the dupatta over their faces, but being usually diaphanous it made only a formal kind of veil, while Muslim women wore burqa, which covered them from head to foot, with a piece of net or lace sewn in the portion over the eyes. But in Muzaffargarh the purda was more strict, and while the Hindu women did not actually wear burqa they often wrapped a sheet round themselves and had a thick veil over the face. Across the Indus even the Hindu women wore burqa.

Muzaffargarh was on the edge of a desert which began only a mile away on its western side. It was a desert of sandhills and valleys. Some hills were more than fifty feet high, and changed their shape whenever the wind blew hard. The sand shifted from day to day and gave them ever-changing contours. The landscape had a strange beauty of voluptuously curved hills, bare and soft, with the sand on the surface furrowed by the wind. In the summer it burnt during the day; at night it was cool and fresh, lapped by a caressing desert breeze. In the winter it was cool by the day and freezing by night. The landscape had a great variety of moods, expressed in colours, changing during the day and from one season to another. It was remarkable how the one single tone of grey could change into so many colours and tints with the sun and the moon. It was at its most spectacular in the hour before the sun rose and after it set, the hour between the day and the night. On the nights of the full moon the landscapes almost ceased to be earthly.

It became our favourite touring country. We insisted on accompanying father as often as we could. It lacked the lushness of growing crops on the rich, fat lands of the perennial canals, but it offered something new, the sand desert and the Indus country.

We never forgot our first introduction to the desert. My brother and I strayed from our dak bungalow one evening and roamed into the dunes. We walked up the hills enjoying the feeling of treading on soft sand which gave way underfoot and left a large trail behind; we rolled down the slopes like logs, and we ran after the camels that had brought the camp baggage and were now turned loose to graze. We chased them through the valleys and up the hills, laughing at their ungainly long-legged trot. As the sun went lower in the sky we were amused at our long shadows, which looked as if we were walking on stilts and made us appear as long as the camels. Occasionally we stopped to pick the small pink and yellow succulent peeloo fruit from the gnarled, thin-leafed bushes, the only thing that bore fruit around here. When we were tired and felt we had enough of the camels and the sand, we decided to return home, but now all the dunes looked alike. A brisk wind had sprung up as the sun went down and it had covered our tracks with new waves of sand. We became frightened because we knew we were lost and we had walked a long way from home. We wandered about, and luckily in the end we were picked up by the camel-drivers, who had strayed in our direction looking for their beasts which we had driven away. They delivered us back at the bungalow from where rescue parties were setting out with hurricane lanterns. Our worst punishment was however to come the next day when our ears full of sand began to ache with excruciating pain.

Further west of this strip of desert the country dipped gently to the Indus. The road and the railway line stopped at a small terminal station at the village of Ghazi Ghat. From here the Indus began, and in the summer it stretched sometimes for nearly twenty miles in width and at places was over fifty feet deep. It was like a brown, muddy sea as far as the eye could see, across which an old paddle steamer used to ferry passengers. In the winter the river shrank to a few shallow streams over which a pontoon bridge of boats was fixed. Elsewhere on the Indus people crossed the river on goat skins. These were sewn up skins, inflated and tied at the neck. On one of them the 'passenger' and on the other the ferryman would lie on their stomachs and paddle their way across. The ferryman used his feet as rudder while he paddled. The passenger was sort of towed along. Occasionally one could see crocodiles basking on sandbanks in the morning sun. The country along the river banks was thickly overgrown with reed and abounded in game: deer, hare, pig, fox, jackal and porcupine, whose quills we greatly prized for making pen-holders.

A great sport in Muzaffargarh, and a quite unusual one, was camel fighting. The animals were specially bred for it, and the fights took place in a sand valley with a ring of high dunes forming a vast natural amphitheatre. They were held on Sunday afternoons and were free to the spectators, who settled down on the slopes of the hills, safely out of the camel's way. Two fighters would be led into the arena and let loose. Their docile and placid look was misleading, for the fighter camels were a vicious lot and fought with tremendous anger. They growled and made the most weird noises, they kicked and bit each other savagely, but mostly they fought with their long necks, and blood streamed down their heads till one of them had had enough and ran away from the arena into the desert, followed by his angry owner. The victorious camel ran around, now growling happily as he was dragged away by his master to make room for the next fight. People bet on their favourite camels and jeered as the vanquished one ran away. There were many other side-shows, cock fighting, quail fighting, partridge fighting and wrestling. The bird fights were clean sport, unlike the gruesome ones I saw in Manila years later, where they put long, razor-sharp spurs on the cocks so that the fight ends in a kill in a matter of moments. Our birds fought with their bare claws and the fight would last a long time, till one of them ran away. There was rarely a kill.

Life in Muzaffargarh did not always run evenly. There was great commotion when one of our classmates was murdered. He was the son of the municipal dai, a widowed woman with only this child. She had delivered a young woman who died in childbirth. The girl's father, who also had only this one child, began to brood over his loss and imagined that it was the fault of the dai. People tried to dissuade him, but in vain, and his belief gradually took on a hideous shape. One afternoon, as school was closing, he met this boy and told him that he had been asked by his mother to fetch him. The boy happily went along and lured by sweets accompanied him to the dunes outside the town. There he was murdered near a water hole. The demented man choked him to death as with a pencil he stuffed his nose and mouth with mud. Such a tragic and cold-blooded murder the town had never known before. We all flocked to the sessions court on the day the judgement was to be delivered. The judge, one of the first Punjabis to hold the post, was a very impressive looking man in a black closed collar coat and a white turban. He spread a black handkerchief over the turban when he came to delivering the sentence. 'Bhai Amir Chand. . . .' In chaste, well chosen Urdu, beginning with the common appelation of brother, he went on impassively to analyse the evidence, deliver the judgement and to sentence him to death. Amir Chand showed no signs of shock, or a trace of emotion; he had probably totally forgotten the young boy and was only thinking of his daughter; he perhaps even welcomed the sentence. The judge must have been moved by this because he ended softly by asking Amir Chand to forgive him.

In Muzaffargarh I saw the British for the first time in numbers. So far one occasionally saw an Englishman, seldom many together except when the governor visited, but now a British regiment had camped outside the town. On the first evening when the British soldiers came to town in twos and threes, in their immaculate white walking-out uniforms, with well pressed forage caps at jaunty angles at the parting of their fair hair, with swagger canes under their arms and in shining black boots, we just stared. We sat on the school compound wall, discreetly out of the way. Their faces and bare knees, the red colour of newly burnt brick, were strange, but the strangest thing of all was that they all looked alike. We could not understand how their officers distinguished one from the other. Someone suggested that they were numbered for that purpose. Gradually we became bolder and tried out small English, but neither side could make out much. Their accent we found totally unlike the English we were used to learning. We wondered where they came from. Someone suggested that they were specially bred for the army, which needed so many of them every year, in the poor parts of London; and the theory was put forward that they were all illegitimate and were collected for the army. As we became familiar we began to exchange hockey and football matches. At hockey we managed well, but playing football with bare feet was hopeless against their heavy boots. Gradually there was much fraternising and friendliness as both sides began to make something of each other's English, but it came to an end abruptly. They were fond of visiting the prostitutes' bazaar, and one day one of them stabbed a reluctant girl and the city was put out of bounds. We never saw them again.

Father's usual spell of three years posting was over and we were expecting a transfer any day. There was always a pleasant anticipation about the next post. Would it be back in the jungles or would we get a town? As we were growing up the place we might go to was of great importance for our schooling. Father had been recently selected for what was then called the Imperial Service of Engineers, which was looked after by the Secretary of State for India in London. He was therefore looking forward to his first new posting in this cadre with the important ring, but we were not a little surprised when he received orders to go to Bahawalpur State, where he was appointed as personal assistant to the State Engineer, a Scotsman under whom he had worked before and who had in fact asked for him. If Muzaffargarh was not quite Punjab, Bahawalpur was almost foreign. As a border state between the Punjab, Sind and Baluchistan, its customs, language and way of life was more akin to Sind and Baluchistan, and it had little in common with the Punjab. We were therefore thrilled with the prospect of 'leaving' the Punjab. The anticipation was further enhanced by the first news from father, who had, as was usual on a transfer, preceded us, that our new house had electricity. So far we had only seen it in railway trains and on odd visits to Lahore. In 1921 very few towns in the Punjab could boast of such modernity. Bahawalpur had besides a college, a club, gardens and palaces. Its proudest boast was a Mall Road, which only the big cities like Lahore, Amritsar and Rawalpindi possessed. Based on some legendary origin in England, the name Mall Road spelled urban luxury to us.

Bahawalpur was interesting because it contained in it a world of the past which had died in the British Punjab years ago. It was an unprogressive world, with intrigues and cruelties which had elsewhere given way to reform and justice, but it possessed also colour and pageantry. To us it had the excitement of a real ruler, a king, his durbar and palaces. Its ruling family of Abassis came from further west some centuries ago. With a young Nawab at the centre, the court and family formed a large circle, none of whom did any work. His father had had many wives and each one's family had given up work from the day of the marriage. Royal dignity demanded that they quit work and live on patronage. Then there were the surviving relatives of his grandfather's numerous wives. He himself was a young man, but before he was eighteen he had also been married more than once. His first marriage was with his maternal cousin as was customary among Muslims.

One of the young members of a closely related family was at our school and a person of considerable interest and curiosity to us. It was an unusual decision to send him to school, and he was flatteringly ignored by the teachers and given immunity from studies and examinations. He had a princely disdain for work but realised its onerous nature sufficiently to express his sympathy for us who had to pass examinations. He was preparing to become an aide one day. In the meantime, he was working hard learning car driving, shooting and acquiring the capacity to do nothing for long periods. He was already learning the mysteries of sex and its infinite variations, which knowledge, apart from personal pleasure, he seemed to regard as a qualification. Some senior boys would hear lively descriptions of his affairs with the bandis in the palace.

The bandis, literally meaning 'the tied', were maids in the harem, usually daughters of female servants. As young women they were often a prey to their masters; to the young in pursuit of their initial adventures, and to the old as 'tender morsels' for a change. They would beget children from the family and were usually married off to manservants, often the sons of bandis. The senior ladies of the family tolerated the institution, partly because it was the traditional way of providing cheap household labour, tied to the home because it belonged nowhere else; but they must have seen in it also the additional advantage of keeping the young men from experimental liaisons with growing cousins or from straying out to the courtesans and bringing disease to the cousins whom they would marry in due course. Mixed with members of the family, and with their blood continually freshened from outside, the bandis were usually good looking and robust. Curiously, they seldom formed any long liaisons or exercised any influence upon the men in the family. There were cases of women, even courtesans, rising to positions of great influence upon rulers, but one rarely heard of a bandi rising to a position of eminence.

A matron with the help of a wise old bandi might arrange to place a young woman in the way of an exploring adolescent. Our unsuspecting schoolmate prince talked of his first affair in terms of a great exploit with this 'reluctant' innocent bandi. Later as the emboldened youth really began to exploit, when he visited his estates, the village girls would be kept in purda for fear of his depredations. If one of them took his fancy he might marry her and put her behind the high walls of one of his many palaces and mansions; or having had his fill of her he might return her to the family with some money. The family could gnash their teeth if they liked, but they could do no more. Being poor and simple, they accepted their fate and were happy if the girl was kept in the harem. Occasionally the patrician would cast his discretion to the wind and show illicit interest in a woman in one of the other households. Such an insult would be avenged by intrigue, not openly, but usually by poisoning. The little wheels of intrigues would move fast but quietly on such occasions, for if the slightest scent of the plot reached the threatened party, wheels on his side would move faster still. The story went of a patrician of long ago who saw one of his young companions coming surreptitiously from the harem. He declared that very day that while in the past he had hunted wild animals with his dogs, on the following day he was going to try the variation of hunting a man. The whole retinue was commanded to witness the spectacle which, everyone knew, would consist of burying the man up to his waist and setting the dogs on him. The young aide immediately scented the danger, and as it was now his life against the master he moved with a speed born of despair. With threat and bribery he and his friends reached a point where hatred and frustration had simmered for many years. Although this deep wound had healed on the surface and was forgotten by others, now given the chance to open, with just the right pressure from someone who had remembered its existence, it gushed and took its long-stored poison in one dart to the masterful victim. The story went that before the night watch went on duty, within barely six hours of the uttering of the threat, the great man lay gasping for life, begging for water, but help had already been ruthlessly barred. The heir was not altogether sorry to succeed the next day to the riches of the estate, innocent though he was of the misdeed. The windfall of power banished any thought of investigation and revenge. Prudence also demanded a discreet acceptance, for a re-opening might lead to another desperate throw of the dice, and this time perhaps also a bid for power. Securely guarded in high-walled harems, the women on these occasions worked side by side with men with even greater boldness and cunning.

The women of the harem were well guarded from public gaze. Soon after our arrival we heard that the ladies of the palace were going to move from Bahawalpur to the old family seat. Years of drill had trained the police in a smooth operation of this exercise. The town criers went about with their drums, and wherever they stood and beat them a crowd collected to hear that on the afternoon of the appointed day no one should be on the road which led from the palace to the railway station, not even on the connecting roads. As far as the eye could see on this route no human being should be visible, not even a woman, in case that was a ruse. People whose houses even distantly overlooked the road were told to stay inside the rooms on the ground floors. All these precautions were taken notwithstanding the fact that the ladies were in any case going to travel in purda cars, completely screened from outside.

Two hours before the appointed hour the police began to clear the roads and order people to shut all doors and windows which could be seen from the roadside. They blew whistles and shouted at anyone they saw from the road. Soon a deserted silence descended, of a kind that was unimaginable. It was eerie because it was in broad daylight and carried with it a threat of the dungeon and even death. We two brothers could not restrain our curiosity to see what exactly was going to happen. We went on the terrace and crouched behind the brick grill of the parapet wall. Mother called us down when she discovered this, but did not dare to go up the open stairs nor shout for fear of the police hearing as it was now close to the hour.

Suddenly the police whistles began to blow, and as each man sounded the signal he about-turned and stood motionless with his back to the road and his head bowed. A cavalcade of cars rushed down the road with their special dark glass windows up and thick cotton sheets tied around them, exposing only the windscreens for the drivers to see through. The partitions between the driver and the rear compartment in which the ladies sat was of course also screened by a blind, and so was the rear view window by the sheet outside. As the procession went out of view the policemen blew their whistles again and life began to creep back to the roads. At the railway station the cars drove up to a separate purda siding which had been built for the purpose with high walls on both sides. The cars went up the platform to the waiting private saloons with closed venetian shutters. Out of the front cars rushed some old bandis to hold sheets and form a purda lane between each car and the railway coach. In the meantime the motor drivers had walked away out of sight. When the ladies were safely in the compartments, the doors were closed and police guards stood watch outside with their backs turned and heads down. Shortly a railway engine came and took the coaches away. At the other end the same exercise was performed to take the ladies from the station to the palace, and once they were inside their one annual excursion was over. It was the only 'outing' they ever enjoyed.

The sisters of a Nawab, according to custom, were not permitted to marry. In the north the word for wife's brother, sala, has somehow become a term of abuse. The Nawabs therefore considered it an unbearable insult to become a sala to someone; they would rather not marry their sisters. But it was a risk to keep them in the palaces for fear of some scandal arising, and they were therefore banished to an old inaccessible fort in the desert. There, under a heavy guard, they lived their long lonely lives like prisoners, lost to the world and looking back to their childhood, the only short spell of happiness they had ever tasted. Relations rarely came to see them, and thus condemned they could only have received scant attention from the fort authorities. But stories went about of strange happenings in this fort of the living dead.

The fort of Drawar must have been built centuries ago. It was twenty-six miles from the nearest town and was surrounded by a featureless desert which had no roads and little life except herds of deer and some wandering camel tribes. We once visited it by car, an old 'T' model Ford, which with its high chassis and light weight was then the only thing on wheels that could have done the journey. Every now and again its wheels would get stuck in sand and we had to get out and push, sometimes literally lift it out. Deer stood observing us innocently and at some movement on our part would bound away, carrying their fat sleek bodies gracefully over mounds and bushes on their ludicrously thin legs. In this barren country of camels and lean men they looked oddly fat and well fed. Drawar rose suddenly out of the desert as we reached the brow of a hill; a magnificent fort built of mud and yellow stone. Its walls rose sheer out of the sand. From the main wooden gate you entered into a scene of centuries ago. With small mud houses, narrow winding lanes, and people walking behind their donkeys or leading camels, the scene looked older than anything one saw in the Punjab. They were tall, proud men with sharp features, thickly bearded and dressed in loose baggy trousers and long kurtas, usually dark blue or black, their loosely tied turbans of a dark red colour. The women, thin and tall, dressed similar to the men, were equally striking. Some men carried swords, others old matchlocks. We passed by a group of rare interest, a very tall, handsome man of erect and proud bearing and his family group of a small son, wife and camel. He was wearing a turban printed with a hand-block design of red with small white squares, a long white shirt to his knees, with silver chains and tassels to the buttons, a red velvet waistcoat whose edges and pockets were trimmed with gold, a blue salwar and black gold-embroidered shoes. A sword hung from his waist in a red velvet scabbard. In his arms he was carrying his young son, gorgeously attired, his eyes thickly dabbed with kohl. The boy had long black hair, like his father whose long hair curled at the ends into ringlets and fell over his shoulders. They were combed back over the ears and came out as a full plume from behind his turban. His wife had an arched red mouth, deep kohled eyes and hair intricately woven in long plaits falling over her ears. She walked proudly behind him, holding the reins of their dromedary equally well decorated with red tassels and a handsome saddle. They must have been going to a wedding.

The population of Drawar was small because water was a great problem. They collected it in underground holes from the odd showers they had during the year. In the fortress apart from the royal virgins there lived also some forgotten men locked up at the ruling family's pleasure. Some had been sent up years ago because they had incurred the momentary wrath of a Nawab. And today no one remembered them. The Governor of the prison fort himself must have felt condemned and no better than the inmates. It was not exactly a prize post and could only have been earned as the result of some lapse or by the successful intrigue of some opponent. This is what Drawar was, one of many picturesque forts in the desert east of Bahawalpur and in west Rajasthan.

The young Nawab, Sadiq Mohammed Khan, was a very handsome youth of finely chiselled sad features. He dressed like the people and wore his curly hair long. They flowed out of his turban in a well-oiled pack of ringlets. He was intelligent and had considerable charm and must have had to fight against the family tradition. With not enough to do and with no scope for his energies, he was restless and sometimes petulant, as when he would stop his car to berate someone who had not alighted from a tonga as he passed by. He had a special type of horn fitted to all his cars. It consisted of a rubber bulb with a long chromium-plated tube on the outside of the car ending in a horn in the shape of a crocodile's head fixed on the fender. It uttered a deep melodious sound, and as his car passed you were expected to get out of your vehicle and stand respectfully by the road. Sometimes one barely recognised the car as it majestically swept past in a cloud of dust, but you nevertheless got out in case he noticed you through the rear view mirror. On a rare occasion he even whipped people for their disregard of this elementary courtesy. Being a charming and courteous young man himself, he could not stand discourtesy in others. Once we had literally to drag our mother out of the tonga, but we managed it just in time. He possessed a magnificent variety of cars, Armstrong Siddeleys, Daimlers and Rolls Royces, all custom-built jobs, but unfortunately for the people, they were swift and silent, and as he was frequently on the road travelling between his country palace and Bahawalpur, at all hours of the day and night, one had always to be alert. But he soon began to lose interest in the manners of his people and did not care whether they stood to attention or not.

When he reached the age of eighteen the Government of India agreed to install him on the gadi, and Lord Reading, the Viceroy of India, came to perform the installation ceremony. There were great preparations. The railway station, where the Viceroy was to arrive in his special train, and the entire route of the drive were scrubbed clean and decorated with arches, plants, flags, festoons and mottoes of welcome. The guest palace was re-furnished. Plans were made for a great durbar at which the ceremony of investing the Nawab with the full powers of a ruler was to be held. Arrangements were made for a banquet that night, and for the sake of His Excellency and the British officers and their wives, who were going to be present, Goan cooks and waiters, complete with the ingredients of the meal, were specially brought from Lahore, two hundred and fifty miles away. It had to be an English meal consisting of soup, tinned paté, salmon also out of a tin, with white sauce, a variety of roast birds, caramel custard pudding, Kemp's bottled coffee and a savoury on toast. The Indian guests were greatly disappointed at the Goan cooking which they considered tasteless. Boiled fish and white sauce with boiled eggs chopped in, unsalted and unseasoned roast meats and baked pudding served with an array of unfamiliar instruments was quite an ordeal. They longed for the spicy, saffron-tinted cuisine of the famous palace cooks.

The durbar was an occasion for felicitation and expressions of loyalty. Honours were conferred, and the young Nawab became His Highness, Nawab Sir Sadiq Mohammed Khan, K.C.I.E., etc., ruler of Bahawalpur State and entitled to a salute of fifteen guns. His privy purse was raised to Rs. 3 lakhs out of the State's total revenues of Rs. 40 lakhs. In addition he would, of course, enjoy many amenities, and everything was tax-free. The Viceroy particularly commented on the young Nawab's progressive outlook. The day before he had lain the foundation stone of a public library, an institution whose fulfilment was postponed for a number of years.

On the following day there was a duck shoot. Detailed arrangements had been made well in advance. A list of the bags was drawn up; the Viceroy would have the biggest bag of several hundred ducks; the Nawab would follow with a slightly smaller bag, decorously conceding the lord's greater prowess at shooting. The protocol continued down the line, zigzagging between Indians and Englishmen. But to make sure of such a vast number of duck special arrangements had to be made. Large nets were spread over the jheels and hundreds of birds were snared. Their wings were gently clipped, so that for some days they would be unable to fly strongly when disturbed. The arrangements worked well, and on the day of the shoot there was great carnage. Thousands of birds were shot, and with great mounds of dead birds in front of them the Viceroy, the Nawab and their party, dressed in khaki shooting clothes and leaning on their guns, were photographed and filmed. A special film unit had been brought from Bombay to prepare a record of the installation ceremonies.

This was the world of the ruling family, a world of the past in which the only new touches were the Rolls Royces, occasional trips to Europe, some new gee gaws for the palaces. Favourites came and favourites went; they came into power overnight and they left just as quickly. Once a venerable, white-bearded old chief minister, illiterate but astute, rose to great power. There was no question with him of any delegation of authority or sharing of responsibility; everything went through the one man. Even the lowliest jobs were filled at his recommendation. His word decided everything, and nobody acted until he had spoken. But one afternoon, at the height of his power, he was told to quit the State within the next few hours. By midnight he was in Multan, impoverished, finished, and soon to be forgotten.

The wheel of fortune never stopped turning. One day a man was right on top and the next day he might touch the hard floor. Those who got on it knew what they were in for and accepted it philosophically. Those who fell off it tried desperately to scramble on it again, and those who reached the top tried vainly to stop the wheel. The game of intrigues was played not only for the results, but also for its own enjoyment. There was the case of an Accountant General of the State whom a contender challenged for the job. That the new man had no qualifications was beside the point. The incumbent was a man of great integrity, but word was gently passed around that he was getting too old. One day, at the end of a busy day's work, when he was anxious to leave office, a sheaf of cheques was brought for his counter initials. The clerk on duty, with a blotting-pad in one hand, very cleverly made him initial them without much scrutiny. Among them was one cheque deliberately filled in for an astronomical amount which would have emptied the State treasury for many years to come. The treasury immediately returned the cheque, and word was taken to the ruler at once that the finances of the State were in the greatest of danger. This was proof that the old man was indeed becoming senile and unfit for such a responsible task. He was promptly retired.

Another man, a minister, again totally illiterate, had the habit of denying instructions whenever anything went wrong. On one such occasion the written order was produced with his signature underneath. He had learned just enough writing to doodle his signature. He cunningly asked for the paper to be shown, held it in front of his face and quickly licked off the signature with his tongue. He then berated the subordinate for falsely issuing the orders, when he had not signed anything of the kind. There was an Inspector of Schools who had also learned to sign his name at the time he was appointed to this job. An Inspector General of hospitals had before been in charge of a jail. Qualifications for a job were trifles that never stood in the way of selection; what mattered was boldness and influence and a courageous assurance that they could do anything.

Administration in the State was based on the most advanced lines, years ahead of the Punjab, at least on paper. There was a cabinet of ministers, if such a mixed set could be called a cabinet. Each pulled the ruler his own way, and everybody interfered and intrigued against the others. The portfolios were Home, Finance, Law, Public Works and others, but the formalities of either the division or the sharing of responsibility were barely observed. Then there were the secretaries, including one for Foreign Affairs, who was supposed to deal with outside affairs of the State, though in fact that was the close preserve of the British Resident, and one on which even the Nawab dared not trespass. The Resident was a jovial and well-fed Irishman who had earned an odious name as a Deputy Commissioner during the martial law days. His visible interests in life were eating roasted quails whole, drinking whisky and nursing his gout; and his work was mainly keeping an eye on the ruler. The Residents were usually men of great administrative ability, and with one or two advisers they could have exercised much constructive influence. Their colleagues in the Punjab with much less powers were rebuilding the country. These Residents seemed only to aim at maintaining a medieval museum, making sure that nothing was disturbed, like in Bahawalpur's Noor Mahal palace where illuminated calligraphed Qorans, Persian rugs, swords and armour of ancestors buried centuries ago, heirlooms for which bloody battles had been fought, were on display alongside the oleoprints of their Britannic majesties and pictures of race horses and champion dogs cut out of the Sketch and the Tatler and framed in gold.

When time came we children were sad at leaving Bahawalpur. The Nawab Sahib, his ever-changing motor-cars, palaces, durbars and processions, elephants and dromedaries, polo and tent-pegging, the stories of court intrigues; all this we were going to miss at father's next posting in some staid British-organised district. But times were moving; we had sold our tonga and the mare, Bijli, lightning, who could march to music, salute by lifting her right leg and put all her four feet on a low stool a foot square; and we had placed an order for a new Chevrolet car for our next station. We might now have electricity wherever we went.

From Bahawalpur I went back to Gujrat to join the newly-opened Intermediate college, and after two years I went to Lahore, where I stayed another two years to finish my degree.

CHAPTER ELEVEN

LEGEND HAS it that Lahore was founded by Lav, son of Rama whose other son Kush founded Kasur, a small town about thirty miles away. Whatever the truth, it must be a very old town. In our days there were actually two Lahores, the Lahore of the Lahorias, people who lived inside the old walled city; and the Lahore of the ring of suburbs that grew after the city began to respond to the new peace and order. This new Lahore belonged to the Punjab and was the centre of the life of the new province. The two Lahores were quite different in appearances and character.

The old Lahore was like Gujrat on a bigger scale, except that it was quite flat. It had a city wall with several gates and a fort inside. Its narrow streets and lanes, its fortified mohallas, whose large wooden or iron gates were stoutly barred every night, its many bazaars, each specialising in a different ware, its busy and crowded markets for cloth, jewellery, embroidery, metal work, household ware, fish, vegetables, dry groceries: all seethed with vitality and colour. On the high road to Delhi and at the ford of the Ravi, Lahore must have felt the shock of untold waves of invaders as they advanced and retreated, but it had learned not to be overwhelmed. Its people likewise learned to combine a mixture of meekness and bluster. They were meek before a powerful invader but full of bluster to the one licking his wounds as he retreated. They were resilient like all Punjabis, but whereas in the countryside people could scatter Lahore was a concentrated target which had learned to suffer and to rise again. Self-commiseration was no part of the Punjabi character; much less of the Lahoria. To watch him in a fight was really to know him. While the going was in his favour, he was bold and on the offensive, but the moment he felt the ground slipping he became the personification of tact and reasonableness. 'Oh kings, why do you not listen, why are you getting upset? I am only doing the talk of your benefit.' And if the tide turned slightly in his favour he was up again. 'Look, everybody, look, darkness has descended; I was doing the talk of his benefit and he comes riding on my head. Hold me back, people, anger is coming over me.' He lay low to let the invader continue to Sirhind, and to strike the best bargain he could with him, but if the stranger was staggering home, reeling under the blow of the defender, I am sure he pinched his pocket.

Circumscribed by the city wall the people of Lahore led a self-contained life. They were born, bred and married in their mohallas, and upon death they were taken outside to Ramu Gardens on the banks of the Ravi for cremation. They had so lost touch with the country, that the Lahoria children proverbially asked how high was a wheat tree. In times of trouble the city closed within its shell. Every house had its store of wheat, pulses, ghee and sugar; every mohalla its own well; the mohalla gates were barred, and the stout erls were pulled behind the studded door of each house; the mohalla defence squads kept vigil; and every home kept its pots full of boiling water and oil. Trouble had always been part of Lahore's life, but for a period of sixty years, from the time the British took it from the Sikhs till they put it under martial law in 1919, it enjoyed uninterrupted peace. Then its life of trouble began again, first the martial law and then the communal riots, ending with the conflagration of 1947, and the Lahore we had known and loved was gone.

Although they belonged to our castes and sub-castes, the Lahorias were different. They seldom married outside, and their customs bore the stamp of the city. In Lahore they never entertained at weddings. When the barat arrived at the girl's house, they would do the milni and then bow to the guests and say, 'Achha Maharaj.' This was a signal for the barat to turn back from the door, and only the groom and members of his immediate family were admitted in. Lahore had certainly learned not to waste its food in communal feasting. Their living was frugal, and to us they appeared self-centred and mean. Some of the richest men of Lahore were famous misers. One philanthropist was commonly reputed to collect rental in annas and pies from beggars and lepers who sought shelter at night in a serai he had built. Could you marry among people like that? Your daughter would starve among them, was the attitude of the outsiders. But there were also families in Lahore who had settled from the districts, in some cases for several generations, and they still continued to practise their original customs. These outsiders either looked for a match in another outside family or in the town they had come from. Intermarriages between Lahorias and non-Lahorias began only in recent times.

Like Gujrat Lahore could not have changed much in a thousand years. If one overlooked the signs of electric supply the city must have been just as Bentinck saw it when he called on Ranjit Singh, or even Babar when he hurried past it to meet Ibrahim Lodi. Apart from fires and house collapses, destruction by invaders, and a slow and imperceptible change in the style of houses, the city must always have looked the same. Though built in the style of Gujrat, it was even more congested. With not enough light and air the Lahorias had a distinctive pallor, unusual in the Punjabi. The only 'open spaces' inside the city were the markets, the most spacious and colourful being Hira Mandi, the area of the courtesans, euphemistically called the gem market. It was an institution to which there was nothing similar elsewhere.

Whereas in Gujrat the courtesans lived in a small lane, here it was a whole district, with bazaars, gallis and squares. Hira Mandi by day was quiet and deserted, but after the sun went down it came into a dazzling and brilliant life. It was typical of the old Punjabi way of containing different aspects of life that even in Hira Mandi there were middle class residential areas in which people of all communities lived in streets adjacent to those of the courtesans.

Late in the afternoon the girls would wake up from their slumber and loll about the house comparing notes, sometimes cursing the race of man, sometimes praising a kind exception, or looking at their wardrobes and cosmetics. Some strayed down to the bazaar and walked about desultorily in their slept-in clothes, untidy in appearance, or stood in front of a pan-biri shop chewing pan and smoking. The mirasi musicians and the kanjar drones, also loafing about and taking the air, might make some rude cracks, which the girls were well able to answer, for after all they were the breadwinners. Slowly they would drift back to start the evening toilet, which was a long and careful process. A scrub and bath, frequently a shaving of the whole body hair, enjoined by Muslim custom, powdering, rougeing, perfuming, hennaing, combing and plaiting, and a careful choice of clothes would finally be set off by passing the silver stick dipped in kohl powder between the eyelids. All ready, they waited for instructions from the mother or the mistress, hoping against hope for that rare treat of an evening's assignment away from the house, at some men's quarters, or more exciting still, a secret rendezvous, when a girl might be taken in purda to remain unseen. But the best treat of all was a journey away to somewhere in Kashmir or some other distant holiday place as an ostensible wife trying to look homely and domestic. However hard their life they were naïve and simple at heart, and while there was hope they prayed for a love affair, one that might even lead to marriage, which might be rare but was not unknown. When that happened they could make truly great wives.

The principal of a college, whose son was at school with us, had made such a marriage. He was an aristocratic man with the great Muslim charm of the culture of old Delhi. He had fallen in love with her while he was still at college and she was just starting. She must have been deeply devoted to him because even now, over twenty years later, you could still see a worshipping look in her eyes, which seemed never to have quite lost a touch of some inner anxiety. She was a woman of extraordinary grace and beauty, and dressed in dupatta, kameez, chooridar pyjamas and embroidered shoes she looked like a late eighteenth century Moghul princess. Her daughter, an image of herself, and her son, who was tall and lanky like his father, were brought up in the old Delhi tradition. It was altogether a charming family and, in spite of its antecedents being common knowledge, cultivated by all. Our mother had no hesitation in getting to know them, and their son was our playmate. I think she also felt that playing in their house would have a good influence on us because they were so cultured, in a way that we Punjabis never were.

As the evening darkened, lights began to go up in the houses and balconies and the girls took their appointed places. There were four classes of houses: the very select ones of the well-known singing girls, those of the nautch girls, of the special courtesans, and of the common prostitutes. There were of course different grades within each category. The leading singing girls lived in luxurious homes and enjoyed a measure of respectability. Their names usually carried the courteous suffixes of begum or banu, and if they were Hindus, as they sometimes were, bai. They were frequently invited out to weddings and other functions; they sang for the recording companies, and later for the Lahore Radio, and still later as playback singers in films. To visit their houses was quite respectable. They received in the hall, a long, well proportioned room with an ornate ceiling and painted walls. The floor was covered with thick quilted mattresses, spread with spotlessly white sheets. Against the walls there were white or coloured velvet cushions, with low carved tables and polished brass spittoons. You sat relaxed along the walls and were served pan supari. The singing girl would prepare the pan herself from her fretted silver box, and a maid would pass it round with scented betel nut and little wads of cottonwool dabbed in attar on a silver tray.

The formalities of reception and the pleasantries over, she would sit surrounded by her musicians, usually three men, one playing the harmonium, another the sarangi, and the third the tabla. She led. After a lot of tuning of the sarangi and the tabla, the musicians would slowly begin. They carefully watched her right hand and its outstretched little finger, as she slowly conducted them in a song-symphony. Years of meticulous training had given her a flawless diction, and each word was uttered with beautiful precision. The opening movement, the alap, might take ten minutes or more, going slowly and repetitively over the scale and gradually culling out the theme in a very relaxed way, till she and the musicians all floated in unison on the wave of melody. As she sustained a long note, the harmonium merely followed in a single low resonant note, the tabla whispered in little taps, but the sarangi sometimes followed and sometimes led her through alternating variations and quick glissandos through the second movement, the vilambit, till both of them, she and the sarangi player, gazing at each other in ecstasy, slowly lost themselves. The tablawala then came in to gently waken them by a slight but compelling change in rhythm, and slowly he took her over, while the sarangi hovered in the background. He would fix his eyes on her, beseeching, cajoling, waking her from the deep reverie of her song which was called khayal, 'thought'. A great khayal was a great thought on the part of the singer, something personal, something uncharted; it was a dream thought which the accompanying musicians sometimes found difficult to follow. Lost in her reverie, they did not know where she would come up again; so they retired muted into the background, not daring to disturb her, but on hand for her return. And slowly a smile flickered on the tablawala's face; he shook his head with the quickening rhythm as each beat, louder than the one before, brought her back to their midst. The sarangi now sang joyously because it had recovered the leader again. It talked tremulously and petulantly to her, dancing around her in sheer happiness; but melting into pure adoration as the khayal built to its cadenza, the tans in drut, the musicians appeared not quite certain of themselves till the finish. They beamed with relief as she gave them a tired smile that conveyed her appreciation.

The audience woke from their own dreams as she gently lowered them to earth. They uttered decorous wah wahs and offered silver coins and notes, which they would pass round the head of the girl before offering them. And then began a chaste appreciation of the song in Urdu laced with pure Persian, carefully savouring the melody, the words and the subtle thoughts behind them. They would go over a single line or a phrase, analysing its construction and poetry, and congratulate her on her delicate interpretation. The servants brought drinks, sherbets and whisky, and perhaps the amber-coloured Rajput-Moghul liqueur, when the weather was cold. It was made from saffron, pigeon and partridge blood, and a variety of spices. It was served only in thimble glasses, and a few drops of it were enough to produce a wonderful feeling of warmth which spread through the body and made one feel hot on the coldest night. Conversation went on in polite tones, and requests were discussed for the next song; was it to be a thumri, a dadra, a kajri or perhaps another khayal in the rag? There were ragas for the sunrise, for the lighting time, for the rains, for all times of the day and for all seasons. And on their merits the discussion continued till the tablawala started his taps again and her right hand began to sway tentatively.

In their humbler homes the courtesan girls, many beautiful even in their prematurely tired youth, would sit on the balconies under a strong light and look smilingly down at the men walking in the lane below. There were jasmine-tinted Kashmirans, wheat-skinned Punjabans, grey-eyed Paharans, delicately modelled Delhiwallis, taut and proud-looking Rajasthanis, an occasional hawk-faced Baluch or a rosy, blue-eyed Pathani. They came from all over the north, from the mountain passes of Karakorum to the hills of Kumaon, from the Nagin of Srinagar to the lakes of Udaipur, dressed in their different clothes and hair-styles. Men from below would look up, vacillating in their choice, till someone would separate from the crowd and dive into the dark staircase, lit by a solitary earthenware lamp. As he entered into the glare of the reception room the girl left the balcony. She would come and sit near the man and they exchanged formal pleasantries, while the maid sat in a corner watching them ingratiatingly and shrewdly. The girl would size up what kind of a man he was and what to ask. Mostly it was a dull routine with a succession of bullying and blustering men, weak and old men, young and fumbling men, mean and demanding men, prudish and hypocritical men, an endless monotony of types that she knew by sight, but occasionally there came a simple man, undemanding, generous, with deep emotions, reaching uncertainly for a fulfilment somewhere but not daring to ask for it, not willing to talk about it. Instinctively she would rise and tell the maid to close the shutters of the balcony, bolt the street door and go away. The understanding mother or mistress encouraged such occasional lapses into humanness because it freshened her up and kept her going. In the seclusion of the reception room, she would talk freely, trying to know him. She would bring him something to eat and drink, and indulge in the beautiful picture that her man had returned home after the day and needed her relaxing care. Almost shyly she would hold his fingers and lead him to her room, both trying to forget themselves and who the other was. Perhaps she even wondered if the time had not come to think of her baby, a thought which had to be faced some day, because if she did not marry, for which the chances were small, she would need the support of a daughter one day.

These girls were superstitious and insisted on some kind of religious sanction. Most of them became Shia by faith so that by a simple invocation they could marry each man as they took him, and dissolve the marriage afterwards. The law of the Shia sect of Muslims permitted marriages of such temporariness.

In the houses of the nautch girls there was much gaiety, music and drinking. But for these girls North Indian dancing might have perished as an art. They were a merry, wily lot who loved dancing and enjoyed their life; they danced and made love because the rhythm in their limbs and their quivering bodies needed a relaxing fulfilment. There were some among them who became famous and kept exclusive establishments like the well known singing girls, but somehow they never quite achieved their status.

The houses of the common prostitutes were gay and busy, men coming and going all the time, and the girls exchanging ribald repartee with them. They were popularly known as the four anna and eight anna walis. Their bodies exhausted, their looks faded prematurely, they provided just satisfaction. When they failed to do even that they joined the ranks of maids, except the few who were shrewd enough to become independent.

This was Hira Mandi, also known as Tibbi, as much an institution of Lahore as Lahore was an institution of the Punjab. Glittering and gay, it had an honest immorality about it. No high-principled finger was pointed, nor had any reformers suggested closing it down. It was there for those who needed it, and such needy ones came from all classes.

Though cooped up in a congested city people had a number of places they could go to on holidays, festivals and fairs in the environs of Lahore. Near the northern gate was Maharaja Ranjit Singh's marble samadhi, where the great Sikh king's ashes were buried. It had become a shrine for both Hindus and Sikhs. Next to it was the Juma Masjid, with its graceful minarets and the open courtyard where the special Id prayers were said. Across the river on the west there was Jehangir's tomb with its spacious park and gardens that offered a pleasant picnic spot; and across the road from his magnificent inlaid-marble tomb is a small ruin of the mausoleum of his queen, Noor Jehan, and her only child, a little daughter. The tragic prophecy of this great Moghul lady, expressed in her own couplet, was more than fulfilled.

On the grave of us poor, neither a lamp nor flowers;
Neither the scorching of the moth's wing, nor the sound of a nightingale.

On the eastern side of the city there was Shalimar Garden, also made by Jehangir, and patterned on the famous Nishat and Shalimar Gardens of Kashmir; the samadhi of Haqiqat Rai, a young martyr who was buried alive in a brick wall by a fanatic qazi; Shahu di Garhi, the shrine of a Muslim saint; and the more recent British addition of the Company Gardens, named after Lawrence, containing parks, zoo and an ornamented hill.

Lahore, despite its frugal habits, knew how to enjoy itself. Added to our many Punjabi festivals it had a number of local fairs, the big fair at the samadhi of Haqiqat Rai, and a particularly beautiful one called the Mela Chiraghan, the fair of lights, which dated back to Jehangir's days. It was held at the Shalimar Gardens, on whose walls, pavilions and canals thousands of earthenware oil lamps were lit, to make the whole garden look like a fairyland. People of all communities came to this fair, and an interesting feature was the Mina Bazaar, held on the third, the last day of the fair, which was attended exclusively by women. Visitors and stall holders were all women. No man was allowed inside, but every year some daring young men would enter, dressed in burqas. Some would invariably get caught and be given the traditional shoe beating by the women. The wretched youths were turned out of the garden to a jeering crowd of men waiting outside the gate for their womenfolk.

The favourite sports of the Lahorias were exercises at the wrestling pits, the akharas, and flying kites and pigeons. Every evening young men, amateurs and professionals, would go to the akharas of well known old wrestlers, to do hard massage and exercises and practise wrestling. Occasionally great champion wrestlers came for tournaments. Each wrestler was taken in a procession through the city by his special followers. With the garlanded hero walking in front, followed by a drummer, the procession would go through the bazaars introducing the wrestler to the city. There was great enthusiasm on the day of the matches, and thousands would collect at a large akhara outside the city to witness the giants battle. These wrestlers were man mountains of tremendous strength, and they followed a complicated etiquette and ritual in both their daily life and their fights.

The kite flying season commenced on the day of the spring festival, Basant, when the sky would be covered with thousands of yellow kites of all shapes and sizes. One usually flew kites from a roof terrace, and in the excitement of the fights the sport always took its annual toll. The cord used with the kites was prepared by dipping it in a solution of powdered glass and glue which made it stiff and sharp. A kite flyer would get his kite high up in the air and then challenge another kite. After considerable manoeuvering you got your kite to do a roll under the other kite, and as it came up you pulled it jerkily so as to cut the other kite's thread. There would be an uproar from the neighbouring roof tops, as the beaten kite floated helplessly downward, and people tried to snatch it with long poles.

Flying pigeons was another old aristocratic and expensive roof top sport. It required a lot of patience to rear and train the birds. The pigeon loft was made from a long bamboo pole with a split-bamboo square platform on top of it, and was fixed on a roof terrace where the pigeons alighted to rest at night, safe from the cats. In the late afternoon the pigeon fanciers would get their flock up into the air and fly them as a team in a circle. The owner gave commands to the pigeons in long whistles, and they would wheel round and round in wider or narrower circles according to the varying tone and length of the whistle, till they were told to settle back on the loft. This daily routine combined training and exercise for the birds. Sometimes there were competitions with other owners, when you made your flock gang up with another flock, or a part of it, and entice it back to its own loft. The decoyed pigeons stayed as part of the winning flock until their owner could decoy them back.

Outside the wall Lahore had developed very pleasantly into

spacious parks, gardens and suburbs. Two famous features were the shopping centres of Mall Road and the legendary Anarkali, and the numerous schools and colleges.

Lahore was the first town to start schools and colleges, and although educational facilities eventually spread all over the Punjab, higher education in arts, science, medicine, law, engineering, teaching and veterinary science was concentrated in Lahore. Each generation, my grand-uncle, father, uncle and we ourselves, studied at Lahore. When you settled in a profession or service, most of your colleagues were old friends from Lahore; you married into some family whose sons and daughters had been to Lahore. Gradually people also began to retire to Lahore. Thus Lahore came to acquire a very special position in our society. There was an overall class of Punjabi professionals who had been educated at Lahore, and this was not a caste of birth and inheritance, for in many colleges, especially those started by charitable trusts, there was a large number of students from humble homes in towns and villages. Punjabi parental ambition to give their sons, and soon their daughters, higher education was indeed great, and often touching. It made Lahore such a large centre of university education with about twenty-five colleges and well over ten thousand students, both boys and girls, more than thirty years ago.

The shopping centre of Lahore was another institution that made it the centre of Punjabi life. There was a range of shopping facilities which no other town provided. Inside the city there were bazaars that specialised each in a different kind of merchandise. In Dabbi Bazaar you could go from one shop to another, all selling only textiles, cotton, silks and woollen, from all parts of the world; you compared, bargained and chose from a competitive variety offered by a hundred shops. If you wanted a bamboo you could go to a bazaar where shop after shop sold nothing but bamboos of all sizes and lengths. But quite different was Anarkali, the street of pomegranate blossom, named after the tragic courtesan girl who was Jehangir's calf-love. Legend has it that Akbar had her murdered to make the young prince Selim forget. The bazaar was built close to her small tomb, and it was not just a bazaar of Lahore, it was a bazaar of the whole Punjab. Sitting in Malerkotla, Muzaffargarh or Mianwali, you talked of having bought this or that in Anarkali in a manner that seemed to convey that Anarkali was a bazaar in your own town. Generations of college students had gone to Anarkali, and they continued the habit throughout their life. At shopping week-ends in Lahore you met old friends and their families in Anarkali. The wives became acquainted and called each other behnji, and sometimes it resulted in future relationships. The shopkeepers remembered you from college days, and you lightly taxed them for charging you just as high prices even though there was no longer the same fear of defaulted bills. And then like good Punjabis you all adjourned to the latest popular restaurant. The old Kesari's, once the pioneering catering establishment which always served the latest in coloured fizz, was still going strong. You stood in the gutter and tried Kesari's latest concoctions in gas and liquid. Then came Stiffles, Kailash's and Standard's, leading in a wide range of eating places, down to the snack shops outside the Shalimi Gate, to satisfy the Punjabis' insatiable love of eating. You took your choice, and while the women talked about the homes they came from and about their children and compared notes about marriageable brothers and sisters the men went back to their college days and exchanged sly references to the places they used to visit in search of varied fare.

It is a charming trick of fate that poor Anarkali, who was poisoned lest she became Jehangir's spouse, is commemorated by a bright and gay street, while Noor Jehan, who ruled both Jehangir and Hindustan, lies in a silent, lonely ruin hidden in the reed thickets on the bank of the Ravi, with only jackals and bats to keep her company.

Next in popularity as a shopping centre was the Mall. In a magnificent curved sweep it began at the foot of the Government College hill, wended its way through the Gol Bagh, and at the Bhangi Gun developed into a wide street flanked by the Arts College, the Science Laboratories, the Senate Hall and the Museum. After that it became a shopping centre. For two miles it proceeded as a wide boulevard with handsome shops of western type, where the British from all over the Punjab came to do their purchases. At its western end were a number of motor-car showrooms, hotels and restaurants, and thereafter the Mall merged into the Lawrence Gardens and some very charming, leafy suburbs.

I came to Lahore in 1927 and managed to enter the coveted Lahore Government College, the first stage of the Punjabi middle class ambition in those days. The second stage was entry into the Indian Civil Service.

Entry into Government College had become a masterpiece of complicated official planning. A few boys were taken in because they had topped the lists in the examinations; thus high merit was unquestioningly rewarded. Some were admitted because they were outstanding in sports and athletics. If they were good enough to get into a college team, no further questions were asked. After having assured the academic élite and the leading athletes the complicated ritual of selection began. There were many areas for reward: families from the states, titled families with record of loyal service to the British Government, sons of high officials and zamindars, nominees of the Political Department, a few Christians and Anglo-Indians and an odd Parsi. The English principal carefully went through the applications, also considering any secret reports that might have come in from the police about a boy's or his family's political leanings. In fact, we all had to sign an undertaking that we did not possess nor would acquire any interest whatsoever in politics. Lastly, a few boys, I among them, were admitted who possessed none of the above qualifications but somehow appealed to the principal because their sheer mediocrity might hold some unsuspected promise. Patterned on Oxford and Cambridge, with a number of British and British-educated Indian professors and lecturers, Government College aimed at giving an all-round education. Its academic standards were naturally high because of its well qualified and handpicked staff which belonged to the well paid senior cadres of government educational service.

Despite Government's attempts to keep politics out of students' way, our interest in it was daily growing. Some of the attempts were pathetic. After one summer vacation two boys were called up by the principal who thrust some papers before them. These were the statements they had signed when they joined college, agreeing not to take part in any political activity. The principal reminded them that on a certain date they had attended a political meeting. With difficulty the boys recalled that out for a walk one day they had seen a crowd collected in a street and had stopped to look. It was a small labour meeting protesting about something or the other, and they moved on. Such strict surveillance however missed the point. It overlooked the fact that what was making real headway was the simple moral of Gandhiji's teachings that we should be independent and free, which one did not have to learn by participation in politics, and which was amply demonstrated by all that we read in English political and literary thoughts; and those few who were attracted by active politics were not to be defeated by threats of expulsion anyway. Politics was permeating our daily discussions at home and outside, which mattered more than what appeared to bother the government–the terrorist movement among young students. The Punjabis, with one exception, made poor terrorists anyway.

CHAPTER TWELVE

ONE DAY in 1928 my father asked me if I had decided what I was going to do after finishing college next year. To three generations of young Punjabis the unquestioned choice had been the Indian Civil Service, and I assumed that this was what my father would expect of me. I was therefore taken aback by his next question. Did I see any future in the I.C.S. or, for that matter, in Government service? I took in his point, but I was surprised that political doubt had crept in even in my father's mind. I had not expected this of his generation. In someone as disinterested in politics as my father any question about the future of government service was indeed a sign of change. I had till now thought that he would see it in the elementary terms that the British had brought peace and development, and while some administrative concessions and improvements were necessary here and there, the question of independence and freedom had no meaning. And yet he said that though the present agitation would no doubt die down, how long would the British be able to carry on? Although he would not admit it, I feel that these thoughts came to him as a result of growing personal frustrations. This I could only guess.

I think these doubts in father's mind began not from any growing political conviction, because apart from what he read in the daily bible of the educated homes, the Tribune, he seldom read about politics or discussed it, but from a change that was taking place in the relationship between his generation and the new generation of Englishmen coming into the department.

I think father's contemporaries had learned and worked unquestioningly for long enough. At first they were grateful for the opportunity, but as time went on they became proficient at their jobs. They had grasped the opportunity well and made a success of the chance afforded them, but naturally time came when the sense of gratitude wore off and they judged themselves on their own merit. Also, by now, young Englishmen were being put under them, and they in turn became teachers. And there was much to be taught, because the specialised nature of the type of work that was peculiar to the Punjab meant imparting training which these young men had not received at their engineering colleges in England. Besides, they were not the pick of the British universities, whereas the young Punjabis from Roorkee were better than ever since the competition for entrance had become so stiff that only the province's ablest youth gained admission.

Furthermore, the English newcomers were not the pioneering type of fifty years ago. As our knowledge of English grew, their facility in Hindustani and Punjabi began to diminish; the ease of travelling and the spread of amenities helped to weaken their interest in the land. Twenty years earlier, when they came on tour they travelled for several days by horse and tonga, spent much time with each assistant and in his area, and stayed a day or two at each dak bungalow, which gave the neighbouring farmers a leisurely chance to meet them. When the motor-car arrived, the superintending engineer could tour through his whole circle of a radius of a hundred miles or more in two days. The amenities of the headquarters towns, the club, electricity, ice and fans, made them reluctant to travel. The new generation were also beginning to send their wives home to look after the children's education, which naturally made them lose interest in the country.

Three or four of father's earlier chief engineers had settled in Mussoorie, where they had bought houses while still at work. There they sent their wives every summer except in the years of furlough, of which there were only four or five in over thirty years of service. They were born here, had studied at Roorkee, married and worked, and here they died and were buried under the thick spreading branches of the rhododendron trees in Mussoorie facing the perennial snows of the Himalays, which fed the canals they had built and run. Their children mostly returned to India and also married and worked here. Father had enjoyed working under these men, sharing language, food and hardships. Mother knew their wives well too, for usually also born in the country they spoke excellent Hindustani, and often Punjabi as well. When they came on tour she would specially cook and send them their favourite Punjabi dishes; they would teach her knitting, crochet, embroidery and making curtains and cushion covers, or cutting khaki shorts for us. She felt at home with them, and the men felt at ease in one another's company.

The new generation came from the British universities, men coming out to India for the first time. Mostly prospects had brought them out: good salaries, quick promotion, liberal leave, concession passages and an early superannuation offered an easier career than at home, at least to the mediocre. While the I.C.S. may still have attracted a type that was interested in India, I doubt if that could be said of the engineers any longer. And they were formal men, with different values, ambitious to get on and perhaps not specially interested in the Punjab. In father's kind these new men found little in common or of interest. They found them industrious but dull, interested only in their work, and I think father was quick to sense the change. He was an old-fashioned Punjabi whose only modern sophistication lay in his skill and social thought. He did not belong to the newly westernised class of Punjabis, nor did he have any problems on that score. He was not eager to be cultivated socially by the British colleagues or to become a member of their club. He was quite satisfied with his own ways and equally with the changes that the British contact had made in him. He wore his turban, but accepted English trousers and coat for working convenience and lived at home in simple Punjabi style. But while between the older generation of the English and his kind there had been a kind of bridge; with the new generation there was no link outside the work. I think the attitude of the new lot hurt him. They stuck to their own ways and made little attempt at understanding his. He had a feeling that they did not think of him as an individual beyond his industry and integrity. They probably found him even a trifle ludicrous, and what the older generation had considered attractive old-fashionedness struck them as backwardness. He never gave expression to his feelings, but I know that he felt it. He also began to resent their assured and privileged position. For an ordinary engineering graduate, with no training in irrigation engineering or building work, to start ahead of the highly trained talent of Roorkee in the name of a 'ratio' seemed indefensible. To spend some years in training such raw youths and then to watch them maintain a lead all their life seemed all wrong. He felt the unfairness of it and equated it with the injustices that the political leaders were speaking about. This wrong belonged to the bigger wrong, the exploitation of the country. And as time went on many wrongs began to appear in his department. Indian engineers, even the ablest in the department, never got beyond a point. Somehow when they came near to the top post of the chief engineer something was found wanting in them. In this race for the top only the English seemed to win, not through declared policy but by the frustrating process of knocking out each Indian contestant individually. Father, of course, was not in the running, or anywhere near it. At the beginning it was accepted that Indians could only go so far; later frustration was avoided by the barriers being successively lowered; but now with plenty of able Indians crowding in at the penultimate post there was growing bitterness at being deprived of the goal.

By the late twenties social tensions also began to appear. In Sargodha, where father was reposted while I was studying at Lahore, there were two clubs in the Civil Station. The Sargodha Club's exclusive Europeanness had been slightly modified by admitting a few senior Indian officers and some big zamindars like the Tiwanas, but not their wives, on the ground that most Indian women were either in purda or socially too backward to be admitted. As a result a separate club had been started by Indian officers and city professionals. The interaction of the two clubs on the Civil Station was interesting.

The Sargodha Club had at that time two Indian officers, the deputy commissioner, an Indian Christian, and the sessions judge. The deputy commissioner accepted the honour but seldom visited the club, but the sessions judge was unsure of himself and felt that he must go there regularly to keep the privilege alive. He played tennis there every evening but felt diffident to join in the purely social activities, so he always turned up afterwards at the Indian Club for a game of bridge and a chat. We had in the station a young Kashmiri, the first Indian accountant of the local Imperial Bank, who was very westernised, extremely lively and sporting. His English manager had invited him to join the Sargodha Club but the young Kashmiri bluntly refused because his wife would not be admitted, and in any case, he considered the honour dubious. He joined the Indian Club, and with his youthful exhuberance gave the poor old sessions judge a bad time. Every evening as he turned up after tennis the Kashmiri twitted him about deserting his English friends. He would hold forth about the whole Anglo-Indian social problem amusingly, but with much thrust and truth. From there he would stray to politics, and simple old-fashioned people like my father listened with much interest because it added a new dimension to the editorials in the Tribune, a dimension of personal feelings vividly expressed. He was much travelled and well connected, distantly, we believed, to the Kashmiri family leading in politics. He spoke about injustices all round, touching familiar chords and providing blunt answers. This handsome Kashmiri soon became the favourite of the club, the political mentor of father and his contemporaries. He gave shape to thoughts that had hitherto vaguely arisen in their minds, thoughts they had had no one to discuss with.

He was incidentally also responsible for the choice of my career. He suggested that I might think of a new profession of Chartered Accountancy, of which there were so far only a handful in India. Father was willing to consider any suggestion from him. Thus it came about that I set out a few months later for England to serve articles and qualify as a Chartered Accountant. My professors and colleagues were astonished at the choice, and I felt important at almost blazing a trail in careers. The first Punjabi Chartered Accountant had just returned from England, but as he had not begun to work no one was any the wiser about this new profession.

At the age of eighteen I began the long journey from Sargodha to London. I was an immature eighteen, having never been further than two hundred miles from Lahore. Leaving home at two o'clock at night did not make the start any easier. A waning moon cast a gloomy light as the car went down the drive, while I felt waves of sadness, thrill and plain fright. I thought of the unknown prospects and the pledge father had asked me to sign before leaving. It was typical of him to make me promise that I would not drink, smoke, consort with women and thus lose sight of the main object of my journey.

At Karachi I had my first sight of the sea. To a Punjabi who has never seen a stretch of water wider than a river in spate, the sea is beyond imagination; but on the overcast August afternoon it looked not so unfamiliar. It was a vast heaving sheet of brown, not unlike the desert; only it broke against the Keamari wall with a deafening roar, instead of the silence of sand. It was as if the petrified desert had suddenly begun to heave into life and sound, with its hillocks and dunes swaying in rhythmic movement.

The coastal mail boat from Karachi to Bombay rolled and lurched in the monsoon and filled me with a misery I had never tasted before. Home-sickness merged into sea-sickness. I understood how the brides must feel as the doli lurches on the shoulders of the bearers. My little wooden cabin, with the curtains drawn to hide the swinging horizon, was as lonely as the swaying doli. I also longed for the solid home, parents and friends, and wished the journey would turn back instead of leading on. What would England be like and its people? Would they be the forbidding, unfamiliar kind we usually saw in the Punjab? We had heard that even the coolies in England were Englishmen, dressed in coat, trousers and hat. Would I be able to ask one of them to carry my baggage? I had heard from one recently returned that in a public convenience you paid two annas to an English sweeper, dressed in a collar and tie, smoking a pipe and reading an English newspaper; what was more, he called you sir and thanked you if you gave him another two annas. There were girls in restaurants who brought you food, and you did not call them madam, they called you sir instead. You lived in strangers' homes and paid them money, and the lady cooked and washed for you and made your fire. The streets were crowded with men and women rushing all the time, walking very fast or riding on railway trains that sometimes disappeared under the ground. As I lay in the heaving bunk, whose spring mattress added acutely to my discomfort, I tried to piece together a picture of the future life from what I had heard, but it was a flat, unreal picture without any familiar dimensions.

The change from the small coastal boat to the large eight-thousand-ton mail steamer at Bombay made me forget all my misery in a wave of wonderment. The new boat was enormous and luxurious, a maze of passages, stairs and decks. I was a bit cowed by the number of English people about, especially the officers and stewards in starched whites, and it added to my nervousness when I discovered that I was going to share the cabin with an Englishman. Excitement rose as in a confusion of new discoveries and crowded decks the siren blew and Ballard Pier slowly receded from the ship. A number of us young Indians stood together in a frightened herd, taking courage from each other's ignorance. A steward came and announced lunch, my first lunch, for meals had always been meals without names. Hungry and curious, I sat subdued at a table laid with a bewildering array of dishes, glass and silver. The menu card conveyed nothing, and I readily accepted the steward's suggestion to have some cold roast mutton. There could have been no worse introduction to English cooking. Boiled, floury potatoes, raw leaves of lettuce and tomatoes, cold grey and pink, spongy slices of mutton and thick boiled wads of watery cabbage, all unsalted, unflavoured, with doughy white bread and artificial looking yellow butter were as unfamiliar as the thick white soup and the boiled cake pudding. By now the ship had turned round Colaba lighthouse and met the big monsoon waves in the open sea. It began to do all the familiar motions of the Karachi boat, and via the lavatories I hastily made my way to the cabin below.

The next five days were pure misery. With the portholes closed the cabin was hot, damp and smelly. I picked up a pillow and a sheet and went upstairs to lie on a wooden bench in a passage where it was a little fresh and cool. Some other Indian students had also discovered this place and were lying in half-dead heaps, past the stage of feeling sick, past all sense of feeling, while the ship reeled on its course ploughing through mountainous waves. Four of us were Punjabis; as it turned out, three from Government College in Lahore, where we had seen each other. We talked about home, the firm flat land, which however hot or cold at least was always stable under your feet. We longed for the sharp, static horizon instead of this uneven line of grey waves which went up and down like a mad swing in all directions. We went back to our school physics and agreed that the fact that this ship did not sink could only be due to Archimedes being right. Gloomy, wet days merged into night, and as the ship shuddered, reeled, and dived we lay inert, not caring if the storm got the better of the ship.

One afternoon the ship suddenly steadied itself and began to move with just a pulsating sound instead of the creaking and groaning of ploughing through big waves. We got up to look at this miracle, and saw the barren hills of the Red Sea and calm blue water with a white wake, as the ship gracefully cut its way forward. It was a wonderful feeling which dissolved all the gloom of the past week. We rushed down, shaved, bathed, changed and rushed up again to discover the thrills of the voyage. The decks were again full of life and laughter; the passengers bent upon making up for the lost days, and the stewards rushing round happily busy.

I discovered my cabin mate, an English customs officer from Bombay who drank from breakfast till after midnight. He seemed to drink and smoke all the time, except for the few hours he spent sprawled on the bed where the steward dumped him every night. This was the first time I saw anyone drunk; in fact, but for the time when we had that half bottle of brandy in the house I had never seen anyone drink. His only attempt at conversation ended abortively. He asked me whether I was going home, but I could not follow his accented speech nor the reference to home and said the Punjabi 'hain'? He told me to say 'pardon', not that 'hain'. I felt hot with shame, and I think he sensed it, because he never spoke to me again. Such problems were cropping up everywhere on the boat. The older experienced Indians, who were familiar with the English ways, knew how to go about; but we were simple and natural and ran into plenty of minor trouble. Some of the hardy passengers who came up on deck during the storm had objected to us lying in heaps on the benches. Eventually the Captain came, but he must have understood our misery, for he let us lie there till we were a little better. We spoke loudly and sometimes called to each other across the deck; we stared at the make-up and the strange clothes of the women, especially when they put their arms round men and without any trace of shame slid to music across a chalked floor. One of the boys disturbed them during after-lunch coffee by trying to strum an Indian tune out of the piano, and they again complained to the Captain. A Tamil brahmin boy who was going to Cambridge for I.C.S. boldly decided to retaliate by sitting cross-legged on the deck next morning with all the marks and stripes on his arms, forehead and chest, chanting mantras interminably till he cleared the whole deck. He knew that religious practice gave the immunity that he did not enjoy in the state room at the piano.

We were told by experienced Indian passengers that these were the usual tiffs between Indians and British on English boats. It always began from Bombay and lasted till Port Said, but once the boat entered the Mediterranean the atmosphere would change. On the opposite way, a pleasant atmosphere existed until Port Said, and then it would suddenly become stiff and unpleasant as the boat went east of Suez. Although in the second class the English themselves were mostly the lower middle class and even the working type, from the customs, port trusts, telephones and railway workshops, we did not even conform to their standard of social sophistication and behaviour; and being simple themselves they were quick to show it. So we went about in two groups, the English and the Indians, never speaking to each other and with unconcealed mutual dislike. A young Bengali, an art student who claimed to be an ex-terrorist, enjoyed the opportunity of giving us education in politics. He told us that he had been picked up as an experiment by an English police officer, who had recommended him for painting murals in India House in London, in the hope that a stay in England would wean him from politics.

We Punjabis were more than anything else worried by the problem of food. We yearned for our thick chappatis, chalk-white butter and curd, till we decided to go to the crew's quarters and appeal to the Pathan and West Punjabi engine-room men. They understood our difficulty, and in spite of the chief officer's protests we became their regular guests. We were also bothered by the English omnivorousness. They seemed to relish all kinds of animals and all parts of them. We were revolted by ham and bacon, roast pork and beef, steaks and ribs, and we were told they even ate the head, feet and tripe of the unfortunate animal. Surely, we argued, they must draw the line somewhere. One morning as some of us were going up to breakfast, a Muslim boy came running down and shouted excitedly that they even ate that part of the animal, its most private part. He could barely explain with excitement, but as he calmed down a little he informed us that he had just been to the dining-room, and the steward had brought him some liver, kidneys and this extraordinary part of the animal's anatomy. He had not even waited to ask. He swore he was telling the truth, and he was, because as we hesitatingly sat at the table, we saw a plateful of sausages. After that we were prepared to expect anything.

At Port Said we made a bee line for the cook shops, and to the disgust of the Bengali, Gujrati, Tamil and Parsi boys our Punjabi group preferred a solid evening of nan-gosht to the sights of the first non-Indian city. With vast quantities of unleavened chappati-like bread, and meat that tasted like camel we arrived back fortified for the rest of the voyage. But from the next day, exactly as our experienced Indians had forecast, the atmosphere on the boat thawed. The first whiff of cold European air seemed to change our co-passengers from Anglo-Indians to English, friendly and attractive. The strain of several years' heat and work seemed to slide off their shoulders. They asked us about our home, where we were going, what we were going to learn, and gave us advice. We began to feel at home with them. They smiled encouragingly at our attempts at picking up their ways. Being imitative by nature I began to learn rapidly their language and mannerisms, their politeness and quiet-spokenness, and to acquire taste for their food and familiarity with the confusing variety of table instruments; so that by the time we reached Marseilles, I was feeling confident already at steering my way through the new life.

As the boat train reached London each one became absorbed in thoughts about the future. There would be many years in a strange land, away from home and parents; there would be successes and failures, disappointments and crises, all to be faced and settled alone. We would spread all over England, Scotland and Wales in universities, workshops, hospitals and offices, reading a variety of subjects and learning many trades and skills. Some would keep a straight course towards their goals, some through either misfortune or fault of their own would stop half way, some would begin to drift, pleasantly at first, and then get caught in a whirlpool and be cast aside, ending their days in mean jobs, usually as waiters in Indian restaurants, never daring to go back home or even contact other Indians in England. And what would be awaiting us on our return home? That was to be the gnawing fear right through the stay. Jobs were scarce in India. As the boat train rushed through miles and miles of backs of houses with their little yards, all looking alike, we sat awed by the present and the future, till we were spewed forth into the immensity of London.

Everyone had someone to meet him at the Victoria Station, a relation, friend or introduction. I had my elder brother, Manohar, waiting for me, meeting every train from Paris since the morning. In reply to his cable on the ship I had told him the day of my expected arrival, little realising that there were many trains to London in a day. He looked so different from when I had last seen him four and a half years ago that I barely recognised him. I felt a little self-conscious at the difference between us. He looked so un-Punjabi, so English; even his skin had paled several shades; his clothes were differently cut, his soft hat and shoes were unlike what I had specially bought in Lahore; even his Punjabi sounded unfamiliar, its construction distinctly English. We spoke awkwardly about home and the journey. In the taxi I told him about the little problems on the voyage, and he explained to me that I would find the English quite different here, and I must forget what I had thought of them in India.

England was to be my home for the next eight years. I was to discover at the end that I did not care whether I returned; that the people known for their strangeness and formality were sentimental at heart and held back nothing, provided you became one of them, and I did.

CHAPTER THIRTEEN

LONDON WAS just too big for me and the two days I spent there so overwhelming that I was glad to leave for Manchester. My brother had arranged some digs in advance so that I settled in straight away. On the following day I went to meet my new principal to whom I was going to be articled, and then to the University. Life opened at a chapter in which almost everything was new. Whether in the digs, at college or in town, impressons came big and fast. The independence I enjoyed in my affairs, the academic and social freedom of University life, the stimulating lectures and the Union activities gave me a most exhilarating feeling; so much so that I began to have a peculiar nightmare. I would dream that I was suddenly recalled home and had to leave this wonderful new life; I would awake with a sense of great relief that it was in fact only just beginning.

Life had a fullness I had never known before. At college in Lahore, extra-curricular activities had been limited to an occasional debate, with a professor in the chair, and an odd lecture by a visitor, again with a professor presiding. You merely listened because questions were not encouraged. The debates were on strictly non-political subjects and the talks on topics as harmless as possible. And now suddenly I was thrown into an atmosphere of freedom undreamt of and so stimulating that I had to remind myself that it was real. I went around in a maze, attending lectures, debates, meetings of innumerable societies, talks, seminars, symposia, concerts and socials. The days were so packed with interest that the nightmare often returned. But before I could really be part of this life I had a problem to solve.

The habit of sticking together had begun on the boat and continued in England. In class and in spare time Indian boys formed into groups. Whenever you came to the college Union after a lecture you gravitated to a corner where there was a small group of Indians, simply because it needed no introduction to talk to Indians you did not know, nor had you to look for a subject of conversation; an enquiry about home was enough. On the other hand, you could not very well walk up to an English group and introduce yourself; for one thing their conversation was on unfamiliar lines, and their idiom was not always easy to follow. Very soon all Indians knew each other, and some made friends and explored together their new environments. One mutual interest was Indian food, because then there were no Indian restaurants in Manchester. Some practised landladies could produce a recognisable curry, but we mostly learned to rely on our own skill, which with some, especially the Punjabis, was soon quite considerable. But the major link was getting our bearings and testing conclusions on each other, especially on those who had arrived earlier. You could put your problems to them without self-consciousness. But this habit of sticking together had its obvious disadvantages; it closed all windows, except the one to studies. Outside lectures you led a life very little different from that at home. There were few points of contact with your environments other than the simple ones of receiving service. Your observations were dulled by being impersonal, tested only by a point of view that was close to your own. It soon began to pall and made me restless.

Participation in the life of a foreign country is not easy. We blamed the English in India for being exclusive, but, except for the fact that they were the rulers, and therefore created problems by their exclusiveness, there was little difference in our difficulties in England and theirs in India. The question is where to begin and what you consider the trouble worth. Most difficult is leaving your own group, which usually regards such an attempt as unnecessary defection, convinced that it can provide you with a self-contained social life. If you want company to go to the pictures you do not have to look for an English student, there will be plenty of Indians whom you can ask. If you sat with some English boys in the refectory or went out to lunch with them, you were told that you were going over to the other side. Attempts at fraternisation dubbed you as one of them and ashamed of your own people. Many undoubtedly found it flattering to be able to mix freely with Englishmen because of the hidden inferiority complex produced by the English attitude in India which made some exaggeratedly friendly, and others unnecessarily suspicious. Few had a natural poise. The group's general attitude was that as they ignored us in India, why should we cultivate them here.

It was altogether a complex situation which some well-meaning English men and women sympathetically interested in India, tried to improve by inviting us to their homes and social gatherings. I genuinely admired these people because it was not an easily rewarding task. Many of us responded with a sneering attitude, others with long harangues on British injustices. Occasionally, when someone mildly defended or suggested another angle, we considered that the very proof of an imperialist outlook which never saw the Indian point of view. Usually we had a sympathetic hearing, which made us alternately lachrymose and arrogant. Poverty, illiteracy, child marriage, and a host of other Indian problems were placed at the British doorstep; we were the blameless victims of it all. They were to be blamed moreover because they did not put things right by brushing aside our own opposition.

One day I attended a lecture by Lord Meston of Agra, an ex-governor of the U.P. He was a mild old man, and I was struck by his unassuming and modest manner. I met him on the road and he asked me the way to the building where he was to give his talk. To see an English lord and ex-governor walking on a wet pavement in a mackintosh, carrying his own bag, was a sight I could never have imagined. We climbed the stairs together, and when we entered the room he looked hesitatingly about till he was recognised by the secretary of the society. In his talk, which was otherwise balanced and informative, he irritated me by his bland assumption, reiterated more than once, that the British record in India was nothing but good, of which he would like young Englishmen to be entirely proud. Had he been addressing the Primrose League this might have gone down well, but here there were a number of sprouting socialists, I among them, and he got a rough handling during question-time. As he left he whispered to me that perhaps I should not have left India. I never quite made out what he meant.

Soon afterwards I got up to speak at a debate on the British Empire. My heart thumped as I fidgeted in my seat, trying to sum up enough courage, and when I did begin, all the lights in the hall went out. They told me to carry on, and undaunted I continued while the lights came and went. I do not remember what I said but I think I demolished the case for the Empire with a barb or two and much eighteen-year-old earnestness, though with a sense of appreciation of what they had done in the Punjab. I discovered that while these young people could be very patient with undiluted criticism, they much preferred it when it was mixed with some humour and fairness; but this does not come easily to us when we criticise or oppose. We usually like to state our wrongs clearly and unequivocally, without relief of any kind.

After this debate I devoted myself to every phase of university life except earnest work. I marvelled at this freedom where boys and girls could organise any activity they liked, and no one in the University seemed to mind. No professors ever entered the Union uninvited, much less directed its activities; and conservatism, communism, nihilism, Marie Stopes, or anything we wished could be discussed. The culmination was the most hectic and the bitterest of all debates, the one on the King and country motion: 'This house will not fight for its King and Country under any circumstances.' To my joy and horror the motion was carried. It was soon followed by a lecture by Saklatvala, a member of the Parsi house of Tatas who had settled in England and was the first communist member of Parliament. He was brilliant and bold, and there was a near riot in the debating hall. It had been bad enough to hear Englishmen talk heresy about the King, but to hear an Indian, a communist, voted to Parliament by Englishmen and women and, to wit, so amusing, was more than the young conservatives could stomach. 'Never, Sir, in the history of this beautiful hall has so much filth been poured on its walls; it will take years and generations to wash it off,' said one young tory in a voice charged with suspiring emotion.

Both at the King and country debate and at the Saklatvala talk I was too astonished to get up. Moreover, it seemed their own fight. My emotions were mixed. I was happy at the thought of so much freedom; sad that in India we should probably never be allowed to enjoy it. But the Indian problem was fast receding from my mind. I felt a sense of elation I had never experienced before. I was drawn into the vortex of a new life, and I cared less and less for the life I had left behind.

Some Indian boys reacted badly and attributed the change in me to the traditional 'Punjabi loyalty to the crown', which ironically enough was a British expression that we could not live down. Some Bengali boys warned others that I was a spy and came from a family of police service. For a time it became quite unpleasant as I argued back extolling British qualities and deprecating Indian shortcomings. Before we condemned the English so wholeheartedly we must take a critical look at ourselves, I argued. A much older student, a lecturer from Roorkee College, who had recently arrived, agreed with my enthusiasm but warned me that on my return I would find the British there a disappointment.

Time passed very pleasantly now, going from one interesting activity to another, welcomed for an exoticness that had taken roots so naturally and easily. I revelled in adopting their ways. After a particularly thick evening I even relished a plate of tripe and onions. My brother had gone to the heart of his English friends by his genuine liking for Bury black-puddings, something for which I was never able to raise great enthusiasm; otherwise I dropped all my inhibitions. I developed a liking for beer, fish and chips, hot-pot and parkin, smutty stories, soft aitches and broad a's and generally got as close to the heart of Lancashire as one could. But one day I found myself sitting between a Lancashire and a Yorkshire couple at Old Trafford at the annual cricket event. Then I was really lost and walked away disgusted with myself, for I could not raise any enthusiasm for the proper rose in this time-honoured vendetta. But I found I had enough natural affiliation left to give a whole half-crown extra to an old cartman who moved some stuff from one place to another, when he said, 'Give us another half crown, Sir; there is many a time I have sat and watched your great Ranji at Old Trafford. He was a cricketer ba goom!'

Lancashire speech and accent was something I took to, and in those days no one regarded it as a sign of inferior education. At college, lecturers and students all had the soft north country speech with its melodious intonation. The class was full of such names as Walker, Winder, Entwistle, Laithwaite, boys and girls from the valleys of Lancashire and the mines of Wigan, with an unassuming, coarse-spun and direct manner that I found very close to our own. Many of them were practically bilingual, for they spoke an archaic kind of language at home and modern English with a Lancashire accent at college. It was not always easy to get to know them because they were inclined to leave you alone, but once they took to you they gave much genuine warmth.

An embarrassing occasion, whose humour completely escaped me at the time, was when I nearly became a Christian. A family invited me to Sunday tea, and I cheerfully accepted because they had an attractive daughter. After tea, over which the usual polite enquiries were made about India, with assurances that at the proper time, no doubt, India would be an equal member of the Empire, especially when she had more people of my kind, I was asked if I would like to go to church. Of course, I did not have to, but if I liked to accompany them it might be nice. I had little choice if they were all going, including the daughter.

The church turned out to be a tabernacle of some strange order, presided over by a fiery Scotsman. It was a plain hall with a platform on which sat two women, one who played a harmonium and another the violin. I had never before been to a church service, but this was different from what I had imagined. After some lusty songs, rendered with great fervour, the shock-haired priest in a lounge suit came on the stage. He began slowly, discursively as he looked at the congregation, fixing each person with a keen gaze. When his eye alighted on me I tried to look intelligently interested in the proceedings and smiled approvingly. That, I was to discover, was my undoing.

The preacher slowly warmed up, and in rapt silence men, women and children listened to him as if they had never heard him before. Soon his voice was thundering across the hall, hurling bolts at his congregation. His hands in the air, his body quivering with pious rage, his dark hair flying like a sombre cloud, he stood firmly on his feet and threatened his followers, inexorably, mercilessly, without offering any hope. Fear began to permeate them, and as he thundered at them, 'Will ye burn alive in hell', they replied sotto voce, 'No, save us.' In a soft voice, suddenly gentle and reassuring, he whispered, 'Yes, I will save ye.' But the next moment he was back with the whiplash. 'If ye are fit to be saved; if ye want to be saved.' 'Save us,' they pleaded in unison. 'Save us, we want to be saved.'

I was getting lost. I could not understand what had possessed them. What had they done wrong, these simple people, to be afraid of chastisement? And why was he threatening them; and what would he do to save them? He scanned the hall and shouted again, 'I will save ye, be ye white or brown; be ye English or furrin; be ye Christian or heathen.' Now everybody knew, and they craned their necks to see the object of this special reference. Some of them had seen me come in, others guessed. My hosts proudly looked back, and I began to shrink in my seat.

The chase was now joined in earnest. This was going to be a glorious Sunday, with a young brown heathen on the platter. Such a saving had not taken place before. He bullied and cajoled, rasped and whispered as he tried to persuade me to be saved. The whole congregation was with him. Some young men and women got up and offered to be saved, largely, I think, to encourage me. But I had a problem which no one understood. I had a vague idea that a Christian saving meant a baptism and that meant a public bath. For one thing it was freezing cold, and for another, I did not like the idea of undressing in public to be dipped under the gaze of all, so I did not take the risk and held fast.

As I thanked my hosts after the service, they wanly asked me to come again, but it was clear that it had been a great disappointment to everybody. I was miserable too, for I would have liked to make everyone happy.

It was interesting to be in England at a time of great changes. As I got to know the country, its institutions and its people, I could even participate in a way in the intellectual process that lay beneath the change. I got the opportunity of joining a committee on University life, I was elected to the Union executive, led an

Indian debating team to the English Universities, and was invited to participate in many interesting activities. This was also the time of the great depression, the hunger marches and 'Love on the Dole'. Living with a family where the man was thrown out of work brought home to me what unemployment could mean. For a time, while the family pride resisted the dole, I was their only employment.

In this family both husband and wife were staunch conservatives while I was becoming ardently labour. I could follow the process that influenced my own thinking, but I found it hard to understand in the beginning what they had in common with conservative politics. Gradually it became clear to me. It was of great fascination to watch their near working-class way of living and the intense struggle she put up to climb clear of the dividing line; and I think it was that which had decided her to take in a boarder. We at first lived in a street of an unbroken row of houses with backyards and front steps, which she felt as a hateful symbol of working-class living that she must get away from. With a slight improvement in the husband's commission and the apparently quite reasonable amount that I contributed, she felt she could afford to get away to something of her choice. 'The idea of bringing up children in houses with backyards and no front gardens–well, it may not have been posh where I came from, but we at least had a little lawn and a couple of trees at the back. And I am going back to where I belong.' I loved the defiant toss of her head, as she shook her bell-shaped hair, and the sound of her soft Lancashire speech, as she waxed eloquent about each class living the way it was ordained.

After a lot of cogitation my landlady came to the point and asked me one day if I was happy staying with her, because if I was, and as I was paying her well–not that, mind you, she did not give me full value–she would like to flit. She would like to leave this neighbourhood. She had nothing against her neighbours, but she would like to move into a council estate house, with a front and a back garden; a semi-detached house which was 'fit and proper for them and the kids'. I was touched because she had begun to regard me as one of the family, and by the simple though practical manner in which she asked me I felt that I had become a part of the family's progress and ambition. I assured her that as long as I was here I reckoned I would continue to stay with her; but I had already acquired enough northern hard-headedness to add that so long as she looked after me well she had nowt to worry.

So we moved into a council house with its own gate and a wire fence. It had a little lawn in front, a small garden at the back that would keep her man respectably busy mowing and digging his own place instead of going to the allotments like a working man. The house had a proper bathroom with a tub and a separate water closet upstairs instead of a privy in the backyard. It had two bedrooms and a small one for the children, a front room which was allotted to me as my study, a dining-room and a kitchen. There was also a tiny hall and a cupboard under the stairs. The family were in raptures over the house, the locality, the proper road that ran in front of it instead of a street, and the fact that the estate had a name. There was a shopping parade with a Co-op, a public house with a car park and all other signs of class. And if they had a lodger it was a proper Indian gentleman who went both to the city and the college, not just a working man. She would now order her shopping to be delivered and would occasionally include some special things like grape fruit for the gentleman staying with them. The children went to a better school where they wore a uniform. We now regularly had a roast on Sundays and high tea, with canned fruit instead of the cheap fresh fruit in season.

I watched with interest the difference between a thrifty Punjabi woman and my landlady. Where the Punjabi woman would have tucked away small amounts in gold ornaments and clothes, this Englishwoman bought bits of furniture–a half-moon rug, an easy chair, a cupboard. Instead of changing her gold bangles into heavier ones, she traded her dining-room suite for something in better wood. Watching her at work and leisure I learned a new definition of house pride. She worked far harder at polishing and scrubbing than our women ever did. I learned, too, that where our women took pride in discharging obligations and duties to the family and the biradari, this woman lived entirely in the world of her own home. I was surprised at the little contact she maintained with her husband's or even her own relations. She seldom visited relations and they rarely came, except at Christmas and christenings. A question they frequently put to me was whether we attached the same importance to home life as they did, but I realised that home to us meant something different. On special occasions we combined as a family of parents, brothers and sisters, uncles, aunts and cousins even thrice removed, whereas with them years might pass without even brothers meeting. I sometimes wondered whose was the better system; perhaps theirs because instead of dispersing energies and resources widely it concentrated them for the benefit of the immediate family. Their attitude certainly had its advantages when things were going well, but when trouble came, as with the depression, I saw its harsher side. There was a time when I was closer to them than their own relations, to whom it was a matter of hard luck that they had fallen by the wayside. To me it was a misfortune to be shared. While we could rely upon relations, they might turn to a friend, but there was never any question of pre-determined obligations.

The depression began as one of those things that start in the States, but Lancashire soon began to feel it. For a while the blame could be put on the ineptness and inexperience of the Labour Government, and Harry would hold forth at length on what you could expect of ex-engine drivers and miners running a government. You must leave it to the Tories, for they were born gentlemen and knew the job since generations. We would have long arguments about socialism, League of Nations and free trade, all of which he considered unsuitable for the Englishman, though he would not grudge them to foreigners. I was acquiring it all as part of my education. It did not take a young Indian in England long to discover socialism as his political creed. We were vexed by the imperialist attitude of the conservatives, their easy assumption that they were in India and elsewhere for the good of those countries, on a sacred mission, even though the misguided inhabitants did not always see it that way. The socialists on the other hand considered the conservatives as much a problem and a menace as we did. The socialist sympathy for the underdog anywhere naturally appealed to us. They spoke about free trade, equality of races, ridding the world of poverty; and they included everybody in the future hope of the world. At the Conservative Association meetings at the Union the talk was instead about preserving the glory of the Empire and taking a firm line everywhere. India should gratefully wait for a long time to be free, if she did not want to sink into complete anarchy. Conservatism of those days did not seem to be interested in us as a people and had nothing to offer for our problems.

The extent to which Indian political and economic thinking has always veered left must be largely due to generations of young Indians having been influenced by Fabian and socialist thought during their student years in England. They sensed in it a genuine sympathy for Indian aspiration and saw in the doctrine a solution to the problems of India. When independence came it was but natural to turn to a socialist pattern.

As the depression deepened a sense of fear began to spread. Now my landlady would tell me over my meal about Mrs. So and So's husband who had been laid off, and the latest plant to go on short time. Harry's firm was not doing too well, and unfortunately the creeping fear was pushing him to drink. He began to arrive home late even on evenings other than Friday, the pay day. This worried her because drink had run in his family, and she was afraid that if he went too far it might be taken as an excuse by his employers to lay him off. Just that happened. He began to drink during lunch hour and was ultimately dismissed. There followed a grim struggle. Pieces of furniture began to go as they had come; things on hire purchase were returned; and she would spend long hours mending and darning things beyond repair. Pride had ultimately to be swallowed and the dole accepted; but only once during those dismal times did she weaken. She said to me one day, 'Prakash, if only I can count on you to stay with us I am sure we will get by.' The years of depression showed me enough to learn a deep respect for the courage of these people, courage amply displayed a decade later.

CHAPTER FOURTEEN

I TOOK my degree and tried unsuccessfully to do some economics research, but soon strayed into the pursuit of delving deeper into English life. In effect, it meant doing nothing at all, and for more than a year I led a pleasantly aimless existence. I went to Hallé concerts, to the new Reference Library, I read the *New Statesman*, worked on the Union affairs, heard Oswald Mosley, Winston Churchill and Harry Pollit, played games, walked extensively in the north country, and sported a snuff-coloured shirt and green and orange ties. Among my friends were at least three who had been doing medicine for ten years and more. It was an amiable life whose only flaw was the weekly letter home, but the chore done with a routine skill I felt good for another week. My allowance of fifteen pounds per month with a small extra amount once a year was ample for my needs. And so life would have carried on in a lazy current that would inevitably have landed me on the mud flats, if she had not arrived on the scene. She appeared providentially at just the right time. I met her at a student congress at Oxford in early spring. Two days before the end there was a choice of visits to Whipsnade Zoo and Stratford-on-Avon, but as the former was half a crown cheaper I took it. Since almost everybody preferred Stratford, Whipsnade had to be cancelled and I was left with no choice in the matter but to improve my mind. She in any case was full of a Nordic earnestness to follow up her history of literature studies at Uppsala. She was chubby and green-eyed with a flat pale face and sturdy ankles, but what took my fancy was her nose. Its Scandinavian arch ending in an up-tilting tip was something I had never seen before, because our Punjabi noses are often straight, with sometimes a middle-eastern curve, but they never point upward. The following evening, our last in Oxford, I realised that life was beginning to do some complicated zigzags, which I did not seem to mind.

Back in Manchester I tried to sort things out. Sweden was where matches in India came from, and that was about as much as I knew about the country. I went to the library to consult the

Encyclopaedia Britannica, but it could only coldly inform me that Sweden had the highest rate of illigitimate births in the world; otherwise it had timber, iron ore and a long dented coastline. Looking at some typical pictures of lakes and forests it seemed about as different from the Punjab countryside as it was far from it on the map. And she came from a small island in the Baltic, which looked even farther. As usual, I decided to accept life as it came, with her as a part of it. It seemed so much nicer that way. The few doubts I had her Viking romanticism and islander's practicalness soon brushed aside. She seemed atavistically willing to burn her boats behind her, once she decided that she liked where she had landed. She cancelled her plans for the rest of her educational tour to the Continent and wrote home to her mother about it. Drawn from a long line of windjammer skippers from the Baltic, going back, may be, to the adventurers with the long boats, she never suffered from doubt; in fact, her determination and the way she ignored the problems I thought the future would hold somewhat frightened me. Her mother sent back a simple invitation to bring me back for summer vacation.

Before going to Sweden I took her to a favourite spot of mine where I turned up for a week-end whenever I could manage it. It was a Quaker guest house in the Ribble valley, on the border of Lancashire and Yorkshire, an old converted farm-house with a magnificent view. Living in Manchester always made me long for a distant horizon, and whenever I could not stand any more the interminable rows of houses, wet pavements and the glistening tramlines, I would pack a small bag and take a bus to this place. The greyness of Manchester continued in another thirty-odd miles of Bury, Bolton and a string of other towns, until the road came out of this industrial tunnel into the open air of the valley of the river Ribble. Now it was a clear sky, green grass, the light and the smells of the country. From the sleepy cobbled little town of Clitheroe, where the bus dropped me, I would walk along a lane that climbed past fields and farms, inhaling deeply the English country smells with their infinite variety of shades.

Hay's Farm was situated well above the valley and commanded an extensive view of the land as it dipped into the wooded hollow that was the river valley, and rose again on the other side through woods and farms to the noble form of Pendle Hill. At the back of the house there was a beautiful old English garden which in early summer was alone worth coming all the way from Manchester to see. The friendly Quaker who was in charge of this guest house told me that during his visit to Lancashire at the time of the Round Table Conference Gandhiji had stayed a night here. He arrived in the evening in his chappals, dhoti and white woollen shawl and took a walk in this garden which just then was in the blaze of its full glory. It had astonished him that Gandhiji did not even seem to notice the flowers. I consoled him that it was quite characteristic of Gandhiji, that though he passionately advocated a return to nature he completely lacked interest in its beauty.

A sense of peace used to fill me as I walked through the garden and stood on the terrace looking at the valley and Pendle beyond. I had got to know every fold and contour of this hill, its every shade of colour through the four seasons, and the changing lights of day and night. I believe I loved it in a peculiarly personal sort of way so that I felt I should do some detransference, and thus it was that I brought Gärd here. Before she introduced me to her country there was a small part of England that I wanted to show her first. We walked through the woods and ravines formed by the streams and brooks that drained the hills into the Ribble. From the valley we climbed the Pendle and roamed for hours over the sombre moors where the wind always blew hard. We sat on an old stone wall and watched the seagulls poised on the currents in the air, occasionally uttering their primitive cries. I had often slipped away from the guest house and climbed the Pendle alone; today I felt a different kind of exhilaration, for the mountain seemed to matter less.

I gazed through the window of the train from Gothenburg to Stockholm at the long succession of outcrops of granite, still blue lakes and silent pine forests. Every now and again you saw a factory in a forest clearing, usually on the edge of a lake, but the train never ran through miles and miles of smoke-stacks with the houses of workers clustered around them. I looked at her face in the opposite seat, and at the faces of other passengers, pale and impassive, with calm blue eyes. They looked so placid and yet you felt underneath there was a strength of passion that I had already recognised in her. It looked all so far from the Punjab, so different, and yet I sensed a commonness and felt at home. As I got to know them well I realised that we were both products of essentially rural societies. Like us, they were a rural people, to whom land and family ties still meant much.

We spent a few days in Stockholm, a city of elegance that blended its architecture, both old and new, so naturally with its fresh and clear waterways and surrounding forests. She happily showed me around its palaces, galleries, parks and linden avenues, the old city and the new town hall, its statues and, what to the Punjabi in me made a great appeal, its variety of restaurants and food. Hand in hand we roamed about from early morning till late at night, and she felt a new thrill of seeing it through my eager eyes. The evenings were long and the nights short, when the sun left a velvety purple dusk behind and soon returned to a rosy dawn which turned into a silvery day. To us even the long days were too short.

In the mornings we met outside the Concert Hall to watch the fountains play on the glistening wet bodies of the indescribably beautiful group of Milles' 'Orpheus Waking up the Dead'. We would wander among the flower-sellers with their gay tulips, narcissi and hyacinths, and decide that what we needed more immediately was breakfast. We would sit in a 'Norma' with a variety of breads, cheeses, butter and milk between us. We then walked along the river where on a little island stands the Singer to the Sun, lifting his arms to the sky in the gay ecstasy of a Swedish summer.

On the last evening we sat on the slopes of Skansen watching a deepening blue mantle gently descend over the city. The brick walls of the Town Hall changed from red to purple, the surrounding waters became a blue black, and the three golden crowns on its main tower stood burnished by the last rays of the sun. Stockholm spread below in a blue shadow. We looked back on the last fortnight and were reluctant to leave. Later in the evening we caught the boat train for the night steamer to Visby on the island of Gotland.

In Stockholm we could get lost, but now it was going to be different. Gotland is a small island and Visby a very small town. On her mother's side her family had lived there for centuries. Her father had migrated from the mainland and had taught generations of schoolboys at the Cathedral school. Her mother's father had been captain on the Gotland–mainland boats and his father before him had perished in a sailing ship. Girls from the island had often married men from faraway countries, but this was the first time that one of them was bringing an Indian home. News had already spread of this unprecedented happening. The moment we stepped on board the mate saluted smartly, an old schoolmate of hers, and disappeared to tell the Captain who graciously waddled down to welcome little Ingegärd and her Indian boy on his ship. Almost everybody, except the mainland tourists knew her on the boat as a schoolmate, or as the daughter of the old teacher, Dr. Skoglar, and Tante Hedvig, and I was lost in endless handshakes, bows from the waist and välkommens to Gotland.

At midnight the boat left Nyanäshamn and on a mirror calm sea set course for Visby. We sat on the top deck watching the beautiful phenomenon that is a northern summer night. To me, coming from the lower latitudes, it had a strange beauty about it. The long twilight reluctantly dissolved into a soft darkness which the sun seemed to insist on keeping in a loose embrace. A pale orange light travelled from the point where it had set and edged along the horizon, never letting the darkness assert itself. I thought of the contrast of our Indian-ink nights where, its job done, the sun was so firmly excluded and pure darkness prevailed. Here sun and darkness mated in half-somnolence, till he gently pushed her aside and began to rise out of the sea. The darkness slowly melted away, lingering for a while in a colourful dawn. By two o'clock he possessed the earth in broad daylight. The sea and the sky were now tinted a china blue, and another Nordic summer day had begun in its resplendent glory. I shivered in the early morning cold and moved closer to her. I wondered why they had shed their worship of the sun when we still held it a god.

The chalk cliffs of Gotland with Visby clinging to their slopes now rose out of the sea. The city wall, the black spires of Santa Maria, the Hanseatic ruins, and the red and green sloping rooftops drew nearer as the steamer swung in its course towards the narrow harbour entrance. I waited to see the vista life held around the next bend. She pressed my hand to reassure me but it somehow felt a little unsure.

Many years later Gärd was to tell me, when she first visited the small town near Lahore where my parents had settled after retirement, how much she felt at home, adding that I must have found the same familiar touch on my first arrival in Visby. In a small town in Sweden, as in a small town in the Punjab, such arrivals were everybody's business. I realised that I had become English enough to find it tiresome at first, but I soon got used to being on display and bore it patiently. From the moment of my arrival Mamma's coffee-pot did not stop boiling for days. She and the maid must have spent days baking cakes to serve all the callers. Mostly women, they came singly or in small groups, and each time, to the delight of everybody and Mamma's special pride, I faultlessly went through the Swedish formula for introduction and farewell. My fixed smile had to make up for my lack of speech. They commented, according to Gärd, on my regular white teeth and my thick unruly black hair, and asked innumerable questions about home which she blithely answered in Swedish without referring to me, though now and then she paused to tell me what the question had been.

I had had advance tuition on the Swedish Lloyd steamer, and had learned the drill well. Each time a guest came I stood stiffly to attention, with the heels together, to shake hands, and bowed from the waist, bending my head so that the hair fell into my eyes. I remembered this vividly when years afterwards, back in Sweden, I saw her giving a gentle push to the heads of our little boys to make them give a correct performance. Most charming was the way girls and young women curtsied to their seniors by bending at both knees, and how the little boys clicked their heels and jerked their heads in a bow. I had also learned that with coffee you had to take one cake of each kind of a whole array, and if you helped yourself to another the hostess took it as a compliment. But you needed some practice to consume so much confectionary. We then had to return the calls, which meant more coffee ceremonies.

In Sweden, besides the many holidays and festivals of religious origin, though more observed for their special fare, there are also those of purely gastronomical significance. Such is the first of August, the feast of the crayfish, when the night is already dark, and in gardens, week-end cottages and outdoor restaurants Chinese lanterns are strung in their honour. Crayfish parties go on through the whole month of August, while it is permitted to catch them in the brooks. I had my proper initiation in Swedish eating and drinking when we were invited to the crayfish party of the local Yacht Club.

The Visby Yacht Club was a truly democratic institution. Anybody who owned a boat, whatever its size, or regularly sailed with friends, could become a member. The president was the jovial Herr Vice-Consul for Latvia, who besides a yacht also owned what must have been the last commercial sailing ships of Gotland. He was there with all his family. The owner of a big store brought also his assistants who used to take turns as crew; a bookseller who employed only girls brought them all along. It was quite a cross-section of small town society, for when it came to boats all were brothers.

The party lasted all night. Swedes have retained the sensible habit of eating and drinking together, but how much they could eat and drink was another matter, and it was hard for a foreigner to keep pace. Before the scarlet guests of honour, the crayfish, arrived on the table there was a prodigious smörgosbord accompanied by the fiery brännvin. You lifted a glass of this unmatured spirit, faintly flavoured with aniseed, and tilted it with a smart jerk so that the entire contents went searing down your throat to explode in a muffled wallop at the pit of your stomach. With the crayfish the time-honoured rule is 'one for every claw'. Through the night drink followed drink and everyone wanted to say skol to the foreign guest. When so addressed, you look straight into the other person's eyes, raise your glass, drink, hold it in front of you again and look again into his eyes before putting it down. With so many drinks everybody started remembering snatches of school-book English and happily engaged in conversation with me. In between bouts of food and drink we went out to dance in the open air, and Swedish dancing was full of vigorous abandon.

I somehow lasted the pace, and the next morning, which was Sunday, agreed to go sailing to the club meet down the coast. There was a high wind, and few set sail, but Gärd and her brother, Sune, put their yawl to sea. Had I remembered my lesson from the Arabian Sea I might have treated the Baltic more respectfully. Last night's crayfish and raw spirit, the kerosene and linseed smell of the boat, the high seas and the cold wind soon showed the whole family that there was a long distance between a sea-faring Gotlander and a land-locked Punjabi. I hardly heeded Sune's assurance that the yacht was specially constructed to ride storms and had seen much worse. Only three boats arrived at the meeting place, and an enormous lunch remained uneaten. I said I would rather walk the eighteen miles back to Visby. Mamma decided to keep me company, but luckily we caught a bus.

Gärd and I went on a bicycle tour of the island starting out on the road that follows the coast to the north of the city. It was a rugged country of pine forests, spruce and juniper, and chalk cliffs. The sparse soil on the stony shore had a violet shine of the thyme that filled the sun-drenched air with its scent. The wind-bent fur trees turned all their branches towards the land, while the low stunted spruce spread like a carpet in the shelter of the rock. Below the cliffs the tideless Baltic lay calm and inert after its last summer storm. When evening came we had to look for somewhere to sleep, so like all wandering youth we walked into a lonely farmhouse and asked the farmer's wife if she could put us up for the night. It turned out that the farmer could speak English as he had been to America in his youth. Most Swedes had kinsfolk in the States, but this man was one of the few who had turned back from there. While Gärd and the farmer's wife busied themselves upstairs fixing the beds he told me about the girls he had known over there.

Our hostess treated us to the best supper she could produce at such short notice, and coffee in the morning, and when we left she would not hear of payment. She asked us to call on her sister a few miles up the road, which we did and were asked to stay to coffee and cakes. And so it was always; whether it was a small farm like this one, or one of the stately stone houses in the rich farmland further south in the island, you were offered free hospitality wherever you went. I was also struck by the way you could trust everybody. One of our bicycles broke down and we just left it on the roadside, without there being any doubt about picking it up the next day. Anything you left by the road was safe. The farmers built little wooden platforms where their approach roads joined the main road. On it postmen and delivery truck drivers left parcels. Crime was virtually unknown, and the small jail in Visby was rarely inhabited.

We had another home in Sweden, the farm her father came from which is still in the family, in the county Dal, near Sweden's biggest lake, Vänern. A road leading to the lake divides the estate; on one side is the garden where four century-old linden trees flank the gate. The path leads to a white and yellow wooden house with grey slate roof; on the other side are stables and barns. The fields are a clearing in the pine forest, the main source of the farm's income.

I first saw Hultet in darkest winter, a darkness yet unrelieved by the snow. She had met me in Gothenburg and we were on our way to Visby for Christmas. I had not realised before what winter darkness meant. Apart from a few hours of grey twilight, impenetrable blackness ruled over the country. In the house the lights burned all day. In the early morning of Saint Lucia's day, which heralds the long Swedish Christmas, her youngest cousin in a long white nightgown with a crown of lighted candles on her yellow head went round the bedrooms. She carried the coffee tray, with saffron bread in the shape of the swastika, the ancient symbol of sun worship the Scandinavians shared with us.

I saw Hultet again in early summer when the scent of the linden blossom floated in the air, weighed with the heavy perfume of the honeysuckle that swarmed all over the veranda. The garden contained many trees not usually found in that latitude, yew, copper beech, walnut that did not fruit. They had been planted by her father who loved the soil he had left. In late summer the forest was full of red and black berries, and all hands not needed for farm work were sent out with baskets to gather enough for jams and juices for the long winter. This was also the time when the local school children arrived to help with the replanting of saplings to replace the trees felled during the winter.

I began to understand the progress of Sweden as I sensed its sturdy society, firmly rooted in the soil and untouched by feudalism, free from inhibitions, and with sex morals that must date back to pre-Christian times. The Swedish tolerance of pre-marital relationship was often mistaken by foreigners for laxity. Here in a corner of Swedish countryside, which was at the time deeply religious in an old-fashioned Lutheran way, it was considered the natural thing for a young couple occasionally to spend a night together at her parents' farm, provided their relationship was accepted by the neighbourhood as one meant to end in matrimony. Any suspicion of wantonness was frowned upon. Sometimes for obvious reasons marriage came sooner than intended. When for practical reasons, such as the youth waiting till he could own his own farm, the engagement had to last long, it could be borne without frustrations. The boy and the girl worked contentedly through the week, and without a sense of guilt they could meet on Saturday night. A sane and practical outlook seemed to be common among the Swedes.

After the long summer in Sweden and a return at Christmas, Gärd, who had left Uppsala the year before, decided to return to her studies. This seemed a signal for me also. For over a year I had done no work, and unless I returned to my articles now it might become too late. It was a stiff enough course if you stuck to the rigorous discipline of work and study, but the way I was going, my Yorkshire principal with a tongue like a cat-o'-nine-tails told me, I had no chance at all. In any case, he wondered if I would ever die a qualified accountant, even if I lived to be a hundred. Stung by this, next week, dressed in my striped trousers and black coat, and for a while, as an earnest of my intentions, with a bowler hat as well, I returned to the office and somehow stuck it for three years. It was difficult to get away from the college Union altogether because these were the exciting days of Mussolini, Hitler, the wars in Spain and Abyssinia, but generally I immersed myself in unexciting things like executorship law and consolidation of balance sheets. Occasional visits to the Hallé, the bawdy Hume Hippodrome, the last musical hall left in Manchester, and the Rusholme Repertory theatre helped relieve the monotonous attempt at belying my principal's gloomy prognostication. Once in a while I managed to escape to the Ribble Valley.

As five, six, seven years passed since I had left India, I began to feel not so much the absence of home as the strain of living in a large town, with a damp and chilly climate. In spite of its smoke and grime I loved Manchester, but the absence of sun and a yearning for the open sky over a flat country began to tell. During the wet, foggy winter months I used to look every morning at a rowan tree outside my window. If the berries were profuse and bright red it was said to mean a severe winter. They seemed to last a long time, till the back of the winter was broken and the bushes on the small road island in front of the house showed small swellings on their bare twigs. My spirit would begin to rise at this first sign of the coming spring, but the liftman at the office damped my enthusiasm. 'You don't know our weather; you don't know our March and our April; we won't be through till May is out, and then tha can cast tha clout.' He was a lugubrious looking man, completely hairless and wore a red toupee, and he was usually right. I laughed hopefully at his gloomy prediction as, during my last winter, one mild February day followed another, and the little rowan, despite the warning of its own red berries, started sprouting little silky green leaves. I looked at its progress every day and thought that perhaps in this unpredictable climate spring might have come early for once. But the liftman was right, and both the rowan and I were proved hopelessly wrong. Winter came back, the greyest, chilliest winter I could remember. The leaves of the brave little rowan shrivelled with the frost, and I sat down to the hard grind, determined to make this my last winter.

The examinations over in a November week of dense fog and marrow-chilling cold I left Manchester to await the result in Visby. Such a luxurious sense of the job-done descended over me that I stayed on in Sweden through spring and summer. Gärd was now teaching at her father's and her own old school, and I spent the months contentedly going through his sizeable library. Hitler was becoming menacing, and I had left behind the first air raid protection posters in England. Even in this peaceful island war seemed inevitable, and I wondered sometimes whether Gärd would ever be able to follow me to India. I let the months lazily go by till time came that I must return.

CHAPTER FIFTEEN

THE FUTURE was already casting a shadow, the big question of finding a job on my return home. So far, Government had been the only employer of managerial talent in the Punjab, where there was no industry or commerce, but Government service was getting riddled with caste and community considerations. There were ratios for Hindus, Muslims, Sikhs and others; there were weightages for all but the Hindus; preference was given to agriculturists; and on top of all that there was pull and favour. And it did not stop there, because all through the service promotions, and even postings, were beginning to be made a communal consideration. Government service was thus ceasing to be the attraction it used to be. I decided to look for a job in the commercial and industrial Bombay or Calcutta.

Before leaving England, I had applied through the University Appointments Board to a number of British concerns operating in India. One or two suggested I contact their local management in India, but an oil company asked me to come for an interview. My hopes ran high, as this company was reputed for having taken a few Indians at salaries equalling those of the I.C.S. But the interview intrigued me. The man seemed totally uninterested in my qualifications and enquired only about my family connections and background. He asked me if I thought I would fit in well. I said I imagined so, though I did not know the work involved and their accounting methods. He looked bored and said he meant, was I able to fit in with their people and senior government servants in the station. This alarmed me. I did not care for this criterion of ability; and I also expected social problems, especially with the general English prejudice against inter-marriage. The inaffable interview came to an end, and a few days later I received a short note to say that they had nothing to offer, though I might call at their local office and pursue the matter. It was quite plain that they had no interest in me.

Something that followed came as a shock. As I happened to be in London I called at the Indian High Commissioner's office for advice about jobs in India. In those days this office was Indian only in name; except for the High Commissioner it was run mostly by British officials who seemed generally uninterested in the needs and aspirations of Indian students. At my arrival, eight years earlier, I had gone there only to get my Punjab University provisional certificate endorsed. Since then I had had nothing to do with them, and I was therefore astonished to find that the man who received me had in front of him a thick file of papers with my name prominently on its cover. He had nothing to offer by way of help or advice, but I left his room puzzled. We knew that Indian students in England were kept under careful watch, but I could not understand what valuable information could have made such a thick dossier on me. Apparently my every movement had been recorded. Next day I left for home.

The journey back by P. & O. was uneventful. Although it was a one-class boat, the English tried to segregate themselves into two classes, according to the cost of the fare. The fact that everybody was doing it cheaply did not prevent those who paid fifty pounds from feeling superior to those who paid only thirty-two, but between the English and Indians the atmosphere seemed generally a lot easier than eight years ago.

The Indian passengers were returning students, and a few not so prosperous businessmen. They mixed more freely and easily. I discovered that after years' lack of practice I felt awkward at speaking Hindi and Punjabi, and I had to try quickly to improve at least my Punjabi before meeting my parents. We mostly discussed politics and the prospect of self-government and Dominion Status; total freedom was still so distant a dream that we did not think of it seriously.

My cabin mate was a mild-mannered Bombay businessman who had gone to Europe to pick up new ideas. He discussed at length a particularly lurid one. He had his eyes on the Juhu Beach of Bombay where thousands came for fresh air in the evenings. He wanted to fill its entire length with hoardings to convey the latest marketing messages to the backward masses. He used to wax eloquent on the moving signs and neon lights of Piccadilly Circus and the lovely posters along the British roads. I ventured a suggestion that Juhu was probably a pleasant palm-fringed beach that might look well as it was. This made him sad. The whole trouble with India, he said, was that things had been left alone for too long. I had the chagrin of meeting him again on the same subject.

Back in India I called on a European working in a Bombay firm with a letter of introduction from a mutual friend. He was very frank and painted a discouraging picture. His own firm, like others, he thought was not yet ready to take Indians in management. An odd young Indian had been engaged, but only because of influence or because he was an Oxford or Cambridge blue. There was the further complication of my proposed marriage. European firms might not like it. In their own firm they had taken on a highly connected Indian married to an English girl, and this had created complications and much unhappiness to the couple. Among his colleagues there was an unspoken disapproval, expressed in a social taboo which the girl felt keenly.

So things stood, and I felt it might be best to join an Indian firm, where such problems would not exist; and somehow the prospect of working for the good of India had its attraction. I heard from a friend of my father that a big Indian company, interested among other things in shipping, were looking for an accountant. There was no question, however, of just walking up to their door and asking for a job. One had to know the manager, preferably belong to his community, or at least know someone to whom he was under some obligation. Why should he throw a good job away on a perfect stranger, when he might oblige a friend or relation by employing somebody equally well qualified.

Armed with an introduction, I went to see the general manager. A shock of a different kind awaited me. This man only wanted to know the minimum salary I was willing to accept. I said rather naïvely that I was keen to join an Indian firm, but had no great interest in the starting salary, so long as there was scope. If, after a time, they found that I possessed ability, they would no doubt offer me a decent pay, but until then the salary did not matter much. This seemed to annoy him, for he delivered a long harangue on the exaggerated notions of people with foreign qualifications.

Did I think that this was the I.C.S. where I could expect a big salary? I tried to protest that I had not even named a figure yet, but he had me out of the room soon with sound advice to be modest in my demands and drop swollen ideas. As to my desire to serve in an Indian firm, I must not exploit such a sentiment. So the interview ended, and I left him more confused than ever.

It was no use trying to obtain an interview with the only other large, Indian firm, because I had exhausted my only contact. Furthermore, they were said to favour their own community. So I decided to call on some European firms. Here I found I could walk in and send my card to the general manager and be called in. Most of them said that their head offices were in Calcutta and I would have to go there; others had no interest, but all received me encouragingly and seemed to imply that they were perhaps not ready to start Indians in management, although Indianisation was not far off. One manager showed some interest and asked me to see their chief accountant. This highly competent looking person, with a broad north country accent that made me nostalgic, also gave me short shrift, for he had no use for qualified accountants in industry. With tactless innocence I asked how else they managed to run their accounts. Once again there was an abrupt end to the interview, and I was told that they built up their accountants the hard way and did not believe in high-fallutin degrees and qualifications. He reminded me so much of my Yorkshire principal whose exterior belied his heart. I reported laconically to the manager that they apparently had no need of an accountant. I think something must have touched a sympathetic chord, because he said it would seem a pity to let me go; could I return the following day? He would like to think it over.

He was a sensitive looking man, with a surprising decisiveness in his speech and manner. He outlined a proposition to me with just the right touch of knowing his mind, but with a fine sensibility to my interest. They were going to open a new department in marketing research, which someone from their head office was coming to start, and they needed a young Indian to receive training under him. The prospects would be just as good whether I began in advertising or in accounts, but I would be making no use of a specialised training of many years. The chances of going into their accounts department were obviously small, he added, with a frank grin. He suggested that I think it over and meanwhile go to Calcutta to try to find something in my own line. I travelled across to Calcutta and began the search again, but I wandered through Clive Street and Dalhousie Square with some experience and confidence gained from Ballard Estate of Bombay. There were few Indian firms of sufficient size or inclination to offer employment. The British business houses were polite but reluctant to try out Indians as managers. An influential youth had been taken on here and there, but Indianisation as a policy had not begun yet. A rubber company chief accountant told me that they had recently employed an Indian chartered accountant at two hundred and fifty rupees per month. 'You may have noticed him sitting outside my office, as you came in. We will see how it works.' The practising firms were cold and aloof, and their partnerships were sacred. The managing agencies sent for young commercial officers from home!

I summoned enough courage to call on the oil company again, and the chief passed me on to their accountant, an Australian who had served his articles in England. This time I got on well. He asked me for several interviews, mainly discussing where we thought the profession would lead to in the future. I became greatly enthused over this subject; and he seemed to enjoy listening to a newcomer in the profession. We hoped for the time when accountants would leave their ledgers and take their share in operating management. Finally he told me that if I could wait for two or three months they might have a position to offer, but would I let him know if I accepted the Bombay post in the meantime. I asked him whether I would be required to fit into the firm and its environments socially. He said we would have to see that, but added slyly that as an Australian he saw my point.

I decided to join the firm in Bombay. The people I interviewed were likeable; they manufactured in the country; and they seemed earnest in their desire to experiment with Indianisation. What attracted me no less was the accent and manner of the north country origin of the firm reflected in many of them. Work seemed their principal concern in life, and that was the criterion I had inherited from my father. There would be a long process of adjustment and many problems and pains, but being the first in their experiment was in itself stimulating, and leaving my training behind me gave an edge to the challenge.

This great problem out of the way, I went to Lahore to meet the family.

CHAPTER SIXTEEN

FOR THE first generation of professional men in the Punjab it had been the natural thing after retirement to go back to the place they came from, and spend their last years as respected elders in village or small town society. But father's generation had grown away from their background, for them it was a question to find a congenial place to settle down. While I was still in England my father retired from service, and built himself a house in Model Town, a suburb six miles out of Lahore.

Model Town was a place, the like of which had never been and will never be seen again. It was almost entirely populated by retired government officials, who all addressed each other as Rai Sahib, Rai Bahadur, Khan Sahib or Khan Bahadur, Sardar Sahib or Sardar Bahadur.

Somebody had conceived the idea in 1925 of acquiring a big tract of jungle wasteland, a few miles out of Lahore, dividing it up into plots, and constituting it as The Model Town Co-operative Society. Everyone who bought a plot became a member with a vote in the Society. The plan of the town was completely geometrical. It had a series of concentric circular roads, crossed by four main roads at right angles, and smaller roads in between, all beginning from the inner circle and dividing the area into equal segments. The roads had no name, but the blocks were alphabetically numbered, so that our address was 12G, while the house opposite was 12F. To the old school of thought this was quite enough to paint on the gate. Later arrivals started giving their homes poetical names.

The big circular area in the middle was common property and traversed only by footpaths. Only thorny shrubs grew there, but it was intended to become a public park. On its periphery were marked the sites for library, school, barat ghar for housing wedding parties, and other public institutions. Only the club, the hospital and dispensary, and the women's club had been built so far. There were several private schools. Special areas were set apart for markets and shops. There were a mosque and a temple, perhaps the most attractive examples of modern religious architecture I have seen in India, and a Sikh Gurdwara. For practical measure there were also cremation and burial grounds.

On paper it looked a picture of complete equality, but Model Town already from the beginning had its distinctions. On the site of the club had originally stood a dak bungalow, and the road leading up to it was flanked by beautiful tall trees. As it was also farthest away from the main market and the road to Lahore, the areas on both sides of this road became the exclusive part of the town. The blocks diametrically opposite, clustered along the road to the city, were to a great extent taken up by shopkeepers and people who had business or work in Lahore.

Regular and well ordered as Model Town looked on the map, so were the lives its citizens lived. The transition from active working life to a retired existence was made easier by the pleasant task of first having to build your own house. One after the other, old engineers, army doctors, retired civilians and sessions judges arrived on the spot and started laying their foundations. The results of their efforts were all curiously alike, because they were all patterned on the government bungalows which had been their homes, and the dak bungalows which had been the scenes of so much of their activity. Each house was divided into two parts by a huge vestibule in the middle. On one side were dining and drawing-room and an office room; on the other side the bedrooms, with dressing-rooms and bathrooms. The front verandah overlooked a lawn surrounded by flower-beds and cypresses. Here male visitors were received. On the other side was a verandah, where meals were served except on winter evenings, and an enclosed paved courtyard, the women's domain, with kitchen and storerooms. Then there were the servants' quarters, spacious kitchen gardens and usually a small orchard.

Our house was a real work of love. All father's skill, conscientiousness and care for detail went into it. It had enormously thick walls to keep out the summer heat, and consequently it was like an icebox on near-freezing winter evenings, when father with his spartan outlook did not condescend to use the fireplaces. The house had three suites of rooms so that all the brothers, at a future date, should be able to live in it with their families, which as it happened never came to pass. Once we all three brothers had a holiday there together, but then the youngest one was still unmarried. It was typical of father's foresight that, although he sold his car when he retired, he built two garages. One of the garages was filled with beds, so you could put up any amount of people. In summer, there were three terraces for your choice to sleep on, the lower one over the back verandah, the main one, and a small terrace on the top of the barsati, a covered shelter from the rain. In its own way the house was like the British bungalows in front and grand-uncle's house at the back.

The furnishings, apart from a few sophisticated houses, were also reminiscent of the dak bungalows and strictly utilitarian. The only touch of luxury in our drawing-room was a big Persian carpet, commemorating father's Kashmir holiday. Round this carpet were arranged in precise symmetry two sofas and six chairs and in front of each sofa was a table adorned with tasseled silk net. Gärd always tried to improve it by upsetting the symmetry and removing the silk tassels, but our old servant restored the order every morning till she gave up. The pictures consisted of my brother's wedding, Ravi Varma's Shakuntala, and the Stages of Life, which Gärd recognised from Swedish farmhouses in her childhood.

In the dry climate the upkeep of such a well-built house was easy, but the garden afforded continuous interest. Here too, father's inclination was utilitarian. The few flowers in the front garden looked after themselves, but the orchard included every variety of fruit that could possibly grow in the Punjab. That was in fact its weakness, for as the few of each kind bore fruit at different times, it was not worth guarding them, and apart from the oranges, the parrots had most of it. The vegetable garden was his main interest, and in season it produced more than enough for the need of the house, and father, like a good Punjabi, looked with pride at the size and whiteness of his cauliflowers.

All the old men began their day early. They believed in exercise, and on summer mornings at half past four the circular road was full of early risers doing their 'chukkar'. Then they were too busy to talk, their minds were purely on the exercise. On cold winter mornings you heard father's alarm clock at six, and while you snuggled deeper into your quilt he was fairly running round the circle to keep himself warm. Surely the day was long enough and he had nothing much to fill it with, but it would have been against his principles to get up later. For rainy mornings he had measured up the back verandah to know exactly how many times he ought to walk it up and down.

The evening walks were livelier and reserved for talk. Father used to set out in the company of a neighbour and old friend who had been minister in Bikaner, and during the chukkar they often stopped to talk to other Rai Sahibs and Rai Bahadurs, generally enquiring about each other's health in great detail, recommending cures and comparing notes on the efficiency of their favourite medicines. They were great believers in old herbal remedies. One of the subjects was of course the pleasure-loving younger generation, who–just imagine–wanted to have a cinema in Model Town. 'Not as long as we are alive. It would only make the servants lazy and take the children's minds off their studies.' Most of them had never seen a film. I overheard someone saying in 1942, 'I believe that now they talk all the time in the films.'

But the most absorbing subject was the affairs and politics of the Model Town Co-operative Society. Having spent their lives as officials, they now all tried to run the Society office and its poor secretary, who usually never stayed in the job for long. The retired conservator of forests took him and the malis to task about the trees and road hedges; the engineers, depending upon the branch of P.W.D. they had belonged to, forced their advice about roads, buildings, canal water ditches and electricity; while the retired I.C.S. just laid the law down about everything. When the time came for the annual elections to the various offices, there was hectic activity all round. Father was seen at home only at mealtimes, and spent his day running around canvassing. But he was too straightforward and devoid of all the traits that make a politician, ever to become an office bearer. Gärd, who once accompanied him to an annual meeting, told me that he was very pleased to be asked to count the votes, and that was all his activity. She also got the answer to a question that had puzzled her, why there were ink stains all over the walls. When members got heated in the debate, ink bottles flew in all directions. She was very happy to sit in the section reserved for ladies.

Gärd actually knew Model Town life more than I did, as she used to spend some time there every year until partition. When she had been in Bombay for a few months, got acclimatised and learnt some Hindi, she went to Lahore accompanied by my younger brother, Krishan, whom mother, I think, had sent to look at his new sister-in-law. Father and mother met her at the station, and she was pleasantly surprised to find father much younger looking and livelier than she had expected. Actually, European women always found father charming, for as they did not address him with the respectful restraint enjoined by custom, he also felt at ease with them and could talk very animatedly. Mother greeted her very affectionately. Many women had asked her if it wasn't a shock to her to get a foreign daughter-in-law. In her lovely simplicity she answered, 'Isn't it better that he makes a foreign girl happy than that he should make a Punjabi girl unhappy?'

This was in August, and Gärd, anxious to create a good impression, was quite happy to go for a walk at half-past four in the morning, the only time she could enjoy some cool air. Father introduced her to his old friends and told them she was an M.A. It was a source of pride to him that both his daughters-in-law had double degrees, and he had seriously offered both to study medicine at his expense, as his ambition was to have a 'lady doctor' in the family. They politely declined, but eventually his niece satisfied him.

In the evenings, when the worst heat was over, and everybody had bathed and changed, the women used to call to see the new bride. They sat in the freshy sprinkled courtyard and each gave her two silver rupees, and complimented her on her stuttering Hindi. Whatever their own views might have been on such an unorthodox marriage, the women all did their best to put her at ease and make her feel at home. Almost every evening a neighbour, who was also a Tandon, came with her five pretty daughters ranging from sixteen to seven, all very curious about this new sister-in-law and eager to practice their English on her. In due course mother took her to return the calls, and so time passed, until I arrived for a few days' work.

Now mother got the chance to have a real marriage performed. An Arya Samaj pandit was called in, the sacred fire was lit in the front verandah, and Gärd was first purified into the faith of our ancestors and gurus, as a symbol of which she was given a sanskrit name. Then tied together we walked the seven steps. It was a short ceremony, with only a few friends and relations present, but it made mother happy. She distributed sweets according to custom. It also pleased Gärd who said a registrar's office in Bombay with two hired witnesses does not make you feel properly married, and her mother would also like to hear about the family wedding.

Two days after I left for the station, and to everybody's surprise came back. The war in Europe had broken out, I learnt at the station, so I waited for revised instructions. Next day I was off, and shortly after Gärd left to visit my elder brother and sister-in-law in North Bihar. Soon after her return to Bombay we got a telegram about mother's sudden death following an operation.

Being cast in the stoic mould, father did not give vent to excessive grief, neither did he expect it from his sons. To us he wired, 'Do not trouble to come.' My sister-in-law was there to take charge. After mother's death father continued his old routine, with his trusted old servant Chatter Singh, who had been in the family for fifty years, to look after his needs. He spent some months with us in Bombay after the birth of our daughter, Maya, but apart from us and the baby he did not have much to take interest in, and missed the company of his own age. So he lived on in Model Town, and we sons took turns to send our families to stay with him. Before partition the youngest also had started a family.

Though every day was like the other, Gärd liked life in Model Town. Although she was never hurt by any social ostracism, Bombay irked her as a place dominated by Europeans, who hardly counted Indians as existing, and she felt happier in the completely Indian surroundings of Lahore. The small Swedish community totally ignored her. But from the moment she had unloaded her baggage, ever increasing as the children increased from one to two to three, on the tongas at the Lahore station, she felt at home. And when at last the cavalcade reached Model Town, people on the road welcomed her back. Life in Model Town was more self-centred than ever during the war years. Cars were laid up for lack of petrol; six miles by tonga into Lahore on a hot day was no joke, and the buses had to be booked long in advance. The Model Town buses looked like trucks, and besides their human overload always carried an enormous amount of trunks, bicycles and other heavy goods on top. The 'lorry', as it was appropriately called, had a 'purdah' section in front, and only if that was completely crammed could a woman decently sit amongst the men. Old 'Princess' Sutherland, widow of an English army doctor, and last descendant of Maharaja Ranjit Singh, was heard complaining that she could not get a seat in the lorry, when all Punjab should have been hers! The old lady had settled in Model Town and spent her days dreaming about her ancestral glory.

Model Town was not only a city of the aged, for some old government servants, who had outlived their wives and married much younger women, kept on raising a family long after retirement. Sometimes it happened that there were three happy events in the family when mother, daughter and daughter-in-law were simultaneously delivered. But the younger generation had not yet put their mark on Model Town. Its only social events were weddings and head-shavings. Old women used to come to the house to ask father's advice about a boy or girl suggested for marriage, as he had a wide acquaintance. This always pleased him. If the match came off the same old lady would in due course arrive with a big bag of sweets as a wedding invitation. Father always asked Gärd to go to these functions, not for the pleasure of it, but out of duty, adding that it was a good thing she was conspicuous as everyone would know that she had represented the family.

The two clubs, one for men and one for women, offered facilities for games, but no club life. Once some young people ventured upon something drastically new; a mixed whist drive at the men's club. This did not meet with approval particularly as it ended as late as eleven at night. Another novelty was a tea party the day after a wedding, in the last year before partition. Though there was no purdah, except in some Muslim families, there was no real social mixing of the sexes. Even husbands and wives did not always go for walks together. She would walk with her own women friends in the evening. Even young people home on leave would often conform.

So life would have gone on in a peaceful routine until the end for all these old engineers, doctors and civil servants, if they had not had to pay the price for the freedom of India. A few died peacefully before partition, but most had to start life anew, living in small flats with sons, and sometimes even, swallowing their pride, with daughters. And their wives had to leave their spacious courtyards, where they had ruled over servants and daughters-in-law, to be dependent on a son, and happy if they were a help and not an unwelcome intruder. Wherever they had to go, they were uprooted from the life they had themselves created.

CHAPTER SEVENTEEN

DEAR PRAKASH,

Come and get us out before it is too late.

While the fading paper flags of the independence celebrations were still waving, the horror of partition broke on us suddenly one day when a post-card arrived from Uncle Dwarka Prashad. It contained this single line.

With my younger brother, who was also settled in Bombay, I had discounted the first rumours, while Government tried to tone down the press hand-outs. No one wanted to spoil the music of freedom still in the air. But every day the news became graver, and uncle's post-card told us that the end had come.

In June of 1947, when partition was announced, most Hindus and Sikhs had accepted it fatalistically. 'We have lived under the Muslims before, then under the Sikhs and the British, and if we are now back under Muslim rule, so what? We shall manage somehow, as we have managed before. Nowadays governments are different, they give you some rights, they have to listen to the people!' Fortified by such arguments, people decided to stay where they were and face the change.

In July things began to look menacing, but few thought of leaving. There were sporadic attacks on Hindus and Sikhs, but they were mostly looked upon as signs of another riot. The turn had come of the Punjab, where people during the war years had prided themselves on living in peace while the rest of the country shook with the ugly outburst of Hindu-Muslim violence. As things worsened, father wrote to say that he considered it pointless to leave the house. Even if there was real trouble he would be safe, because he had so many Muslim friends and neighbours. Who would want to harm an old man, semi-paralysed by a stroke? Besides, he was so comfortable with his faithful Chattar Singh, who was on such good terms with everybody, Hindus, Muslims and Sikhs alike, to look after him.

In August law and order of ninety years came to an end.

Elementary civil protection, taken for granted the week before, ceased. Chatter Singh felt that his own family would prove a burden if he suddenly had to leave; and to take care of father would be an added problem. So he appealed frantically to our neighbours to persuade father to go away for a while, till things improved. He was going to move his wife and children to the safety of Amritsar, now across the border. My elder brother wired from Bihar that father must leave, and reluctantly he agreed, whereupon Chattar Singh hurriedly packed him off. Many others were sending their women and children and old people away. Like everyone else, father thought he was only going for a short time, till the riots subsided.

Uncle Dwarka Prashad had remarried some years after Savitri's death and had permanently settled in Gujrat. My second aunt was a very handsome woman in her youth, with long brown hair and a melodious voice. After quite a struggle she had slowly managed to tame uncle. He worked hard, and with his natural ability he soon prospered. He built his own house outside the city wall, conveniently near the law courts, where he had built up a lucrative practice. She gave him two sons and two daughters. The eldest, a girl, urged by my father, had studied medicine. She then married a dentist, and they were both settled in practice in Amritsar. The elder boy had just finished his law studies at Lahore, while the younger children were still at school.

Uncle had always been tough and fearless, and easily persuaded to fight. He had mellowed with the years as he became an elder of the biradari, a senior member of the bar and influential in municipal affairs. He was greatly respected by all communities, and most of his practice came from Muslim litigants in the district. Everyone assured him that he could safely stay, no one would touch him and his family. He wanted to believe in their assurances even as he saw the trickle of exodus gather volume. These others thought it wise to go away for a while; they would all return when everything was calm again. The thought that this was a going away for ever never crossed anybody's mind. A calamity might cause temporary uprooting, but afterwards you came back to what had always been your home.

One day, a train crammed with two thousand refugees came from the more predominantly Muslim areas of Jhelum and beyond. At Gujrat station the train was stopped, and Muslims from the neighbourhood, excited by the news of violence in East Punjab, began to attack and loot. There was indescribable carnage. Several hours later the train moved on, filled with a bloody mess of corpses, without a soul alive. At Amritsar, when the train with its load of dead arrived, they took revenge on a trainload of Muslim refugees. There was also great killing at Sheikhupura, and on the other side in Jullundur. The whole Punjab was in conflagration. Six million Hindus and Sikhs from the West Punjab began to move in one dense mass towards safety, and from the east of the border a similar mass movement was under way in the opposite direction.

Muslim friends came to uncle late one night and said with tears in their eyes that they were unable to offer him protection any longer. The family must move at once, before dawn! Dwarka Prashad now saw it only too well that they had to go away, not for a few days, but for ever. He had in fact been expecting it since the day of the massacre at the station, but the problem had been how to get out; and it was then that he had sent the post-card.

His friends rushed to an Indian military evacuation convoy that had arrived the same evening, and brought a truck. They heaved a sigh of relief as uncle and his family, with two suitcases and a few blankets, drove away. On the Grand Trunk Road their truck joined an unending line of military and civil trucks and cars, bullock carts and tongas, people on horseback, and carried on shoulders. In its long history of over a thousand years this road had never seen such a migration.

As dawn was breaking, they caught the last view of Gujrat through the shisham trees by the road; a view they had so often seen when going to the river Chenab at Besakhi. They looked at the weathered dark brown mass of the city rising as a flat-top cone. My aunt's ancestral house was in the highest mohalla inside the fortress, and she could see almost the spot from where twenty-seven years ago her pallanquin had descended the narrow lanes to our old house inside the Kalri Gate. She wondered what would happen to her house, to her cupboards and trunks full of clothes, linen and utensils, and above all to the buffalo and its calf that she had left tied in the yard. She suspected that in a few hours their home would be swept bare, but she was too numbed to care. Through smoking towns and charred villages the convoy moved like a long dark snake. At one time over the narrow bridge of the Bullokee headworks, where I was born, there was a convoy of over two million people seeking its way out. Through Kharian, Wazirabad, Gujranwala, Emnabad, Gakhar, it heaved forward, swelled by other convoys joining it from the side roads. After delays, alarms and rumours of attack, it reached the Ravi and crossed into Lahore. They were put up at uncle's old D.A.V. college, which had become a vast temporary camp. From here they moved on in smaller convoys, and uncle's party eventually arrived at the new frontier post of Wagah, a tiny hamlet which was now in the limelight as a scene of dramatic activity. As the truck passed the barrier into 'India', they looked back at Pakistan, their homeland which did not want them.

The truck delivered them at Amritsar, and the young Maratha major who had been in charge of their section of the convoy bade them godspeed. He had to rush back, for there were still plenty more on the other side. Uncle tried to express their gratitude, but too dazed still to sort out his thoughts, he could only recall the tense moment when they were held up at a police outpost at Shalimar Gardens outside Lahore, and an ugly crowd collected. The Maratha had leapt down from the truck, drawn his revolver and threatened to shoot his convoy out. The police pushed back the crowd and let the trucks pass. Sitting beside the major, uncle had asked him if he knew our Punjab country. The Maratha said no, but someone in his family had been here very long ago. My uncle did not know that he descended from a distinguished soldier in Bhau Sahib's army, which had tried to bar the way of Ahmed Shah Abdali at Panipat on his return from Delhi in 1761.

They landed at their daughter's house in Amritsar like wreckage from a swollen river, but my aunt's Khatri pride was fierce. After a few days' rest, for which she insisted on paying from whatever money she had on her, she decided that they must move on.

The daughter and son-in-law said she was crazy. Where were they going to? Though they were now in India there was no safety on the roads. The whole of East Punjab was in turmoil. After the first taste of blood there was likely to be indiscriminate murder and looting. But she was adamant, she would not accept a daughter's hospitality.

The family was on the move again and joined another convoy on the Grand Trunk Road to Delhi. And now the rains broke, and to the hatred of man was added the cruelty of nature. Beas and Sutlej rose in an unprecedented flood, and thousands of homeless were carried away by the swirling waters. One enormous convoy had been camping on the banks of the Beas on the night when the river rose in flood. The water had gone down when uncle's party arrived at the river. From a distance they saw a vast stretch of debris dotted with countless black spots. When they came close they discovered that the debris was a mass of bodies with black heads which the subsiding flood waters had left behind.

The journey from Amritsar proved less dangerous, but more tortuous, and they staggered on without knowing where they were heading for. They were carried forward on a human wave. Like a flood the mass migration deposited some here, some there, in towns and villages of East Punjab, in the hastily rigged up refugee camps, till the bulk of them reached Delhi. From here the migrants were scattered all over India, from Cochin to Kohima, and uncle and his family, for no apparent reason, found themselves at Ajmer.

In Ajmer uncle was given some work in a refugee camp by the relief organisation. He managed to find a small house, and they stayed there for over a year. But he found the work unsatisfying, and had the feeling at the back of his mind that this work was only created to boost his morale, and was in fact cloaked charity. He was constantly thinking of ways to start a normal working life, and even toyed with the idea of going into business, though this was something utterly foreign to him. He was then sixty-two, and he had not long before he stood face to face with death in another guise. He was found to have throat cancer, and he came to Bombay for consultation. The doctor examined him and told him frankly that it was a bad case, and the only thing to do was to continue the deep X-ray treatment in Lahore. Something touched the doctor in the way he walked out after the verdict, for he called him back. 'It may seem hopeless and I am sorry that I can do nothing more for you, but, you know, miracles can happen. You must keep courage, and that may help.' And in uncle's case the miracle did happen. After continued treatment the doctors told him some years later, just before the partition, that they could see no signs of the cancer, and in fact it did not reappear.

Uncle therefore did not easily despair and continued his search for a new start. And when he heard about a refugee colony in Karnal, eighty miles west of Delhi, where Government gave land and subsidies to those who wanted to settle and build a house, he took his chance and left his job in Ajmer. He built his house and set up practice again. In a short while he was doing well; in fact, better than ever. He worked like one possessed, but without joy. He was very different from our father; he was a man who had enjoyed life, loved company, and he was an entertaining talker. But when he had to leave Gujrat, something broke inside him, and his new-found prosperity gave him little pleasure apart from the satisfaction of providing anew for his family. Having twice escaped death, he came to a strange and cruel end. His alsatian bitch bit him and a friend. They both received treatment, but it became evident some weeks later that on him the vaccine did not work. Nothing could save him, and he died in agony, conscious till the last moment.

Today we have no one left in Gujrat. All the Hindus came away at partition. It is strange to think that in all the land between Ravi and Chenab, from Chenab to Jhelum, from Jhelum to Indus, in the foothills and in the plain down to Panjnad, where the five rivers eventually merge, land which had been the homes of our biradaris since the dawn of history, there is no one left of our kind.

Partition changed the course of many lives which would otherwise have run in their familiar channels. Most were lucky to find a bank where they clambered up and started afresh; but the real sufferers were those whom the ebbing currents of partition claimed again. When the turmoil was over some well-meaning but short-sighted people tried to, as they saw it, undo some of the evil by restoring abducted women to their families. With grim determination they searched for years for these unfortunate women, and sometimes with pathetic lack of understanding caused fresh tragedies by uprooting them again. Such a tragic story was told me by a second cousin of mine, Hari, a young army officer.

Five years after the partition, in 1952, Hari was posted in Calcutta, and there he and his wife, Usha, got to know a young Sikh who lived behind their house. He was a simple man, but his cheerful ways were very engaging, and they took a great liking to him. Hari discovered accidentally that the Sikh had been in the army, which made another bond between them. One day when Hari was in uniform, the man surprised him by saluting very smartly, and questioned he reluctantly said that he had done so from force of habit. He had been in a Sikh regiment during the war, served in the Far East, and joined the Indian National Army which had thrown in its lot with the Japanese. Another thing the two had in common was their love of the races. The Sikh used to come round regularly to ask for tips. He had a profound faith in Hari's inside information, and once actually did very well out of a tip.

One evening the young Sikh came with a worried look on his face, which was unusual for him, and when they pressed him he told them his story.

After the release of the Indian National Army prisoners, he had returned home to Jullundur, in the East Punjab, to live with his parents. When partition came and everybody went mad, he had also run amuck. He and a friend of his one day saw a crowd on the point of massacring two young girls. They had set fire to a house and killed the inmates as they came out of hiding to escape the flames. These two sisters were the only ones left. Their beauty, and the look of desperate fear on their faces softened him and brought him back to sanity. Without hesitation he called out to the crowd.

'Look, you have burnt this Muslim house and all their goods; you have had your revenge. All the people are dead except these two girls. Why should you kill them? I am a poor man, and so is my friend here, neither of us can afford to get married. Why not hand the girls over to us? We will convert them to our faith and marry them. Instead of killing them wastefully, you will do a good turn to two poor Sikh brethren'.

The crowd had probably done enough killing for the day, and found the argument reasonable, so they allowed the boys to take the girls away. The young Sikh took one of them home to his mother, who instantly liked her. When the girl recovered from fear she began to like the bold boy who had saved her life. They got married, and slowly fell in love with each other. Gradually memories of her parents and her former life faded. They were very happy together, and a little boy was born.

Meanwhile the social workers had got busy recovering abducted girls from both sides and restoring them to their families in East and West Punjab. Many of them were torn away from husbands they had learnt to love, from children they had borne, and handed over to parents who had given them up as dead. From respectable, married women they suddenly became unclean and outcaste, not daring to admit that during the years of 'abduction' they had been happy. But the social workers, many of them, cold, passionless women, were working assiduously, and with the aid of the police and the law tightening their net.

The other sister had not been lucky. The Sikh boy who took her away and married her did not treat her well. She ran away and with the help of the police found her way to her parents in Pakistan. She told them about her sister, and even though she knew that the sister was happy in her marriage, or perhaps just because of that, she reported the matter to the Pakistan police and gave them the address in Jullundur.

Soon the social workers in Jullundur were making enquiries, but the Sikh had got scent of it and ran away with his wife and child to Calcutta. Here he lived happily in hiding for some years, and his only regret was that he dared not go back to visit his parents. But the social workers and the police caught up with him.

They prowled about his house, making enquiries from the neighbours. The poor young man was scared out of his wits, and came to Hari for advice. He wanted Usha to talk to his wife to satisfy herself that the girl loved him and wanted to stay with him. Only then would he ask them for help.

Usha asked the wife over, a pretty girl of nineteen or twenty, quiet and shy. In simple words she bore out her husband's story. She loved him and her child; she was happy, so why did they want her to go back to her parents? Her home was here, with him. She grew eloquent, as she talked about this injustice. She would rather kill herself; they would never take her back alive.

Hari and Usha were deeply moved, young and deeply in love as they were themselves. Hari had also met Usha in the mêlée of partition. They offered to hide the girl while they were finding ways and means of saving her. They approached some friends, they tried to prevail upon the social workers, and they eventually managed to get a stay-order from the court, while the law was taking its ponderous course. Meanwhile the poor youth, afraid of losing her, decided to run away again. The police were bound to get her, he said to Hari, so it would be better for them to go back to some little village in the Punjab where no one would know them, and there would be no police to shadow them. His wife was expecting another baby. Although Hari and Usha were very unhappy about it, they reluctantly agreed that it might perhaps be the best course under the circumstances. They would continue to work for her release order, so that eventually they should be able to live in peace.

More than a year later, the Sikh turned up. They found him waiting for them when they got home late one night. But he was a changed man; all his youthful exuberance had gone. Hari thought he would be happy to get the news that his wife's release had come through. Big tears rolled down the Sikh's cheeks. 'Kaptan Sahib, it is too late, the order is no use now.'

They had settled in a Punjab village, and things went well for a time, till the police arrived again and began to ask questions. His wife was then nearing her time. He left the little boy with his mother, and he and his wife hid in the sugar-cane fields. He dug a large pit, a kind of fox-hole he was used to from his training, and built a barricade. He made her as comfortable as he could while he lay with a gun, waiting for the police, determined not to lose her while he was alive. In the pit he delivered her with his own hands. The next day she ran a high fever, and in three days she was dead. He had not dared to take her to the hospital. He was so afraid the social workers and the police would take her away.

'Kaptan Sahib, thank you for all you have done, even though it is no use now. They will never get her, but at least they have made sure that I shall not keep her either.'

With those words he turned and walked away, and Hari and Usha never saw him again.

EPILOGUE

AT PARTITION we three brothers were already scattered outside the Punjab. My elder brother, an engineer, was working in a sugar factory in North Bihar since before the war; my younger brother, also an engineer, had joined an airline in Bombay. They had both married Punjabi girls from Lahore. Gärd and my sisters-in-law visited Lahore once a year. My brothers would join them on their annual holidays. As business took me to Lahore frequently, Gärd and the children each time stayed on for some months with father. We three brothers had bought small plots of land to build our own houses one day. Our children would probably come to Lahore for their college education. They might scatter still further away in India, but Lahore would always be their home, the Punjab their vatan. The marriages in the family would take place there and some of the children might even settle back, as the developing Punjab was sure to offer more opportunities. As we made friends and formed relationships with sons and daughters of our parents' friends and neighbours, even though we did not live there permanently, so would our children inherit the family connections. And so we pleasantly planned our lives with Lahore always as the centre of it, the place where we would one day ourselves retire.

Partition changed all this. For us there was no more Punjab. Many refugees settled in East Punjab, but to us and many others, it was all over when the West Punjab went, and home was now where we earned our living. Those amongst the refugees who did not find an immediate footing in the East Punjab went all over India. One could not help admiring their courage and enterprise. Simple people, who had probably never been further than fifty miles away from their homes, set off in all directions and landed up in places they had never heard of. An old Sikh, who was our company's wholesaler in Peshawar, came to my office in Bombay because he had heard that we had offered to help settle our uprooted wholesalers and staff on both sides of the border. He walked into my office, worn out and bent, and said that he was going to forget the past and settle anywhere he could. I offered him our wholesalership in Cuttack, a town four hundred miles south of Calcutta and over two thousand miles from Peshawar. He thought that was wonderful, just the place he would like to settle because he was sure that its air and water and business prospects were excellent. He thanked me profusely and said that he and his son would take the first train to Cuttack. But as he was going he turned to ask, 'Tandon Sahib, where is Cuttack, is it on the upper side of Hindustan or the lower; we haven't quite heard of it before in Peshawar.' He hoped I would forgive their ignorance, and it would make no difference to their accepting the offer. It did not matter how far it was but he thought he would just ask where it was.

My younger brother and I decided to forget the Punjab and regard Bombay as our home. We built two small houses next to each other, at the foot of Pali Hill in an area of largely Christian population. We had already lived in this area for a number of years and made many friends. Now, instinctively, we began to throw the roots deeper, and soon we were invited to their weddings and christenings and attended their funerals. They found our Punjabi ways, or Indian ways, as they called them, quaint. Our children went to the local schools where they learned English while they spoke Hindi at home. They never learned Punjabi.

Father divided his time among us three brothers. He stayed with my elder brother for a while in North Bihar, then sometimes with me and sometimes with my younger brother. I think he was never really happy with us because he did not like to be dependent and he always missed Lahore. He missed Model Town and the company it offered of people of his own generation, the retired Government servants with whom he had spent a lifetime of work. He missed the Punjab, its climate, the spacious comfort of his own house. He missed his old relations with whom he could discuss the affairs of their families. He used to liven up whenever we spoke about his early life and service days. He was also very interested in my career, because he said that an executive in industry was something as new today as his own career fifty years earlier.

When my younger brother was later transferred to Delhi father moved with him. In Delhi he felt nearer to the Punjab, and relations and old friends used to call on him now and then. But his life was ebbing, and he was gradually ceasing to take interest in the outside world. On the last day of 1955 the family found him unusually lively. He spent the whole afternoon sitting on the verandah in the warm winter sun, and was happy to receive a visit from his niece and her husband with their children. Krishan thought he had not seen father looking so bright for a long time. After his evening meal he fell into a sound sleep. On New Year's morning, when Krishen and his wife went into his room, they saw that he had again gone to sleep after his early breakfast.

When they returned from some visits, father was still asleep. Looking closer they found that he was dead. So peacefully, without wakening, had he passed from sleep into death.

GLOSSARY

Abassis (or Abbasids)	The second of the two great dynasties of the Moslem Empire.
acharyas	Brahmins who conduct various ceremonies immediately after death, particularly cremation ceremonies.
Ahmed Shah Abdali	Ruler of the Afghan tribes. Between 1747 and 1769, he led more than ten invasions into India. He destroyed Bhau Sahib's Maratha army in 1761 at Panipat.
Akbar	The greatest of the Moghul emperors, he ruled India from 1556 to 1605. During his reign, the Moghul Empire grew substantially and at his death in 1605, his empire was comprised of fifteen provinces stretching from Ahmednagar in the south Deccan to Kabul and Kashmir in the north. Akbar's Hindu policy was conciliatory since he realized that he could not rule India successfully as a proselytizing, orthodox Moslem sovereign.
akhara	A wrestling pit.
alap	A prelude to a raga, which is a characteristic oriental melody.
Ali brothers	These were Mohammed Ali and Shankat Ali who were Indian Moslems and supporters of the Khalifat movement.
amaltas	Laburnum tree.
an	Grain.
Anarkali	The courtesan whom Akbar had put to death in order to make his son Jehangir forget her.

Angrez log	English people.
Angrezi Sarkar	British Government.
anna	One-sixteenth of a rupee in Indian currency.
Arora caste	The merchant and trader caste.
arhti	Middleman or broker.
Arya Samaj	A sect of modern Hinduism founded in 1875 by Swami Dayanand Saraswati which is opposed to idolatry, is monotheistic, and opposes the caste system.
ashirvad	Blessings.
Azadi	Freedom.
Babar	The founder of the Moghul dynasty. He was a descendent of Timur and Genghis Khan, the two scourges of Asia. Ousted from his ancestral dominions in Central Asia, Babar was forced to take refuge in the mountains of Kabul, which served as a convenient base for mounting his attacks on India. At his death in 1530 he controlled the greater part of northern India.
babu	Clerk.
bagh	Garden or orchard.
bag pharai	A special ceremony during the wedding; literally, to hand over the reins of the horse.
Bahris	The first group of twelve Khatri families.
bai	Hindu lady.
baithak	Sitting room or living room.
Bakri-Id Festival	A Moslem festival.
bandis	Female servants in the harem.
banu	A Moslem lady.
baoli	A well.
barat	Bridegroom's wedding party.

barquandaz	Head of the artillery men.
barsati	A covered shelter on the roof of a building.
Basant Festival	A spring festival when yellow clothes are worn. It marks the beginning of the kite flying season.
Bazigar	Acrobat.
begum	A Moslem lady.
behnji	Sister.
Behroopi	A person who performs under a deceptive appearance.
Bentinck	Lord William Cavendish Bentinck (1774–1839). A British soldier and administrator whose many radical innovations while Governor-General of India (1827–1835) made him one of the most influential figures in the development of modern India.
Besakhi Festival	A thanksgiving festival celebrated at the end of the harvest.
Bhand	Clown.
bhangra	A vigorous folk dance done by the men of the Punjab.
Bharat	Son of Kaikeyi and stepbrother of Ram in the Indian epic *Ramayan*.
Bharat Mata	Mother India.
Bhau Sahib	Leader of the Maratha army which was defeated by Ahmed Shah Abdali at Panipat in 1761.
bhayya	A villager from the province of Uttar Pradesh.
bheeri galli	A very narrow lane.
bhocha	A traditional ceremony in which the bride's parents send gifts to the bride-groom's mother prior to the wedding.
biradaris	Local brotherhoods; the members of a

biradaris (*continued*)	lineage segment who live in the same village and who are able, therefore, to cooperate effectively in daily life.
Brahmin	The highest of the four Hindu castes; originally the priest/learned class.
brinjals	Aubergine or eggplant.
bunds	Earthen banks.
Bunjahis	The second group of fifty-two Khatri families.
burqa	A special gown worn by Moslem women covering them from head to foot as a part of semi-purda.
chandni	A special white sheet; literally, moonlight.
chappals	Sandals.
chappaties	Unleavened bread.
charpoy	A cot of woven jute string with a wooden frame.
Chelianwala	A site in the Punjab which is famous for a battle between the Sikhs and the British.
choora	Red painted ivory bangles traditionally worn by a bride.
choutha	Fourth day after death when the bones and ashes are collected after the cremation.
chowkidar	Watchman.
chownk	Inverted cup-shaped ornament worn by women on the top of the head.
chukkar	A circular walk.
College Party	Liberal wing of Arya Samaj.
dadra	One of the traditional forms of Indian melody.
dai	A midwife or nurse.
dain	Witch.
daj	Dowry.
dak bungalow	Government rest house.

dakshina	Special gifts given to the priests.
dal	Pulse.
Damyanti	A beautiful female character in the legendary episode of the lovers "Nala and Damyanti" from the Indian epic *Mahabharat.*
Dasarath	King of Ayodhya (Ondh), father of Ram in the *Ramayan.*
Daswan	Tenth day after death when certain ceremonies are performed.
D.A.V.	Dayanand Anglo-Vedic High School and College in Lahore.
deohri	Entrance hall of a home.
dhak	The tree called "flame of the forest."
dharamsala	A temple inn.
dhobi ghat	Location where washermen launder clothes.
dholki	An oblong two-sided drum.
dhoti	A length of cloth, usually white, tied around the waist and hitched up between the legs.
diwala nikalna	To declare oneself bankrupt.
Diwali Festival	The festival of lights in October/November to commemorate the homecoming of Ram after fourteen years of exile in the Indian epic *Ramayan.* Also the Hindu New Year Festival.
Diwalia	A person who goes into bankruptcy.
diwas	Earthenware cup-shaped oil lamps.
doli	The ceremony of the daughter leaving her parental home after the wedding; literally, a palanquin.
dupatta	Veil.
durbar	Court.
Durga	An earth-mother goddess, symbolizing nature in all its aspects. Her worship is in part designed to avert evil.

durrie	Cotton rug.
Dusserah Festival	A festival in October when the battle between Ram and Ravan from the *Ramayan* is enacted on the amateur stages of India.
erl	A wooden bar placed across a closed door to fortify it.
fursat	Leisure.
gad	A prewedding ceremony during which the bride's parents send gifts to the bridegroom's parents.
gadi	Throne.
galli	Lane or narrow street.
gana	Ceremony of tying a thread on the bride's wrist.
gao-dum	A long tubular bolster; literally, a cow-tail.
Gao-Mata	Holy Cow.
gatka	A sport in which one man fights with one or more opponents with short sticks.
ghagra	A voluminous full-length shirt.
ghar	Home.
ghee	Clarified butter.
goondas	Vandals, scoundrels.
gram	Split peas.
granthi	A Sikh priest.
Granth Sahib	The holy book of the Sikhs.
Grihalakshmi	The goddess of the house.
Gujars	Herdsmen.
gul araz	A rose-hued, pale pink complexion.
gulli danda	A game played with a wooden rod and small stick sharpened at the ends.
gulu band	A necklace fitting snugly around the neck like a collar.
gur	Unrefined cane sugar.
gurdwaras	Sikh temples.

Gurmuhi script	Punjabi script based on Sanskrit.
guru	Teacher.
Gurukul Party	The orthodox wing of Arya Samaj.
halva	A sweet dish made from flour, sugar, and clarified butter.
halwai	A confectioner
hamam	Steam bath.
Handa	A charitable offering of cooked food.
Hanuman	Monkey god associated with the exploits of the divine hero Ram.
Haqiqat Rai	A young martyr buried alive in a brick wall by a fanatic Moslem priest in the 17th century.
Hari Singh Nalwa	A famous Sikh general known for his march into Kabul in the early 19th century.
hartals	Strikes.
hattis	Ledges on the wall.
hawan kund	An iron receptacle in which the holy sacrificial fire is burnt.
Heer and Ranjah	Legendary lovers in Indian folklore.
Holi Festival	Spring festival occurring at the full moon in February/March. During this festival people throw colored powder and water on each other in a light-hearted spirit.
hooka	Hubble bubble.
hooka pani	To socialize.
huzoor	Sir.
Ibrahim Lodi	The last sultan of the Lodhi dynasty, who was defeated by Babar at Panipat in April 1526.
Indrajit	Son of Ravan.
Ishwar	God (in Punjabi).
jajmani	A traditional social system according to which the lower castes are bound to serve the landowners and receive

jajmani (*continued*)	in return a share of the harvest in the form of fixed quantities of grain.
Jallianwala Bagh	An enclosed garden in Amritsar, Punjab, historically famous for the massacre of Indians by British troops under General Dyer during the Indian Freedom Movement in 1919.
janab	Sir.
janj ghar	A hall built by the community for the reception of marriage parties.
jantri	Almanac.
jats	Villagers of the Punjab.
Jehangir	Son of Akbar, ruled from 1605 to 1627. He neglected his administration and was subservient to his favorite wife, Noor Jehan. Jehangir is mainly remembered for his self-revealing memoirs from which it appears that he was a drunken despot, subject to outbursts of fiendish cruelty.
jheel	A lake.
Jhewar	A caste of professional cooks and servants who help at weddings and ceremonies.
jhoonga	A small measure given free in addition to the purchase.
jhumke	Earrings.
junglis	Wild people.
kababs	Barbequed spiced ground meat (as lamb) marinated and cooked with onions and tomatoes on a skewer.
kabadi-kaod	An Indian game explained fully on page 52.
Kaikeyi	Third wife of King Dasarath, stepmother of Ram, who persuaded Dasarath to grant her a long promised

Kaikeyi (*continued*)	boon through which she demanded the banishment of Ram for fourteen years and the appointment of Bharat, her own son, as heir apparent in his place.
kajri	A traditional melodic form.
Kalal	Liquor or opium dealer.
Kal Yug	The era of falsehood, demoralization, slavery, and poverty.
Kanjar	A community that breeds prostitutes and dancing girls.
kanungo	A junior official of the Revenue Department.
kanyadan	The gift of a daughter; to give one's daughter's hand in marriage.
Kathas	Religious discourses.
Kewra water	The essence extracted from the Kewra plant.
Khan Bahadur	A title conferred on Moslems by the British.
Khatris-Kshatriyas	The second of the four Hindu castes (originally the warrior class).
Khayal	A special piece of music in the style of a thought; literally, thought.
Khazana	Treasury.
Khilafat	The Khilafat movement aimed at the preservation of the Turkish Empire and restoration of the caliphial powers to a supreme Moslem authority in Mecca. This movement was another source of anxiety to the British Government in India. The movement was frustrated in its endeavors and subsequently joined hands with the Nationalist Party under Gandhi in subversive agitation against British rule.

Khuda	God (in Urdu).
khurli	Mangers for cattle.
Kirar	A derogatory term for Vaishyas, Hindu merchants of the southern Punjab.
Kirya	Thirteenth day after death when prayers are offered for the departed soul. This marks the end of the official mourning period.
Krishna	An incarnation of the god Vishnu (the Preserver). Krishna appears as the teacher in the Bhagwat Gita.
kullar	Saltpeter or potassium nitrate.
Kumbh Karan	A demon in the *Ramayan*. He was the brother of Ravan and known to sleep for half a year and remain awake for the other half.
kurta	A long shirt.
Kurukshetra	Battlefield of the great epic *Mahabharat*.
Kush	The son of Ram.
kutcha	Unpaved, unfinished, raw.
laddus	A sweetmeat.
Lala Lajpat Rai	(1865–1928) An Indian politician and extreme nationalist who was born in the Punjab. After entering politics, he became associated with the extremist wing of the Congress Party and Balganga Tilak. He was deported from India without trial for his participation in Punjabi political agitation in 1907. On his return, he became president of the special session of the Congress Party which launched the non-cooperation in 1920. Later he was imprisoned for seditious activities, released in 1923, and died in Lahore in 1928.

lakh	One hundred thousand.
Lakshman	Brother of Ram, whom he accompanied into exile.
Lakshmi	Spouse of the god Vishnu.
langoors	Baboons.
laong	A nose ornament; literally, a clove.
lassi	Buttermilk.
Lav	Son of Ram and brother of Kush.
Lohri Festival	A festival in January when large bonfires are lit and firecrackers are thrown into the fire.
Madari	A juggler.
Madar-i-Hind	Mother India.
Mahabharat epic	One of the two great epics of India which depicts the struggle between two rival families—the Kauravas and the Padavas—before the tenth century B.C.
mali	Gardner.
mandi	Market.
mandir	Hindu temple.
mangna	Engagement, literally, to ask.
mantra	A short repetitious prayer.
Maratha	A member of the Maratha caste famed in history as yeomen warriors. Their homeland is the province of Maharashtra.
maunds	Weight measure; one maund equals eighty two pounds.
mayan	A period before the wedding during which the bride is dressed in old clothes.
Mehra	A professional cook akin to the Jhewar.
Mela Chiraghan	The Fair of Lights.
milni	A ceremony of formal introductions of male members of the bride's and bridegroom's families before the wedding.

Mirasis	Moslem musicians and comedians.
mohalla	A block of houses built around a courtyard and constituting a neighborhood unit.
mouli	An auspicious red and white thread.
mullah	A Moslem priest.
munshi	An accountant-cum-secretary.
Nadirshah	(1688–1749) Shah of Persia from 1736 to 1747. In 1738/39, Nadir invaded India. His forces defeated the Moghuls at Karnal and marched on to occupy Delhi. They returned to Persia with booty of almost incalculable value, including the famous peacock throne of Delhi and the diamond, Koh-i-noor.
nan-gosht	Baked unleavened bread and meat curry.
nans	Persian oven baked bread.
nautch	Dance.
Nawab	A Moslem prince.
niwar	Wide cotton tape.
Noor Jehan	Wife of the second Moghul king, Jehangir. She not only ruled her husband, but his empire.
Padre Sahib	A Christian priest.
Paharan	A hill woman.
pala	The end of a veil.
pan	A special leaf wrapped around various ingredients which is chewed as a digestive or stimulant.
pan-biri shop	A shop where tobacco and pan are sold.
pancha	A village council member.
panchayat	The village council; literally, a council of five.
pandit	A learned person.

Panipat	A historic battlefield near Delhi where the fate of India has often been decided.
pansari	A seller of spices and herbs.
pan supari	Pan, beetlenut, and other ingredients.
paonchies	Anklets.
parathas	Unleavened bread cooked in fat on a griddle.
Parmatma	God (in Hindi).
Parsi	A Zoroastrian of India descended from the Persian refugees who fled Mohammedan persecutions in the seventh century and settled principally in Bombay.
Pathan	Native of northwest frontier province of India—now in Pakistan.
patwari	A local official appointed by the government to keep detailed records and maps of the ownership and transfer of immovable property.
peeloo	A succulent berry.
persian wheel	An undershot wheel adapted to raising water from a well using radial floats.
phool	Small silver ornaments which women wear on the sides of the head.
phulkaries	Embroidered tapestries customarily used as shawls.
pies	Indian currency; one half of an anna.
pinnis	Cookies pressed in the shape of small spheres.
pirhis	Low stools.
prashad	A small portion of the offerings to the gods, redistributed to the congregation as blessed food after prayers.
puja	Worship performed in the form of prayers, hymn singing, offering of flowers, and burning of incense.
pukka	Fast or dark colour, burnished.

purda	Seclusion of women from public view.
putra	Son.
qatil-e-am	Massacre of the public.
qazi	A Moslem priest.
rabi	The winter crop.
Rai Bahadur	A title conferred on Hindus by the British.
Rakhri—Raksha Bandhan	Festival in August when sisters tie a band around their brothers' wrists in return for a pledge of protection.
Ram	An incarnation of Vishnu and hero of the *Ramayan*.
Ramayan	The Indian epic (Life of Ram) by Valmiki.
Ram Leela	Dramatic performances of episodes from the Indian epic *Ramayan* enacted during the festival of Dusserah.
Ram Rajya	The rule of Ram in the epic *Ramayan*. During this period there was peace, freedom, and plenty.
rani	Queen.
Ranjit Singh	Maharaja Ranjit Singh (1780–1839). Leader of the Sikhs, and known as the Lion of the Punjab.
Rasdharis	Actors and dramatists.
Ravan	Demon king of Ceylon who abducted Sita, wife of Ram.
Ravi Varma	A famous Indian painter of the royal family of Travancore state, who depicted many mythological scenes at the end of the nineteenth century.
rayat	Public.
rupee	Indian currency.
salwar kameez	The Punjabi woman's dress consisting of a long shirt and baggy trousers.

samadhi	Memorial.
saman araz	Jasmine hue—pale complexion.
sandhya	A prayer.
Sanjivani herb	A legendary medicinal herb.
sarangi	Bowed reedy-toned fiddle.
Saraswati	The goddess of learning and the arts.
sarbhala	Best man at a wedding.
Sarin Khatris	The third group of Khatris.
Saroop Nakha	A character from the *Ramayan* whose nose was cut off by Lakshman because she had harassed him.
Sarson sag	Mustard greens.
Sassi and Punna	Legendary lovers.
satyagraha	Non-cooperation; civil disobedience.
Sat Yug	Era of truth, justice, and prosperity.
savan	The monsoon season (July/August).
seer	Weight measure; one seer equals two pounds.
sehra bandi	A wedding ceremony in which special headgear with flower garlands is placed on the bridegroom prior to the departure of the groom's wedding party to the bride's residence. It is reminiscent of the crown used in the old days.
semi-purda	Partial seclusion of women from public observation by means of concealing clothes, e.g., veils.
serai	Rest house.
shagan	Earnest money given by the girl's parents to the boy's parents to confirm a marriage proposal.
Shakuntala	The heroine of Kalidasa's classical drama *Shakuntala*. Kalidasa, Indian poet and dramatist and the most distinguished figure in classical Sanskrit

Shakuntala (*continued*)	literature, is generally assumed to have lived about A.D. 400. *Shakuntala* was adapted from an episode in the epic *Mahabharat*.
shanti	Peace.
shanti path	Prayers of peace.
shingar patti	Ornaments for the forehead.
Shiva	God of destruction.
Sher Shah	An Afghan rebel who ruled in India for five years after defeating Humayum, the second Moghul emperor.
Sikha-Shahi	Sikh ruler or Sikh supremacy; usually synonomous with high-handedness.
Sikh Gurdwara of Nankana Sahib	Sikh temple in the holy town of Nankana Sahib in the Punjab.
siris	A flowering tree (rain tree).
Sita	Wife of Ram. The ideal of Hindu womanhood, the perfect wife and mother, entirely devoted to her lord.
siyapa	A special mourning ritual performed by women.
snogra	Flax.
Sonar	Goldsmith.
Sohni and Mahinwal	Legendary lovers.
subag de geet	Songs wishing the bride a happy married life.
swami	Holy man.
Swami Dayanand Saraswati	The founder of the Arya Samaj sect of Hinduism.
syce	Coachman.
tabla	Drums used in Indian music.
takias	Pillows or cushions.
tans	Tunes.
tar babu	Clerk in the telegraph office.
Tarkhan	Woodworker.

tehmad	A sheet worn by men around the waist and allowed to drape to the ankles.
tehsil	Subdivision in a district.
thara	Brick-paved platform in front of the house, a patio.
thumri	A traditional melodic form.
Tia	A Hindu community from Cannanore in South India.
Tilak	(1856–1920) As an Indian political leader, Tilak was among the first to maintain that Indians should cease to cooperate with foreign rule, but he always denied that he had ever encouraged the use of violence. Upon his death in 1920, Mahatma Gandhi took on the leadership of the Indian national movement.
tilak mark	An auspicious marking put on the forehead.
Tiwana	A family of Moslem landowners from Shapur district in the Punjab.
tonga	Two-wheeled horse-drawn carriage.
tonga-walla	Tonga driver.
twitarian	Ornamental hair clips.
vari	A gift of clothes and jewelry given to the bride by the bridegroom's parents.
vatan	Homeland.
vedi	A decorated pavilion where the Hindu wedding ceremony is conducted.
vilambit	The second movement in a musical piece.
wali	Feminine ending for an owner, possessor, or profession.
yatra	Journey or pilgrimage.

Yam-doot	A messenger of death.
zamin	Land.
zamindar	Landowner or landlord.
zan	Woman.
zewar	Jewelry.